A Buddhist's Shakespeare

A Buddhist's Shakespeare

Affirming Self-Deconstructions

James Howe

Rutherford • Madison • Teaneck
Fairleigh Dickinson University Press
London and Toronto: Associated University Presses

© 1994 by Associated University Presses, Inc.

All rights reserved. Authorization to photocopy items for internal or personal use, or the internal or personal use of specific clients, is granted by the copyright owner, provided that a base fee of $10.00, plus eight cents per page, per copy is paid directly to the Copyright Clearance Center, 27 Congress Street, Salem, Massachusetts 01970.
[0-8386-3522-9/94 $10.00 + 8¢ pp, pc.]

Associated University Presses
440 Forsgate Drive
Cranbury, NJ 08512

Associated University Presses
25 Sicilian Avenue
London WC1A 2QH, England

Associated University Presses
P.O. Box 338, Port Credit
Mississauga, Ontario
Canada L5G 4L8

The paper used in this publication meets the requirements
of the American National Standard for Permanence of Paper
for Printed Library Materials Z39.48-1984.

Library of Congress Cataloging-in-Publication Data

Howe, James, 1944-
    A Buddhist's Shakespeare: affirming self-deconstructions / James Howe.
      p. cm.
    Includes bibliographical references (p.) and index.
    ISBN 0-8386-3522-9 (alk. paper)
    1. Shakespeare, William, 1564–1616—Religion. 2. Drama—Religious aspects—Buddhism. 3. Buddhism and literature. 4. Self in literature. 5. Deconstruction.
PR3011.H68 1994
822.3'3—dc20   92-55109
                                                                     CIP

PRINTED IN THE UNITED STATES OF AMERICA

To the goddess Diana
in all her forms

Contents

List of Illustrations / 8
Preface / 9
Introduction / 13

1.	Pacifying Action in *A Midsummer Night's Dream*	27
2.	Awakening: The Sword of Prajna in the Visual Arts and in *Richard III*	51
3.	*The Merchant of Venice* as Sword of Prajna	74
4.	The Cause of Suffering and the Birth of Compassion in *Julius Caesar*	96
5.	The Emptiness of *Différance* and the Six Samsaric Realms in *Antony and Cleopatra*	114
6.	Prince Hal's Deferral as the Ground of Free Play	146
7.	Further Glimpses of Free Play in *Hamlet* and *King Lear*	168
Epilogue: *The Tempest*		191

Appendix A. The Sword of Prajna in the Visual Arts of the Continent ... 200
Appendix B. Shakespeare's Access to Renaissance Practices in the Visual Arts ... 223

Notes / 228
Glossary of Buddhist and Buddhist-Related Terms / 253
List of Works Cited / 256
Index / 270

Illustrations

Portrait of Elizabeth I, attributed to Nicholas Hilliard, c. 1575.	62
The Empress Theodora, San Vitale, Ravenna, sixth century.	63
Wall fresco, *Sala dei Giganti,* Giulio Romano.	139
Ceiling fresco, *Sala dei Giganti,* Giulio Romano.	140
Maestà, Duccio di Buoninsegna.	205
Madonna di Crevole, Duccio di Buoninsegna.	206
Section, *Battle of San Romano,* Paolo Uccello.	209
Sir John Hawkwood, Paolo Uccello.	210
The Trinity, Masaccio.	215
Ceiling fresco, *La Camera degli Sposi,* Andrea Mantegna.	216

Preface

It seems fitting that this book begin with an expression of gratitude to those who have helped me complete it. To the friends and colleagues who were kind enough to read sections and comment on them, the debt is obvious. In successive stages, Tom Lyon, Jim Holstun, and Roxanne Lin forced me in this way to rethink what I was doing. However, many who nurtured this project did so inadvertently, simply by being the good people they are, by encouraging me to learn and do and be more, and by confronting me with my ignorance. Their number is too great for me to name individually, but my gratitude to each of them is profound. In particular, my many helpful colleagues at the University of Vermont and my fellow members of the Burlington Dharmadhatu family have a very large place in my heart and mind.

The burden of such an enterprise as this falls most heavily on those closest to it. I wish to thank my wife Diane for bearing it so gracefully so long. It has been said, perhaps truly, that one who chooses to marry a Buddhist must already be enlightened.

A Buddhist's Shakespeare

Introduction

I

This book is a partial record of one American Buddhist's transaction with particular Shakespearean texts. The version of Buddhism that underlies this transaction is therefore the one I myself practice: I am a Mahayana student of the late Chögyam Trungpa, Rinpoche, a teacher in the Kagyü lineage of Tibet who was abbot of Surmang monasteries until 1959 when, like the Dalai Lama and many others, he fled to India after the Chinese invasion. Then nineteen, he was appointed spiritual advisor to the school for young lamas in Dalhousie by the Dalai Lama; four years later, having learned English, he began several years of study at Oxford University. Gifted with the knack of translating traditional Tibetan beliefs into Western terms, he was unusually well prepared to do this work when he came at last to North America in 1970. Gradually, the network of study and practice centers which he established here has come to span the continent, and has spread to Europe and beyond.[1]

Because Trungpa's teachings are at the center of this book, it is important at the outset to acknowledge the fact that the term "Buddhism" is an extremely general one. It encompasses extraordinarily diverse religious practices and beliefs, and these religious forms are inextricably linked to an equally diverse group of cultural forms. For the purposes of this argument, I have tried to use only those aspects of Trungpa's teachings which seem to represent the kinds of attitudes and beliefs on which nearly all Buddhists would agree. None of his tantric teachings, and very little Mahayana that could be specifically distinguished from Theravadin teachings, have been employed. Although, as a result of this selection process, no single version of Buddhism is fully represented here, I hope none is done violence. By using the term "Buddhism" as if it referred to a unified set of beliefs, this selection creates a useful fiction which makes discussion of an important subject possible.

I should further warn the reader that this book records a transaction that is still unfinished; it is not the last word on its subject, but merely a resting place within a history that continues to unfold, a history that has been completely rewritten eight times already. By the middle of the last chapter, each previous version felt like a falsification. My way of reading Shakespeare had changed in the writing, and the manuscript had to be rewritten yet again.

At the time of this particular rewriting, I have been teaching Shakespeare for over twenty years at the University of Vermont. In the middle of this academic career, at a point when my previous assumptions about myself and the world seemed to be in transition, a friend introduced me to Buddhist ideas and meditative practices. Somehow, their approach to life seemed more true to my experience than anything I had known. I began a two-year program of study, primarily in Burlington, Vermont, at one of Trungpa's local study and practice centers; in 1982 I formally became a Buddhist.

As I read and reread Shakespearean texts over the next few years, they seemed to change; perhaps not coincidentally, they seemed to change in directions that paralleled the changes I could see in myself. Each time I congratulated myself on the achievement of a new level of wisdom, Shakespeare seemed already to have been there. Gradually, the truth of an observation by Stephen Greenblatt (1980, 6) became obvious: inevitably, our valuations and interpretations of Renaissance texts are our own inventions. However, to me this recognition does not at all imply that any "reading" will do as well as any other. Quite the reverse: it positions the reader's once-hidden agenda in the foreground of his consciousness, so that he is constantly challenged by his awareness that this agenda always informs his interpretations. Rereading Shakespeare in this spirit, in the spirit of opening oneself to the possibilities within the text which do *not* fit one's personal agenda, becomes a continuous process of self-deflation. The imperative for self-discipline becomes not less obvious, but more.

Still, even in this spirit, only very gradually did I discover that I had been working toward a Buddhist vantage point all along, and even after this discovery I resisted the idea of writing a Buddhist's view of Shakespeare. The ideas seemed too arbitrary, too obviously my intervention into a writer whose intentions must have been otherwise.[2] And yet contemporary criticism has deconstructed not only the idea of authorial intentions (let alone our ability to know them), but also the very idea of an author's authority and the stability of the texts in which this authority might be vested. Equally, it has become clear that *any* interpretation is a reader's "reinvention" of the chosen text, and that the primary function available to a critic is to record his or her transaction with it.[3] At last I came to accept the necessity of my Buddhist vantage point; as I did so, possibilities that I had earlier denied arose in the texts.

I use this word "transaction" to characterize my experience with the texts because it seems more accurate than, for example, the more traditional "reading." It implies reciprocity, a mutually dependent exchange: for the texts, a renewal of power, a new intervention into the life of a reader; for me, a challenge to be open, to attend to the extraordinary diversity of voices in the Shakespearean texts, so that the process of reading could challenge what seemed fixed, could lead to deepening self-awareness. Because a major part of the Buddhist project is to become open in this way, the lure of Shakespeare's unique challenge is, at least to this Buddhist literary critic, irresistible.[4]

As the recognition of diverse voices within the texts implies, and despite the apolitical reputation of Buddhism, my transaction with these texts most certainly contains a political dimension as well. This dimension takes into account not only the presumed meaning of the words on Shakespeare's page, but also those social negotiations that exist in the margins or between the lines or, as Frederic Jameson suggests, are implicit as their "absent cause" (1981, 102).[5] These negotiations themselves have two sides: the influence of society on the texts, and also the texts' influence on their society. If the reader is to have a transaction with these texts, then, he must acknowledge their specific political nature in their specific culture as one of the sites of that transaction. Indeed, not to do so is to give free rein to, and hence to risk losing track of, subjectivity; it is also to deny otherness to the text itself, thus erasing whatever value on either side the transaction between reader and text might have.

At the same time, there is another site as well. These reciprocal political relations between play and society are mirrored in the reader's transaction with them. As we know that there is not one history, but many, and not one text of a particular Shakespearean play, but many, and indeed not even one meaning to an individual word, but none (or as many as there are contexts in which *différance* can play), we know too that a reader's subjectivity cannot be edited out of his reading. Therefore, as Jameson argues, any reading is an appropriation (1981, 9–10). Like the writing on which it focuses, reading too is a political act.

This political activity exercised by a reader upon a politically charged text is complicated in still another way by the necessity of imagining this text within its own theatrical moment. To imagine how a play's text might have functioned within its culture seems to require imagining its enactment in a theater at that moment, and this act seems in turn to require imagining an audience and its response. As usual, accuracy (objectivity) is impossible, and so it is important not to invent an ideal audience, for that audience will merely be a projection of one's own ideal self-image into a believed construct, obscuring the subjectivity of its invention. As before, it is crucial to place this fact of the reader's subjectivity in the foreground. In this study, then, I will try to imagine an audience with as much specificity as possible, while keeping its created quality squarely before us. I will try to imagine myself, a creature of Burlington, Vermont, USA, 1993, with a particular and (at least to me) known personal history, seated among an essentially similar group of people, transported to the specific cultural and theatrical place in which the play in question was originally performed (insofar as scholars have been able to describe it).[6]

There are several political dimensions to this reading, then. However, they are all consistent with the Buddhist project discussed earlier. Indeed, it may not be too much to say that these political dimensions are simply different aspects of this Buddhist project. Our awareness of the degree to which our personal agenda informs our interpretations might alert us to that agenda's political and theatrical implications. To see the political implications of our reading/staging might even revolt us. We might be changed. Our next transaction with the same texts might be different. To the degree that our consciousness is a function of our society, we might also see that society more clearly, as well as our relationship to it. Our continuing social transactions might change. This complex process of reading might then have fruitful implications for society in general.

II

However, a Buddhist transaction can also engage socially significant issues more directly. For example, for several centuries Buddhism has been deconstructing conventional ways of organizing experience very much in the manner of Jacques Derrida. In addition, it has a twenty-five-hundred-year tradition of describing the fruitful aspects of the experience of "presence" in "absence," an aspect of Derrida's thought with which he is much concerned, but that he has had difficulty expressing.[7] Perhaps because of this difficulty, scholars like Michel Foucault and the new historicist Stephen Greenblatt use several of Derrida's ideas in their social interpretations of texts and in their interpretations of society, but reach conclusions that seem to diverge from those implied by Derrida's thought. Buddhism, with its tradition of describing the fruitful side of "absence" (of *sunyata,* the fullness of emptiness), seems to offer a model by which textual transactions might follow the social implications of Derrida's theories more closely.

There is little question that Foucault has given us a primary intellectual building block in our attempts to understand ourselves in relation to our often mystifying world. He has given us a clear vision of our place in the field of power relations within society: "The individual is an effect of power, and at the same time, or precisely to the extent to which it is that effect, it is the element of its articulation. The individual which power has constituted is at the same time its vehicle" (Foucault 1980, 98).

Although this vision clearly places us, it places us in a disempowered position. Foucault makes this problem particularly clear when he writes of the author, that individual who is conventionally assigned the greatest power of creativity in our society:

> Suspicions arise concerning the absolute nature and creative role of the subject. But the subject should not be entirely abandoned. It should be reconsidered, not to restore the theme of an originating subject, but to seize its functions, its intervention in discourse, and its system of dependencies. We should suspend the typical questions: how does a freed subject penetrate the density of things and endow them with meaning; how does it accomplish its design by animating the rules of discourse from within? Rather, we should ask: under what conditions and through what forms can an entity like the subject appear in the order of discourse; what position does it occupy; what functions does it exhibit; and what rules does it follow in each type of discourse? In short, the subject (and its substitutes) must be stripped of its creative role and analyzed as a complex and variable function of discourse. (Foucault 1986, 147–48)

The possibility of a "creative role" for the "subject" is not denied, but it is specifically ignored in favor of more urgent imperatives: "not changing people's consciousness, . . . but the political, economic, institutional regime of the production of truth" (Foucault 1980, 133). Because discourse levels are created by forces larger than the individual, it is such larger forces that must be changed if individuals are to have access to "truth," and thus to the possibility of changing their lives.

Jonathan Dollimore, echoing Marx, explains why this is the case: "Human consciousness is determined by social being rather than the converse" (Dollimore 1984, 35). This explanation, however, again implies our dilemma. We are at once the effect of our society's organization, and its agents. We ourselves express the very organization and values that determine our consciousness. Ironically, to the degree that we are mentally imprisoned, we are *self*-imprisoned. If the contents of our thoughts are determined by this prison, we are the ones who perpetuate and even reinforce it. Our attempts to think our way out of it are limited by our own mental walls. We run in circles within them, deluded by movement into an illusion of progress.

This bleak assessment seems to apply to the literary criticism of the new historicists generally, despite Stephen Greenblatt's continuing exploration of the possibilities for a more optimistic view (see Greenblatt 1988b, 2–3). In *Renaissance Self-Fashioning,* for example, he aims at developing a *"poetics of culture"* (Greenblatt's italics) and, linked to this poetics, an "anthropological interpretation" of texts which "must address itself less to the mechanics of customs and institutions than to the interpretive constructions the members of society apply to their experiences" (Greenblatt 1980, 4). This formulation allows room to explore the creative powers of individuals within society, to explore their choices and their reasons for making them. But in practice, once again it is clear that society sets the terms in which the subjects live and determines the discourse options with which they express themselves; in short, it is the field of power relations by which they are bound. In his introduction to *Representing the English Renaissance* Professor Greenblatt, echoing Foucault, writes of the human faculty that above all others was once thought free, "the artist's imagination," that in reality "in its materials and resources and aspirations, [it] is already a social construct" (vii). In Greenblatt's hands this idea is far from simplistic. Nonetheless, it clearly implies that even when an individual rebels against society and its authority, that rebellion will express itself in terms society has taught. Individuals can struggle, make choices, and change their behavior and even their beliefs, but this "self-fashioning" occurs entirely within the terms of their entrapment. In broadest terms, they are caught in the assumption that the only mode of being is oppositional. Caught in a field of power, they must always be for or against, winning or losing, defending or attacking (or, in a blissful but inevitably temporary private moment, escaping from this underlying "reality"), forever in an adversarial relationship with the circumstances of their lives. The only alternative seems to be acquiescence to enslavement, a loss of dynamism and will.[8]

Nor is there a way back to an earlier optimism. Foucault speaks for many of us when he asserts the bankruptcy of older assumptions:

> "Tradition," "essential humanity," "spontaneous fullness of being," far from being affirmations of "life," seem now more like a fear of it—in particular a

fear of contamination by difference and otherness, a fear of disintegration through democracy and change. (Foucault 1980, 267; see also Sinfield 1983, 2, 6, and Said 1983, 10–30)

Yet such assertions get rid of one problem only to replace it with another. [Although Foucault, the Marxists, and the new historicists have made immensely important contributions to our thinking about the power relations within society, including those involving artistic production, they all seem to agree at last (though they would not state the case this way) that we are bound within an endlessly repeated, unavoidable circle of frustration. Their powerful critique of mid-twentieth-century thought does not seem to empower the individual to find new patterns, any more than did the older assumptions that they attack.]

However, this critique has performed a crucial service: its denial of individual empowerment has opened our eyes to our dilemma.]Indeed, at least in the case of Foucault, this dilemma may be intuited, for Uta Liebmann Schaub suggests that there is a hidden aspect of his thought which seems to have a Buddhist orientation. She argues that Foucault disbelieved in "Western strategies of control," questioned the belief that self and world are "knowable through reason" (Schaub 1989, 308), and believed that the Western preoccupation with "the eternal other" is unproductive. Instead, she writes, he moved toward a "nonpositive affirmation" grounded in Buddhism, which could offer

> support through denial of support, operating around an empty center: *nirvana, sunyata.* Because this center is at the same time full of presence and empty of content, the "other" can remain empty, open, unthinkable, and unspeakable while providing the ground for a critique of its counterpart. (Schaub 1989, 309)

This view has interesting implications for language:

> Foucault does not take seriously speech acts that claim to establish truth. . . . He takes very seriously language forms that do not assert anything but, rather, display the tentativeness of all discourse and show the essential insufficiency of language for expressing truth. (Schaub 1989, 315)

If we were to see this orientation as the main thrust of Foucault's work, we would see him to be closely connected to Derrida's ideas, as well as to Buddhism. However, in Derrida's linguistic model, with the world and the idea of a text set up as analogues, their uncentered and therefore unstructured natures are far more explicit and emphatic than they are in Foucault. To Derrida, they are characterized primarily by their constituents' free play, by a "field of infinite substitutions" of signifiers whose meaning is unfixed and indeterminate (Derrida 1986, 91). These ideas deny our ability to control language, to assert our will by the strategic deployment of words, to state and therefore to have meaning. They threaten our conventional assumptions not only about texts and language, but also about ourselves and the world. No longer can we anchor ourselves to a self-image, to an idea of ourselves, to an "identity," and this is so regardless of whether the identity we conceive is self-sufficient or tied to our place in the world. Implicitly, at least, the idea of a field of power relations is as meaningless as any other definition of the world or of society; the presumed oppositions themselves are empty of meaning and identity. Even the idea of an "identity crisis" is out of order if there is no such thing as "identity." Free play must therefore seem anarchic, perhaps so disorienting as to be frightening. If Foucault gestures in the general direction of Derrida's Buddhist deconstruction, certainly it is left to Derrida himself to work out this direction's negative implications. However, working within the anarchy of language, even he cannot do more.

It is precisely here that the Buddhist "view" positions itself—where all "meanings" must acknowledge themselves to be already subverted by the very assumption of indeterminacy that seemed to nurture them in the first place.[9] [It is central to the Buddhist path *not* to set up a system of beliefs, but rather to learn to live with dignity and joy in a situation without ideas about what things are, or about why they are, or about how they should be.] This may seem contradictory, for by the act of naming a religion, we seem to imply that there is a system of belief to which we can give a name. [From this point of view, we might think of Buddhism as *a system of contradictions,* a systematized denial of the validity of all systems. It is always subversive of established ways of thought, its own as well as others'.] Much of the teaching of the Dharma is about techniques for cutting through all preconceptions and all systems, for coming to occupy a mental space of conceptual emptiness. At such a point, as a famous sutra (the *Hridayasutra*) says, there is no Dharma either, no Truth, nor any sense of having arrived (see Edward Conze 1959, 162–63). One simply is here.

[Buddhism teaches, then, that the act of putting preconceptions (beliefs or intellectual labels) on our experience is a way of falsifying that experience, and is a primary cause of our pain in this world.] Instead of trying to categorize and stabilize experience, Buddhism teaches us to let the flux of our experiences flow through our open hands like grains of sand. It teaches us to be fully alert to this flow, yet to play in it rather than to try to rationalize or secure it. It teaches us not to expect stability, firmness, and security, nor to think of these qualities as particularly desirable. To insist that our world make a particular kind of sense (no matter what kind) is to assume that we know better than it how it keeps itself turning.

Buddhists do not underestimate the importance of human intelligence; however, they have their own idea of what its fruitful uses are. It is not fruitful to use it to impose meanings on our experience or our world; one of its major fruitful functions is ceaselessly to uncover our constant invention of meanings, ceaselessly to dissolve our conventional assumptions about the world and ourselves. Indeed, given our experience in this century with the rationalizations of authority in all its forms, including the discourse of literary critics as well as governments, all believing themselves to be the "center" of their worlds, the free play of anarchy could feel instead like an outbreak of sanity.[10]

III

In part through the metadramatic qualities of his plays, Shakespeare frequently performs the Dharmic/Derridean function of dissolution. He often subverts not only the apparent meanings of his texts, but also their authority *as* texts, thereby disrupting their "normal" relations with their audience (or reader), and changing his role as author by making it visible. René Girard asks,

> Will a critic do to Shakespeare what Derrida has done to Plato? Shakespeare has already done it to himself. We might see him perhaps as a Socrates who would be his own Aristophanes, and more besides, as a Plato who would be his own Derrida. Where does that leave the rest of us? (Girard 1973, 38)

It may leave us without our conventional critical authority, but it does not leave us functionless. It might be that by recording Shakespeare's many forms and kinds of subversion, we could learn not how to be more powerful but, what may be more crucial, how to evade the clutches of both society and its agents, ourselves. Indeed, empowerment may not be natural to us. The very desire for it may be self-defeating.

This study, then, will privilege those voices and modes of presentation in a limited group of texts that seem to present a radical critique of conventional patterns of thought and being. It will also investigate the possibility of perceiving a Buddhist view in these texts. The various aspects of Buddhist thought that are included in the study are explained in detail as they become relevant to the discussion of particular plays.

The texts themselves were chosen in part for their apparent receptivity to this form of interrogation, although from this point of view the list could easily have been lengthened. They were also chosen so that collectively they would seem at least roughly representative of the variety of Shakespeare's work. And they are ordered in such a way as to present the most basic Buddhist ideas first, and the corollaries and elaborations of these ideas later. Although this plan may therefore seem to indicate a progression in Shakespeare's development of attitudes that parallel those a Buddhist might hold, that is not a stance I should like to defend. What I do want to illustrate is that each of his genres, and every period of his career, rewards an approach that joins self-deconstruction to Buddhism.

The first chapter examines a comedy of Shakespeare's early maturity, *A Midsummer Night's Dream*. At the center of its metadramatic situations is Bottom, a character who (despite obvious differences) has some qualities that Buddhism associates with wisdom: he does not intellectually categorize experience; he lacks desire; and he has a nonadversarial relationship with all aspects of his world. Uniquely, he is rewarded with the love of the queen of the fairies and, without trying to, uses a play to pacify his ruler from self-righteously rational rigidity into participation in the "lunacy" of both art and love. He illustrates the real power theater can have when it has no pretension either to "reality" *or* to power. However, the play as a whole does not fully realize this power. As we in the audience see that Bottom's (and Puck's) power derives from the dissolution of the boundary between "reality" and "play," we are likely to retreat from the loss of stable selfhood which the dream/forest seems to imply, into conscious self-subjugation to a now demystified ruler. [Buddhist-like awareness is inevitably perceived by the conventional self as a threat.]

The second chapter argues that, like Shakespeare's *Dream,* the Western tradition in the visual arts, and particularly that part of the tradition that Michel Foucault terms "the art of resemblance," has even from earliest times implied its own emptiness of "reality." It also argues the paradox that, like *Pyramus and Thisby,* this art is at its most powerful when its emptiness is most emphatically presented; thus, it helped to keep available in the West the potentiality for a Buddhist-like critique of our conventional notions of what is "real" and "true." Diego Velázquez, Hans Holbein the Younger, and Nicholas Hilliard illustrate this point here, while Appendix A illustrates the variety of visual forms that function in this way. The play *Richard III* suggests Shakespeare's analogous use of dramatic forms by presenting a royal portrait with qualities very like those created by the visual artists. Richard exemplifies the Buddhist view of how we "normally" operate in the world, constructing and projecting an image of the world that confirms our own sense of ourselves. Richard also exemplifies the Buddhist view that there are inevitably discontinuities in these projections and therefore also in our self-images; that we see these discontinuities, and panic; and that as a result we may become paranoid, and project our worst fears outward as "reality." Because Richard is a character who is constantly playing a role, he enacts with unusual clarity this view that our sense of having a stable personality is really only our own theatrical construction. However, once again the play offers us in the audience no unproblematized alternative to this threatening vision. Once more we are likely to retreat from this fearful critique of "meaning" into another self-subjugation to Elizabeth.

The Merchant of Venice (chapter 3) seems different in both method and effect. It seems to encourage us to make interpretive choices between "good" and "bad" characters and their values, then makes these choices impossible by associating the "good" with the "bad," and vice versa. Whereas in the earlier plays, both comedy and history, we were *shown* the dissolution of "normal" beliefs within the world of the play, in *Merchant* we are drawn into *experiencing* this dissolution ourselves. This experience is most intense during Shylock's trial: Portia is our wish-fulfilling heroine, our proxy onstage who takes "bad" Shylock's logic even further than he does, thus forcing us to see in her the inhumanity of our own desire, and to see too that Shylock was right, that we are like him too, that there is no essential difference here. We in the audience are forced to see, then, that any interpretation is merely wish-fulfillment. This radical shift in awareness, in turn, undermines our sense of ourselves; it is the prerequisite for any change in us that might evade habitual, socially induced patterns of thought.

The next two chapters are intended to deepen and expand this view by analyzing a pair of Roman plays, each of which shows a different aspect of the Buddha's First Noble Truth and Second Noble Truth: (1) that our suffering in this world is continual, and (2) that its causes are our conventional belief in our "selves" as independent and stable identities, and the desires to which this belief leads. Chapter 4 concentrates on the tragedy *Julius Caesar,* a play which, unlike *Merchant,* does not close down interpretive options but instead presents several cases in which apparently contradictory meanings for the same event are simultaneously "true." Our attempts at interpretation are challenged in a new way: we are forced to abandon the comfortable exclusiveness of "either/or" constructions. However, the three histrionic leaders (Caesar, Brutus, Antony) are not. Thus, like Richard III, they each can believe in their own self-created roles as their "true" identities. Yet we in the audience who have been taught to be different are also forced by Caesar's funeral to concede our common humanity with these figures. We can therefore no longer believe in ourselves—yet here we are. Shakespeare places us in this play on the brink of a void which is potentially the ground of Buddhist fulfillment, prepared for the Third Noble Truth: that our suffering ceases as we accept the absence of self and meaning (or as we accept the opposite side of the same fact, i.e., that all selves and all meanings are equally plausible).

Antony and Cleopatra's characters are still more obviously histrionic, and by the end they still more obviously believe in the roles they have created for themselves. This self-belief is the product of a process of vacillation that takes up most of the play, a process that illustrates the panic we feel when self-belief is threatened by honest self-awareness. The portrayal of this process is also full enough to illustrate five of the six realms of samsara, five of the psychological styles that we typically adopt to entrap ourselves within the self-defeating yet self-perpetuating cycles of desire. The characters' "playing" emphasizes this view of them by deconstructing their roles, Shakespeare's play, and our own self-belief in the audience. The play thus offers a glimpse of emptiness and its fullness (*sunyata*) as well as the close relationship of this Buddhist vision to Jacques Derrida's vision of *différance*. From the political point of view, each of these plays not only exposes the "king's games" that authority requires the courtier to play, but puts us in a psychological position in which we might play these games while laughing at them. The machinery of state is unthreatened, but has lost its ideological foundation. We are not poised for violent revolution, but we *are* poised in a revolutionary frame of mind that is outside the bounds of what society would have us think.

The following two chapters present three positive examples of the fullness in emptiness. Chapter 6 focuses on *Henry IV, Part One*. It presents Prince Hal as a character whose self-definition is based on what he will be; his identity is, as Derrida might have it, "deferred." Thus freed of self-belief in the present, he can "play" in life as a Buddhist might, without needing to judge, without desire. He can enjoy Falstaff, and therefore learn much about the dimensions of "play" from him; yet he can also win in battle, love his father, and generally not close himself off to possibility. Although Hal's free play does not seem the result of Buddhist-style wisdom, but rather of fortuitous circumstance, within his situation the prince offers an example of the fullness possible within the emptiness of "presence." For us in the audience, his nonjudgmental model suggests that it is possible to stand for peace and justice without subverting either authority or oneself.

In *Hamlet* (chapter 7), the "playing" motif is virtually ubiquitous. In this way the play makes its own constructed nature transparent, as well as the pretenses of its characters; it collapses "play" and "reality" into one texture, and shows that both are empty of meaning—that indeed if there *is* meaning, this meaning *depends on the play's transparence,* on our ability as interpreters to see through it to the constructor beyond (or within). This "seeing" gives the "mousetrap" its power, and Hamlet his cue to action in the final duel. In this way, *Hamlet*'s statement about art coincides with the implications traced in the art of resemblance in chapter 2 and in Appendix A. And in this context, the prince's famous delay becomes his *deliberate* deferral of his believed identity as avenger, unlike Hal's *un*chosen deferral of kingship. His frequent self-flagellating soliloquies betray his self-questioning anxiety more than actual delay, however, and it is this painfully honest self-awareness that drives his inconsistencies in character. At last, though, his honest questioning of himself and his situation leads to a change; he comes to accept his inevitable death, loses attachment to a "self," and becomes desireless, goal-less, without plan, beyond hope and fear and guilt, untied either to past or future, fully "ready" in a present emptied of "self"-belief. He exemplifies the relaxed alertness that derives from a vision of the transparence of this world, a vision in which the world is like its mimetic art; it is this relaxed alertness, in turn, which allows Buddhist "skillful means" within this transparent world. Because the play also deconstructs its own truth-value, it places us in the audience at a vantage point like Hamlet's from which we are well positioned to appreciate his example.

A brief section in this chapter also describes King Lear in act 4, scene 6 as a "playfully" wise character while still mad, but who loses this perspective as he becomes conventionally "sane" in act 5. This difficulty of maintaining the Buddhist view is elaborated in the final chapter's discussion of *The Tempest*. Here again a play self-deconstructs, largely through the agency of the master actor/playwright Prospero, who collapses its "reality" into ours such that, reciprocally, our "reality" too becomes "play." The play's close relationship to "normal" reality outside the theater is further intensified by Prospero's associations with both Shakespeare and James, and by his epilogue request for us to take on his roles. However, because Prospero is a problematic hero, we are made aware of the problematic nature of Shakespeare and James—and of ourselves as well. As the play empties itself of truth-value, then, its power to draw us into its deconstructing orbit increases. One valence of this power is our conscious self-subjugation to the problematized king; however, there is also a different one. Our awareness has been raised by the *play's* self-problematizing nature to the Buddhist alternative of not imposing meanings on our (or Shakespeare's) projections; this *différance* remains present "under erasure"—the only way it ever can be expressed. The inherent transparence of the self-deconstructing art of resemblance always keeps this possibility open. In *The Tempest,* Shakespeare gives it unique emphasis.

1
Pacifying Action in *A Midsummer Night's Dream*

I

One of our common assumptions about the meaning of "freedom" is that in some way it is the state of being without limits or boundaries, of being *unbound*. However, if society creates not only the boundaries against which the impulse for freedom presses, but also the terms by which this impulse is defined, then it must create as well the aggressive style by which freedom is sought (the pressing against boundaries). If, in addition, we ourselves are our society's agents, the ones who do its work, it is not surprising that the pursuit of freedom is felt as an endless cycle of frustration. The pursuit of freedom, that is, seems a self-contradiction, an attempt to enhance our lives by escaping from ourselves. To succeed, we would have to discover a state of consciousness, a discourse strategy, and a style of self-enactment that are derived neither from society nor from our conventional idea of individual consciousness.

Therefore, given the convincing ways in which Roy Strong and Stephen Orgel, among others, have demonstrated theatrical enactments to be a discourse of power in Shakespeare's England, the stage would seem to offer a very unlikely site for the pursuit of freedom. On the contrary, a person who joins this discourse seems almost automatically to confirm his subordinate status. Stephen Greenblatt generalizes from his study of Thomas More that this is true even when a play is being subversive: "The theater pays tribute to a world that it loves—or at the least that it cannot live without—even as it exposes that world as a fiction" (Greenblatt 1980, 27; see also 12–14).

It is not surprising, then, that this seems also to be the case with Bottom in *A Midsummer Night's Dream,* and perhaps with Shakespeare as well. Like his author, Bottom works with a discourse privileged by and fully inscribed within the hierarchical organization of his society. He is near the bottom of this hierarchy; he is a laborer in an important Elizabethan growth industry, the production of wool. He is ultimately approved for his participation in the casting, rehearsing, rewriting, and finally the performance of a play before the court because his purpose is to do the court a service: to celebrate the duke's marriage. By playing, that is, he enthusiastically identifies himself within the underclass. His deficiencies in understanding the discourse level he has joined, as well as his deficiencies in acting, emphasize the completeness of this subjugation. He is the "bottom," completely out of his element. At least in conventional terms, it is difficult to imagine a less "free" or independent person. Of course the court applauds his play.

However, his deficiencies also work in the opposite direction. For instance, at each moment during the casting of *Pyramus and Thisby* he would like to be whatever role is being discussed, as long as it seems appealing—as long as he can imagine himself in that role. He does not imagine the difficulty of playing both lovers during their love scene, or playing the lion and Thisby when one pursues the other. He brims over with energy and imagination and spontaneity. He knows no limits. Although he is aware of the hierarchical difference between himself and the duke, he has no sense of his own inferiority.

This is also true of him as playwright. He shows total ignorance of the dramatic conventions on which the success of dramatic illusion depends. He plans to reassure the audience that his character only *seems* to die, that Lion only seems to be a lion but is actually Snug the joiner, and so on. He assumes that his audience will believe in his role, that the boundary between himself as actor and his role, between life and the pretenses of play, are invisible. Therefore, he must revise the play by inserting a speech that will call attention to this boundary. Whether taking a part in the play's casting or in remaking stage conventions, Bottom has no consciousness of the limits of his situation.

He is equally unbounded when offstage in "normal" life. He does not discriminate between the situations in which he finds himself but, as Ronald Miller observes, simply accepts each of them "as perfectly ordinary" (Miller 1975, 260). Just as in the casting episode he can play any role, so in love he needs no magic potion to feel at ease with Titania or to be comfortably familiar with Cobweb. He is equally at home with his fellow players, their audience (to whom he unself-consciously speaks from the stage), and the queen of the fairies. In love as on stage, he is a leveler of categories, in this case of social classes and even of *species*. He travels with aristocrat and plebeian, in city and forest, reality and play and dream, all with equal insouciance.

It is natural to attribute Bottom's unconsciousness of conventional boundaries not only to inexperience in the spheres in which he finds himself, but also to his stupidity. His famous misquotation of 1 Corinthians after his "dream" is over seems to demonstrate both these qualities. Yet he seems not altogether a fool when he says,

> I have had a most rare vision. I have had a dream, past the wit of man to say what dream it was. Man is but an ass, if he go about [t'] expound this dream. (4.1.204–7)[1]

His sensory confusions ("The eye of man hath not heard," etc.) are as real as his aesthetic ones, but there is another, equally real, side to him in this scene. He refuses to try to explain that which is beyond explanation. And of course, this is a kind of wisdom. Whether we conceive of language as a set of conventions imposed on us by society or as a field of signifiers without fixed meanings, an experience that is outside the boundaries of convention—beyond what society has privileged—cannot be expressed explicitly in words. Bottom always acts in a way consistent with this recognition. He is no intellectual; he does not think in terms of analytic categories; he does not tend to reduce his experiences to the compartments of rational discourse.

Frank Kermode, while acknowledging the absurdity of Bottom's speech as a parody of St. Paul, argues nevertheless that the blind love which is its inspiration is of "a higher power than sight" (Kermode 1961, 215). Both Leon Guilhamet and Thomas Stroup also see parallels to 1 Corinthians. Guilhamet (1975, 266) believes the speech to be "suggestive of a paradisiacal order"; Stroup (1978, 80–81) asserts "that the phrase 'the bottom of Goddes secretes'" in Corinthians "is a source, if not *the* source, of Bottom's name." Indeed, Bottom is St. Paul's wise fool.[2]

This kind of foolish wisdom is not uniquely Christian. Although Bottom is definitely *not* an image of Buddhist enlightenment, it is useful to recognize one basic similarity between his mental style and the Buddhist view of things. In speaking of nirvana, Chögyam Trungpa, Rinpoche, describes a state of being "in which all conceptions and judgments . . . pass away" (Guenther and Trungpa 1988, 13). sGam.po.pa, founder of Trungpa's Kagyü lineage, described it similarly in the twelfth century: "all conceptualization has come to an end," "all unrest has disappeared," and "the whole of reality has the flavor of sameness" as if it were "a magic show" (s.Gam.po.pa 1986, 214–15, 259). We have then stopped "reading" our preconceptions—ourselves—into "reality." We have escaped the politics of appropriation in a state of being where there are no categories, not even sensory ones. According to Sakyamuni Buddha in the *Heart Sutra,* there are then "no eye, ear, nose, tongue, body, mind; no forms, sounds, smells, tastes, touchables, or objects of mind" (Conze 1959, 163). Bottom's sensory confusion, then, is a crude representation of this state, a state which is in keeping with his lack of intellectual distinctions elsewhere. For him, everything is raw, uncatalogued experience. Nothing is therefore labeled "right" or "wrong," threatening or nonthreatening, at least in relation to himself; life is ridden "as waves that continue all the time" (Trungpa 1976, 22): one, then another, and another, but no one is counting or cataloguing.

It is this lack of categorical judgment that allows Bottom his equanimity in the face of the extraordinary situations he faces. There is a basic intelligence at work in him. Despite his incongruousness, we are as likely to enjoy him on his own level as we are to laugh at him, for he does not think himself better than he is. On his own terms, he is full of common sense. When Titania awakens, sees Bottom, and croons,

> I pray thee, gentle mortal, sing again.
> Mine ear is much enamored of thy note;
> So is mine eye enthralled to thy shape;
> And thy fair virtue's force (perforce) doth move me
> On the first view to say, to swear, I love thee[,]
>
> (*MND* 3.1.137–41)

Bottom responds, "Methinks, mistress, you should have little reason for that" (142–43). When she expresses a wonderful admiration of her ass-eared beloved—"Thou art as wise as thou art beautiful"—he again responds sensibly, "Not so, neither" (148–49). He may or may not be stupid, but he does know his ordinariness, and he accepts it. Not thinking less of himself for this knowledge, he will enjoy Titania's love. Neither judging himself as unworthy nor taking on a false pride, he accepts the puzzling nature of his world, in which good things come and then fade. Our temptation to judge him is forestalled.

Not forming ideas about what should be, he does not cling to things. Perhaps because of this fact, he has no antagonist, nor antagonism, in the play. Others may judge him, but always humorously, and he is unaware of those judgments; certainly he does not judge himself. He seems to lack the desire to be other than he is. Terry Eagleton (1986, 68) writes with reference to *Othello,* "Jealousy is not a form of sexual desire: sexual desire is a form of jealousy." If we define "desire" from this point of view, the drive to *possess* is more basic than the drive for sexual satisfaction; indeed, the sex drive becomes one manifestation of this need to possess, to be somehow different, stronger perhaps, more exciting, than we perceive ourselves to be in the present. It defines not only our love motives, but our motives for any goal. It *requires* some sort of adversary, some sort of strife, someone or something from which to win or protect our prize, and thus a clear occupation, something to do: the pursuit of victory. It is fueled by dissatisfaction, by boredom or restlessness—at bottom, by insecurity. We need more status, more possessions—more victories—to shore up our sense of ourselves, to reassure ourselves of our importance—ultimately, that we exist.

Bottom, however, seems to have no discontent, no insecurity, no desire. He has spontaneous enthusiasms, but he does not cling to them. He lets them go, accepts their passing, and does not go in pursuit of another goal, except that of giving service. For himself, he is not attached to anything. It is as if he were situated in a landscape of indeterminacy not unlike the one Derrida describes, a landscape of unpredictable events on which it is impossible or unimportant to put a value. He seems to be in free play; he seems to be free in the sense that he is conscious of no need to press against boundaries. He is conscious, indeed, of no boundaries at all. He seems to embody the Buddhist teaching of nonattachment: that our suffering in this world ceases with the attainment of nonstriving, with what the *Heart Sutra* describes as "indifference to any kind of personal attainment" (Conze 1959, 163).

II

Regardless of how ideal this kind of freedom may seem in itself, it seems endangered when considered in its political context. It seems mainly passive, freely allowing power to flow to those who want it, and it is easily exploited by those who *do* treat the world as an adversary. Thus Bottom plays at the royal wedding at the royal sufferance. His simple wish to serve cedes power to the already powerful; he relinquishes control of the circumstances of his enactment to another, to one who can and will appropriate it to his own purposes.

Such "freedom" is different from Trungpa's description of the freedom that occurs when one is enlightened:

> It is an ultimate and fundamental sense of freedom, a sense of humor, the ability to see the ironical aspect of the game of ego, the playing of polarities. If one is able to see ego from an aerial point of view, then one is able to see its humorous quality. (Trungpa 1976a, 45)

Bottom does not have this kind of distance; he does not see his life as ironic. In addition, it is not clear that he makes choices about what he does. Trungpa writes that if one is truly free,

> one is quite free to determine one's way of life, free to determine whether to look at things in a categorical way or an aesthetic way. (Guenther and Trungpa 1988, 28)

Bottom is neither a Buddhist nor enlightened. Nevertheless, because in some ways he finds himself in a Buddhist-like relationship with his world, he is not so fully disempowered, nor are those in authority so empowered over him, as we might expect.

Certainly the play presents an image of authority in society that is repressive. Individual desire is legitimized or denied (as in the Lysander-Hermia-Demetrius triangle) on the basis of patriarchal property rights—the arbitrary exercise of a father's power over his daughter or of a husband's over his wife. These rights are backed by the state in the person of Theseus, a particularly arbitrary situation because Theseus himself has won his betrothed Hippolyta by defeating her in battle, and has a varied sexual history as well (according to Oberon: 2.1.76–80). Male force rules, and this force it is which, in scene 2, we see Bottom and his companions preparing to legitimate with their little play.

The forest is not different, even though its ruling spirits are of a different species. The fairies may at first seem charming in the way of nature spirits, but the wrangling between their king and queen is a repetition of the authoritarian tone of act 1, scene 1. It is another power struggle. King Oberon claims to be Titania's "lord" (2.1.63). As both she (2.1.61, 81) and Puck (2.1.24) point out, his statement about her keeping the "little changeling boy" (2.1.120) out of respect for her votaress, as well as his accusation that she was once infatuated with Theseus, is made in jealousy. Oberon wants his wife to be entirely his; he resents both her old love and her present devotion, even though its recipient is female and dead. As Louis Adrian Montrose observes, all the males of the play who are in authority as rulers, fathers, or husbands try to disrupt whatever strong bonds "their" women have with other women. Hippolyta has lost her Amazons; Titania will give up her votaress's boy; and Hermia will give up her close relationship with Helena—in each case to be married, to take a husband as master.

However, we learn in the forest that this neat male-dominated order has not always been in place. The royal foursome have had past relationships that intertwine them as couples: Oberon with Hippolyta, Theseus with Titania, the reverse of their present pairing (2.1.65–80). This pattern of change behind apparent orderliness is a parallel to the present foreground partner changes played out by Lysander, Hermia, Demetrius, and Helena. Impermanence and change exist at all levels of the world of this play, including at the level of its privileged males. Indeed, as represented by Lysander and Demetrius in the forest, males seem more changeable than females. From this point of view, the order which the male authority figures seek to impose seems particularly arbitrary.

This sense of flux applies not only to the love relationships, but is also extended throughout the play to things in general. At the very beginning of the play, for example, Theseus confesses his reliance on the moon (1.1.3–10). And at the end, after the new moon has arrived and the marriages have taken place, the couples are in bed, presumably overcome by passion, and the fairies have taken over the court. The world's flux, that is, asserts its continuing and overarching sovereignty, despite the appearance the nuptials give that order has been satisfactorily restored.[3]

In between, in acts 2, 3, and 4, in the dark forest world, authority is even more obviously arbitrary. The lovers' changes in affections (on both the human and the fairy level, including Titania herself) are caused by herbal magic, the potion derived from love-in-idleness. This magical power is administered by Oberon to satisfy his passion for revenge because his authority has been challenged by his wife. In the case of his lieutenant, Puck, it is more capricious still; he lacks even the rationale of desire: "And those things do best please me / That befall prepost'rously" (3.2.120–21).

Under these circumstances, change becomes not only arbitrary but incongruous. It is played out to its fullest imagining. Love is rendered ludicrous by having partners change quite literally in the blinking of an eye. The queen of the fairies has a liaison with Bottom, complete with ass's head. The four romantic lovers show the blindness of their love by changing partners in two movements, each with two parts: first each man changes so that he woos the "wrong" woman; then each man woos first one woman, then the other. In this situation, neither woman can enjoy the affections of her truly beloved, even though each keeps her own allegiances constant.

As a result, the importance of individual will and self-determination, even the idea of individual identity itself, is undermined. The lovers change partners without any intention of doing so, and in their love relationships they seem very nearly interchangeable.[4] Each is subsumed into a common irrationality of excess. Each seems capable of the speeches attributed to the others. Demetrius whines, "O Helen, goddess, nymph, perfect, divine! / To what, my love, shall I compare thine eyne?" (3.2.137–38). Lysander had awakened a little earlier to vow (to the same Helena), "run through fire I will for thy sweet sake" (2.2.103). Helena herself, in a less fortunate moment, proclaims her love to Demetrius in similarly extraordinary terms:

> The more you beat me, I will fawn on you,
> Use me but as your spaniel, spurn me, strike me,
> Neglect me, lose me; only give me leave,
> Unworthy as I am, to follow you.
>
> (2.1.204–7)

And Hermia, as early as the first scene, finds once heavenly Athens to be a hell because it cannot compare with the "graces" that "in [her] love do dwell" (1.1.206–7). All four are caricatures of the idealizing lover. They have "lost" themselves.

This sense of lost individual identity is further emphasized by Puck's references to them. When he tells us his plans to lead Lysander and Demetrius "up and down" (3.2.396–99), and when, slightly later, waiting for the four lovers to gather, he comments, "Yet but three? Come one more; / Two of both kinds makes up four" (3.2.437–38), he refers to them more as animals than as human beings with free will. It is their sex ("kind"), not their individuality, which distinguishes them—as if they were horses or cows. They are also his playthings: "Shall we their fond pageant see? / Lord, what fools these mortals be" (3.2.114–15). Their lives are his "sport" (3.2.229, 353).

Human identity is also destabilized by the ironic blindness of the lovers. Hermia, thwarted in her desire to marry Lysander, says, "O Hell, to choose love by another's eyes" (1.1.140). Lysander, when the love potion has diverted him to Helena, not his "true" choice, asserts, "The will of man is by his reason swayed; / And reason says you are the worthier maid" (2.2.115–16). Even the fairy queen Titania has her identity endangered when, in her new delight, she asks Bottom, "What angel wakes me from my flow'ry bed" (3.1.129)?

In this context of the overarching power of love and the moon, any insistence on male-dominated hierarchical order and even on individual human identity—the assumption on which established order rests—seems as ironic and blind as the forest lovers themselves. The forest seems just another version of the city. It subjects the romantic lovers to an arbitrary power that creates chaos in their lives, just as the city did in act 1. But in act 1 that power is exercised in the name of property rights, of law and social stability. In the forest, it is enacted more nakedly as the pure assertion of will: for jealousy and revenge, and for the love of what is "prepost'rous"—of exercising power for the sheer pleasure of doing so. In both, though, reason, sight, love, even identity are always in flux; the forest merely presents this fact with greater clarity.

In this world where dream and reality seem almost to coalesce (as Puck will explicitly say they do in his epilogue), where all existence is characterized by impermanence and flux, where the idea of stable individual identity is a mirage, we are being shown a vision very near the Buddhist view of ourselves and the world. Trungpa explains:

> The experience of oneself relating to other things [the world] is actually a momentary discrimination, a fleeting thought. If we generate these fleeting thoughts fast enough, we can create the illusion of continuity and solidity. It is like watching a movie, the individual film frames are played so quickly that they generate the illusion of continual movement. So we build up an idea, a preconception, that self and other are solid and continuous. And once we have this idea, we manipulate our thoughts to confirm it, and are afraid of any contrary evidence. It is this fear of exposure, this denial of impermanence that imprisons us. (Trungpa 1976a, 13)

After the forest transformations have played themselves out near the end of act 4, it seems incongruous that the prince reappears to insist on concord, truth, and reason. This incongruity grows when he reacts to the forest tales of the four lovers, for Theseus treats them as raving lunatics (or poets—or lovers). They "give to aery nothing / A local habitation and a name" (5.1.16–17); they assume the figments of their minds to have substance, and distort the shapes of *actual* things: "How easy is a bush supposed a bear" (5.1.22). They "apprehend more than cool reason ever comprehends" (5.1.5–6). Although we in the audience must agree that these events in the forest have indeed been very strange, we have nonetheless seen them happen. We know them to have been as "real" as, say, Theseus himself, the "rational" character about whom Titania, queen of the fairies, is asked,

> Didst not thou lead him through the glimmering night
> From Perigenia, whom he ravished?
> And make him with fair Aegles break his faith,
> With Ariadne, and Antiopa?
>
> (2.1.77–80)

We know them to be *more* real than his belief that reason can be imposed on the irrational, order on flux, permanence on the changeable—and than his belief that he is the person to do these things. His belief in his identity as a consistently rational and fair person is necessary for his own self-legitimation as head of an arbitrary hierarchical order. But it is true neither to his past (especially if we consider his warlike wooing of Hippolyta to have been done in the same spirit as his alleged pursuit of Titania) nor to our own reception of the forest experience.

Ironically, he shows the reverse of his intention; he exposes the play's stylized version of a hierarchically organized state to be a function of the ruler's desire, of his need for self-confirmation. As Trungpa explains, "We seek to prove our own existence by finding a reference point outside ourselves, . . . something solid to feel separate from" (Trungpa 1976a, 19). From the Buddhist perspective, belief in this construction is fundamentally unlike Bottom's nonattachment. It is the most basic form of ignorance; it generates most of the other misconceptions from which the pain of anxiety and fear arise. When his construction is threatened, as it is at least in potential by the lovers' tales, one's sense of oneself is also threatened. This perception of threat, in fact, is symptomatic of insecurity, of an intuition that this construction is somehow suspicious—that it *is* a construction. Such an intuition, in turn, can become the seed of paranoia. Self-confirmation comes to require more than an Other against whom we can define ourselves. It requires an adversary, someone or something to which we can be superior. This adversary, though, may often be our Alien, a projection of the part of us we most wish not to recognize. Theseus's denial that the lovers' stories have any claim to truth-value is symptomatic of his refusal to face his own inconsistency, his own irrational acts. As the potential for insecurity grows, so must self-confidence inflate itself.

III

Therefore, Theseus will exploit Bottom and the other players. However, in order to do so, the duke must decide to employ rather than reject the very thing he finds suspect, a production of the poetic imagination. Now in a festive mood, believing himself fully in command at court, anticipating the delights of his wedding night, he is in an unguarded mood. In such a mood, he reads the list of offered entertainments, rejecting them one by one until he comes to:

> "A tedious brief scene of young Pyramus
> And his love Thisby; very tragical mirth."
> Merry and tragical? Tedious and brief?
> That is hot ice and wondrous strange snow.

He then asks a question that is an echo of the one he had asked after hearing the story of the four lovers in the forest: "How shall we find the concord of this discord?" (5.1.56–60). Philostrate's answer describes the little play in a way that reinforces Theseus's attitude toward poetry: that like love it is lunacy, that one need not take it seriously. Although its (fictional) subject is tragic, its effect is comic. Indeed, Philostrate believes, "It is not for you" (5.1.77); it could not please a cultured person used to more sophisticated performances.

He is wrong. It is precisely *because* it need not be taken seriously that Theseus will

> ... hear that play;
> For never any thing can be amiss
> When simpleness and duty tender it.
>
> (5.1.81–83)

Dramatic conventions and forms are to Theseus here as individual identities and affections and even shapes are in the full play to Puck and Oberon, and as young peoples' affections are to Egeus: interchangeable and therefore without truth-value. Thus it is that Theseus believes he can see through the play's mutilated form to its essential "concord": "simpleness and duty." He does with *Pyramus and Thisby*, that is, what Hippolyta urged him to do (but what he could not then do) for the lovers' forest tales: he sees that

> ... all their minds transfigur'd so together,
> More witnesseth than fancy's images
> And grows to something of great constancy.
>
> (5.1.24–26)

Theseus can allow himself to enjoy this little play because he knows *Pyramus and Thisby* to be not only art, but incompetent art done by simple folk with purely "good" intentions. Having no presumption of its own "reality," or even of its own "truth"—of its "seriousness" as art—it can be seen as purely fanciful, as harmless good fun. It does not seem to threaten rationality.

And so he relaxes with it. Condescendingly, he appropriates this little play to himself and his court. He and his aristocratic companions are on the same full stage on which the playlet is presented, and form an audience that cheers the plebeian actors on, just as parents do when watching their children in a high school play. The quality of the play becomes a function of the striving amateur who attempts the role of actor. The audience cheers the actor on by pretending belief in the characters. With Theseus and his followers, this takes the form of direct comment to them, as if they were real people:

> *Dem.* Well roar'd, Lion.
> *The.* Well run, Thisby.
> *Hip.* Well shone, Moon.
>
> (5.1.265–67)

As Theseus and the others in this audience on stage express their disbelief, they actually join into the spirit of the little play. In full self-awareness (their praise is obviously ironic), they pretend to take the play seriously on its own terms. It is as if the characters exist on the same level of "reality" as the audience that watches. The conventional boundaries between illusion and "reality" are dissolved in precisely the way Bottom, in act 2, feared they would be, although for precisely the opposite reason. Character and actor and audience, illusion and "reality," all are collapsed into one another not because the dramatic conventions are well enough maintained to encourage suspension of disbelief but, quite the reverse, *because those conventions are so badly maintained as to be transparently artificial.*[5] Indeed, their artificiality is made explicit by the human speech of Lion:

> Then know that I as Snug the joiner am
> A lion fell, nor else no lion's dam,
> For, if I should, as lion, come in strife
> Into this place, 'twere pity on my life.
>
> (5.1.223–26)

Theseus is put into a playful mood. He answers Bottom's offer of an epilogue with conscious irony that is also an appreciation:

No epilogue, I pray you; for your play needs no excuse. Never excuse; for when the players are all dead, there need none to be blam'd. Marry, if he that writ it had play'd Pyramus, and hang'd himself in Thisby's garter, it would have been a fine tragedy; and so it is, truly, and very notably discharg'd. (5.1.355-61)

Indeed, the sillier the better. Disarmed, Theseus now accepts and even appreciates this tale which imagination produces. If a bush becomes not merely a bear, but a dinosaur, it is equally all right.

We could restate this idea in political terms. In its lack of discrimination among categories of being, between real and imaginary, between person and actor and character and audience, *Pyramus and Thisby* is essentially anarchic. It represents the same openness toward the idea of a play which the forest in the main play represents about love and human identity. Theatrical conventions, like human identity and affection, are here unfixed. They elude the stabilizing categories of analytical thought. This fluidity is further emphasized by the fact that the subject of *Pyramus and Thisby* is the same kind of romantic love that dominates the action in the main play's forest. In speaking directly to the characters, in not only enjoying the play but enthusiastically destroying its boundaries, Theseus refuses to mark it off as distinct from "normal" life. He refuses to marginalize it. Quite the reverse, he *joins* it. The view of the woman Hippolyta is legitimized against reason. Theseus himself unfixes his supposedly stable, rational identity. With no threat, no adversary to best, he is for a moment as free as Bottom. As Trungpa teaches, "There is no need to struggle to be free; the absence of struggle is in itself freedom" (Trungpa 1973, 11).

Bottom himself seems to be responsible for this change in his ruler, since he not only participates in the little play, but imprints his anarchic nature on it. He resembles it in being unaware of any limits, either for himself or for the "reality" of his little play. We have seen this in his desire to be cast in several mutually exclusive roles, in his belief that the audience will mistake theater for reality, in his invention of speeches, and in his love relationship with Titania. Without intending it, he subverts his respectable identity. As actor, he is so bad that his performance becomes a self-parody. He also parodies the profession of acting by taking its conventions, beliefs, and customs to incongruous extremes. The royal discourse is misused, misplaced, misappropriated, just as love seems to be when a queen loves a commoner. He is successful, however, not through conflict and competition, but by pacification.

This point raises a further political issue. To the Buddhist, as we have seen, "normal" life is an ironic game of ego into which he or she may choose to enter, always keeping that sense of irony, never mistaking this "normality" for a *necessary* way of being, or even for one with any particular validity. It is one of many possible choices that can be made. So with service to another. There is power in serving when it does not lead to servility, to the loss of one's personal dignity. One may *choose* to serve, for example, as a way of teaching. Through pacification, the "master" may be disarmed (as Theseus is) and made to see differently, and therefore to rule differently. Perhaps he can even be induced to resign. Thus service, when used to pacify another's need to assert authority or aggression, can be a positive act rather than a passive one.

Bottom chooses to serve, of course, but not for these reasons. Because he seems to have no sense of personal dignity, no clear core of being, certainly no intention to teach, he may be said to be used by the duke he serves. He does not show us an image of a Buddhist, then. But the fact that he wishes to serve and does not feel servile about doing it, combined with the fact that his ignorance allows him to move freely (unconsciously) among different categories of being, allows him to exhibit *by chance* some of the qualities which a Buddhist master might *choose* to manifest. In doing so, he shows the power that pacifying action can have.

Stephen Greenblatt has argued that plays of this era often produce subversive ideas, but usually contain them within their preapproved dramatic format.[6] Walter Benjamin, in writing of a different culture in our own century, gives a similar idea slightly different emphasis:

> The bourgeois apparatus of production and publication can assimilate astonishing quantities of revolutionary themes, indeed, can propagate them without calling its own existence, and the existence of the class that owns it, seriously into question. (Benjamin 1986a, 229)

That is, *ideas* can easily be assimilated. The playlet within *A Midsummer Night's Dream* is different, because its subversive element is not composed of ideas at all. Indeed, the assumptions about heroic romantic love in *Pyramus and Thisby* seem quite consistent with Theseus's sense of his own identity. Even Bottom's unintended parody of such a lover is irrelevant to the little play's subversion, especially since it is obviously contained within the play that Theseus licenses and uses for his entertainment.

What makes *Pyramus and Thisby* uncontainedly subversive is not what it is *about,* but what it *does.* Theseus never recovers himself after it. He goes from the play to its ratification in a dance, plans to continue "nightly revels and new jollity" for another two weeks (5.1.370), and makes his final exit into the (irrational) passions of the marriage night, leaving the court vacant for the fairies to take over. What is decisive is the fact that the ruler Theseus seems to be subverted into a way of being that is anti-rational and anti-order.

Our crucial question then is, how does this subversion occur? How, using the discourse of the ruling class of the dominant culture, can the political implications of this discourse be avoided? How can this incompetent little play accomplish social work that by definition seems impossible? Benjamin is again helpful:

> Rather than ask, "What is the *attitude* of a work to the relations of production of its time?" I should like to ask, "What is its *position* in them?" This question . . . is concerned, in other words, directly with the literary *technique* of works. (Benjamin 1986a, 222)

The little play empowers its subversion, rather than containing it, because the form of this subversion is nonthreatening. As a result, it is sanctioned by the ruling class to dissolve its own boundaries (not attack them, not create an adversary, but let them fall away—Bottom's *intention* in fact being the reverse). It becomes truly a social intervention; it truly impinges on and creates a change in its sanctioners, not by expressing subversive ideas in an approved format, nor by expressing subversive ideas in an alternative format (neither of these options is likely to work— our society has assimilated not only the work of Brecht, but the work of, say, Jackson Pollock). Rather, it works by expressing sanctioned ideas within a sanctioned framework, by being thoroughly conventional, *and then dissolving the whole notion of form and convention.* Its subversion is not in its subject, nor in its form, but in its technique, its *approach* to form.

This use of metadrama is very similar to the Buddhist use of meditative techniques. As Bottom's metadramatic playlet exposes the empty, or illusory, nature of playing, and thus dissolves it, so meditation is a form, a practice, the object of which is to dissolve consciousness of form and hence the need for practice. Each is a form which is used against itself, for self-dissolution. Another way of stating this paradox as it applies to meditation is to say that it is a habit which is consciously adopted as a technique to dissolve habitual patterns of thinking and being. One practices, initially, with the goal of becoming goal-less. However, as the practice becomes habitual, goals drop away and the practitioner just practices; the habit takes over the job of breaking habits, until at last even the habit of meditating dissolves in its own irrelevance, no longer needed. Thus, as Trungpa observes, at first

> we find ourselves doing something fishy. We are doing the same thing we were criticizing. . . . So by sitting and meditating we acknowledge that we are fools, which is an extraordinarily powerful and necessary measure. . . . We begin to see how the techniques function as a crutch. We do not hang on to our crutch or regard it as having important mystical meaning. It is simply a tool which we use as long as we need it and then put it aside. (Trungpa 1976a, 43–44)

Trungpa goes on to clarify:

> Meditation practice is not a matter of trying to produce a hypnotic state of mind or create a sense of restfulness. Trying to achieve a restful state of mind reflects a mentality of poverty. Seeking a restful state of mind, one is on guard against restlessness. There is a constant sense of paranoia and limitation. We feel a need to be on guard against the sudden fits of passion or aggression which might take us over, make us lose control. This guarding process limits the scope of the mind by not accepting whatever comes.
>
> Instead, meditation should reflect a mentality of richness in the sense of using everything that occurs in the state of mind. Thus, if we provide enough room for restlessness so that it might function within the space, then the energy ceases to be restless because it can trust itself fundamentally. (Trungpa 1976a, 48–49)

Bottom's pacification of Theseus through his little metadrama is, though unintentionally, a similar process. It is a demonstration that even an inadvertently free being has the power to change the nature of authority.

IV

If the subversion in Bottom's little play is not contained within the authority structure of Theseus's court, however, this does not necessarily imply that *A Midsummer Night's Dream* is subversive to Elizabeth's. *Pyramus and Thisby* occurs within a larger play that has a larger audience; although it provides a model of how subversion *might* be accomplished, we have still to ask whether this larger play adopts the same strategy in its approach to *its* audience, those outsiders to the stage who populate the rest of the theater. Put another way, we could ask if Bottom, who is not an image of any Shakespeare I can imagine, might nonetheless represent the image of the playwright/player that Shakespeare chooses to project for his audience's consumption.

In this enlarged perspective—that of the theater audience which sees all the action of the play (including a great deal that Theseus does not)—the lower-class Bottom seems to be an even more powerful transformative force. He seems actually to carnivalize both romantic love and theater. In his relationship with Titania the queen, and in his lead male role in the play within the play, he is not only inappropriate but subversive. His first line with an ass's head is, "If I were fair, Thisby, I were only thine" (*MND* 3.1.103). He is, in rehearsal, unwittingly making a mockery of romantic love. Then, very quickly, the rehearsal dissolves and Bottom is in "reality," still with the ass's head on, and almost immediately becomes Titania's "angel" (3.1.129). Since the ass's head is the focus of our attention, his move from play to reality without changing appearance or identity breaks the conventional boundary between them. And in this "reality," as in the little play, Bottom's social class makes his idealistic romantic love inappropriate, as it does his entrance into aristocratic discourse. His social class makes even more emphatically inappropriate his relationship with a queen. The ass's head is a visual expression of this inappropriateness, of his inner asininity. The conventions of romantic love and theatrical discourse are both turned topsy-turvy.

Yet there is a kind of rightness to this inappropriateness. Bottom has been perfected by this ass's head. His outward appearance now matches his inward quality of ignorance. When we consider the resonance of Queen Elizabeth which his lover, the fairy queen, brings to their relationship, we can see both a redoubled sense of inappropriateness and simultaneously the appropriateness of a head of state united to her stomach, to her plebs.[7] In Titania and Bottom a world is unified.

Bottom's ignorance is a precondition for this desirable unity (or else he could hardly accept Titania's love with equanimity); so too is that loyal desire to serve that signals his enthusiastic acceptance of the status quo. He can be the lover of Titania because he refuses to categorize experience and because, being unthreatened, he is also unthreatening. In the context of his relationship with the queen of the fairies, that is, each of these two qualities, his ignorance and his willing subservience, are at the same time supportive and subversive of authority, and both are imaged equally in his ass's head. Peter Stallybrass and Allon White describe the qualities of carnival in terms of a similar ambiguity. In contrasting the "high discourses" of the dominant class with "the low discourses" of the disempowered, they argue that although the dominant class designates "what is to be taken as high and low in the society," the primary site of contradiction, the site of conflicting desires and mutually incompatible representation, is undoubtedly the "low." . . . [Yet] a *political* imperative to reject and eliminate the debasing "low" conflicts powerfully and unpredictably with a desire for this Other. (Stallybrass and White 1986, 4–5)[8]

Bottom as lover with an ass's head, in "reality" *and* in play, is certainly the site of "mutually incompatible representation." He and Titania do not inhabit a "low" discourse, but Bottom as the male lover of the queen does invert the normal class hierarchy, and Titania clearly presents an image of the desire that the "high" may feel for the Other.

Bottom and Titania and, it may be, Shakespeare and Elizabeth, are caught in a circle beyond their power to end: the "rightness" of their union is the precondition for its subversive quality, and vice versa.

Their circle must therefore be dissolved by a power outside it, and this King Oberon quickly does, as soon as he decides that it has gone far enough. The queen's desire is not to be fully indulged. Yet Oberon's act of containment also frees Bottom from his ass's head so that, no longer *appearing* to be subversive, he can in fact subvert Theseus with *Pyramus and Thisby,* a play that epitomizes *A Midsummer Night's Dream* in general: both are potential tragedies about romantic love that turn into comedy. Also, they both show the flux of identity and convention and rational category, thereby discrediting the bases for their own idealization of love and marriage. These parallels between the play within and the larger play that encloses it are further emphasized by the fact that Bottom exists in both with his ass's head, reducing both equally to incongruity, and therefore making it seem little change when he also dissolves the conventional boundaries between the smaller and the greater play. This may be why we in the greater audience are not surprised when Theseus is assimilated into the play within.

Pyramus and Thisby has a powerful effect on the whole play for another reason as well, one that gives focus to these more general similarities. By recasting the original play within in the form of a metadrama, Bottom and his company remind us of its made, artificial nature: not only that there are actors behind its roles, but also playwrights, those who recrafted the script to give the play this form. In metadrama, the author inscribes himself into the text. The fact of artifice implies an artificer. In particular, in *Pyramus and Thisby*, we are intensely aware of Bottom behind (or has he positioned himself in front of?) both Pyramus and "Pyramus."

The process of casting, rehearsing, revising, and finally performing this little play has a similar effect on *A Midsummer Night's Dream* as a whole. Casting begins in the second scene, and the process continues throughout. We are, therefore, continually reminded that a play is put on by male actors, at least one of whom impersonates a woman; that its effect is entirely dependent on its conventions (including the manner of their presentation); and that it has only that "reality" that we in the audience choose to allow it. Bottom's worry in act 3, scene 1 that the audience will be frightened by roles and staged events simply exaggerates a normal assumption about theatrical mimesis; as he reminds us of it, however, he renders the very idea of theatrical mimesis ridiculous.[9] This play within the play seems, that is, to make an active intervention into the main play, to undermine its authority, to show its dependence on conventions too, to render it a transparency through which we can see what lies behind (or, again, in front of?) the roles onstage. Shakespeare, through Bottom and his little play, inscribes himself into *A Midsummer Night's Dream*.

This inscription is etched more deeply still by the play's conclusion. Sidney Homan believes that in this final act we in the audience watch Puck and Oberon watch "the pathetic mortal comedy of Theseus and his court, who, in turn, are watching the pathetic comedy *Pyramus and Thisbe*, staged by Bottom and his company" (Homan 1970, 411). At the end it is these fairies, not Theseus, who rule Athens, and it is their two stage managers, Oberon and Puck, who, fresh from their recent forest manipulations, have the final speeches. The several levels of the play can be said to be arranged in concentric circles, in each of which the metadramatists rule.[10] Puck's final speech confirms this orientation toward the "reality" of the world of *A Midsummer Night's Dream:*

> If we shadows have offended,
> Think but this, and all is mended,
> That you have but slumb'red here
> While these visions did appear.
> And this weak and idle theme,
> No more yielding but a dream.
> ....
> Give me your hands, if we be friends,
> And Robin shall restore amends.
>
> (5.1.423–28, 437–38)

This speech is an apology for the play's unsettling materials. They have undermined the premise of stable human identity on which dignity, marriage, and the hierarchical social order are based. As Bottom has before him, Puck ingratiates himself with his larger audience by explicitly dissolving his world into illusion. It has been as unreal as a dream, he says to us, so do not take it seriously. If it had seemed to threaten, Puck takes that threat away so that his audience can relax, acknowledge its enjoyment, and applaud. If we accept his apology, and hence the play on its own "dream" terms, we *will* applaud. This applause will end the performance. We will be freed to leave the dream world of the play and enter a daylight world outside the theater. The way out of this dream (that is, the precondition for our freedom from it) is to confirm our acceptance of it, to confirm its lack of offense—to confirm our own pacification. The way out is consciously, deliberately, to confirm the power of its illusion. In acknowledging Puck's power to speak directly to us, we dissolve the boundary of the play's conventions. It is no longer "play"—or we all are players.

Before Puck's final speech, the implication of our willing acceptance of this dream has already been rendered political: we approve Oberon's continuing reign. It may be that we are encouraged to confirm this power because it seems benign. The experiences of the forest irrationality have been positive rather than negative. Despite the anarchy in Puck's love of the "prepost'rous," under its influence every "Jack shall have Jill, / Nought shall go ill" (3.2.461–62), and all the levels of lovers are sorted out. At peace with themselves and all the others, Oberon and Titania bless the three marriages. However, the second of these benign blessers of marriages is the same Oberon who consigned his wife to Bottom, and allowed Puck's preposterous derangements, all because he was jealous of Titania's loyalty to another (dead) woman. It is the same Oberon who stopped these derangements only when the premises of authority itself seemed threatened by the general chaos. He is, then, a demystified authority figure: he has been represented as a king motivated by pique, by whim, by self-interest, yet whose power to recreate order out of chaos remains always intact. His is clearly a greater power than that of the pacified and disarmed Theseus, but it is not different in motive or intention. With Oberon (and Titania) authority resumes its reign in the full play, but it is authority unmasked. Our applause for this dramatic illusion seems to confirm our own consciously willed subjugation, our desire to be handed over from King Oberon to Queen Elizabeth, in each case warts and all. Indeed, our consciousness that we acquiesce to the rule of a *demystified* ruler intensifies our statement of willed servility. Reciprocally, it may be, the ruler's awareness that we offer ourselves to her in full knowledge of her limitations intensifies her own sense of power, and therefore the sweetness of our applause. The metadramatic qualities of the play that put us on the same level as the players are crucial to the full effect of the play *and of its audience* on the queen.

If we assume the play's occasion to be an aristocratic wedding, Shakespeare has clearly provided his masters with an "abridgment" for their evening that mirrors that of Bottom's for Theseus.[11] Indeed, if we imagine ourselves to be among the guests at this marriage, then our relationship as audience to *A Midsummer Night's Dream* is the same as the relationship of Theseus, Hippolyta, Hermia, and the others to *Pyramus and Thisby*. As Theseus and the rest of the onstage audience breaks the boundaries between play and life, so do we, seeing ourselves by proxy as the audience on the stage. We are encouraged in this way as well to forget the boundaries between the full play and the "real" life that we presumably inhabit. But even more explicitly than Bottom, the playwright Shakespeare labels his creation an artifact, thereby inscribing himself within it, so that he and it become a joint gift to his superiors in the social hierarchy.

Yet in Puck's assertion that this whole play is "a dream" lies its dissolution as well as its power. The texture of this artifact that we term a play is said to be analogous to the dream world it contains. The container opens. As we applaud, we allow container and contents to pour into our lives. For a brief moment we have a glimpse of a dream life, of an existence unfettered by a stable sense of identity or order, without clear reference points—a life of free play. Through this metadramatic intervention we glimpse, however briefly, a landscape of indeterminacy, the possibility of living a dream. For a brief moment, the play's self-dissolution is also ours.[12]

This is, however, a disorienting vision of our lives. Most of us will retreat from it, preferring the reciprocal vision of willing subjugation to a ruler who will take responsibility for providing order, and who will confer identity upon us through status and occupation. Yet the two visions, like the two sides of the Titania-Bottom relationship, are reciprocally reinforcing, each a precondition of the other. And, unlike the play within, whose effect on its audience is fully shown and contained within the larger play, we are left to consider by ourselves the endlessly repeating circle in which we have been placed by *A Midsummer Night's Dream*.

Our consciousness of being caught in this circular system of polarities is strongly suggestive of the Buddhist view that we have the choice of seeing our placement in this world as either samsara or nirvana. Contrary to common belief, nirvana is not thought of as an ideal place, nor even as an ideal subjective state in the sense that the problems of the "normal" world are escaped. Instead, it is still just the same old world we have always lived in, with the same old ingredients, but seen differently. Seen "normally" (as samsara), this world is the environment on which we project our egos, our assumptions that both we and the objects that surround us have solidity and more-or-less fixed identities, the one in which we build our lives by collecting houses, friends, and other possessions, other extensions of ourselves. Seen as nirvana, this same world is perceived without these projections, without the "normal" assumption that we and it have some kind of solidified existence. It is seen to be characterized by impermanence and flux and contingency, so that there is no stable or even separable being on which to confer independent identity. Nirvana is the samsaric world with all its uncertainties faced so fully that, freed from attachment to it, we can engage it with curiosity and joy.

Thus although these two views are different, they are not opposed. Samsara is, rather, the basis of nirvana; it is not its enemy but the necessary material of which nirvana is composed. Trungpa writes,

> ... without respecting Samsara, the world of confusion, one cannot possibly discover the Awakened State of mind, or Nirvana. For Samsara is the entrance, Samsara is the Vehicle for Nirvana. (Trungpa 1969, 22)

He cautions Western students who have been raised on the moral need to judge positive against negative, good against bad, about the attitude to adopt toward samsara:

> ... we do not have to regard our negative stuff with ... hatred; we could look at it as ways and means of wearing itself out. If you have a pair of shoes you don't like, instead of throwing them away, you wear them a lot. You walk around in them. In that way you can wear them out completely, use them up, exhaust them. (Trungpa 1979, 67)

Gradually, a new view of the samsaric version of the world develops:

> ... your attitude towards the phenomenal world is that it is not regarded as solid and invincible. Instead, the phenomenal world is seen as a dream. ...
>
> Regarding things as dreams does not necessarily mean that you become fuzzy and wooly, that everything has an edge of sleepiness about it. ... Things have a dreamlike quality, but at the same time the production of your mind is quite vivid. (Trungpa 1979, 88)

Yet,

When we look at the root, when we try to find out why we see things, why we hear sounds, why we feel and why we smell—if we look beyond that and beyond beyond that, we find a kind of blankness.... Everything begins to dissolve. (Trungpa 1979, 89)

Clearly, in this Buddhist view of our existence, we are close to the spirit in which Puck can proclaim our recent, quite vivid experience in the theater to have been a dream. And to Bottom's confession about his experience in the forest that he has "had a dream, past the wit of man to say what dream it was." In each case, as in ours in the audience, boundaries have dissolved and alternative visions of human experience have come together in coexistence for a moment. We can be present in our experience without attempting to give it the solidity of a name. And in this position, we may approach Jacques Derrida's belief that it is *not* in naming, but rather in the process of the play of linguistic *différance*, that presence may exist. This is

the play of a trace which no longer belongs to the horizon of Being, but whose play transports and encloses the meaning of Being: the play of the trace, or the *différance*, which has no meaning and is not. Which does not belong. There is no maintaining, and no depth to, this bottomless chessboard on which Being is put into play. (Derrida 1986a, 133)

Shakespeare has placed us in a Buddhist-like landscape of indeterminacy and free play, where categories and names dissolve even as they are asserted. He has presented a play and drawn us into it, then shown us its dream quality and therefore our own. In the process, he has demystified the relationship of the sovereign to the theater, and has also shown that within the theater itself there are political implications: in the relations between play and audience, and between dream and "reality." Yet the conventions of our position in the theater require applause; as we clap, the demystification of these power sources intensifies not only our sense of freedom, but also our sense of willing subjugation. Subversion is contained within an endless circle.

This is not, then, the full Buddhist view, for Buddhism has developed meditative techniques that cut through this circle. However, it is an important part of this view. Shakespeare has, through metadrama, exposed "normal" life for what the Buddhist sees it to be: samsara, an endless cycle of desire that we ourselves create, and from which we cannot escape as long as we believe in our life's primary conventions, the solidity of our own "reality," and of the world's. He has dissolved this apparently solid world long enough to show its gaps, its fundamental instability, and to implicate us in the possibility of disbelief toward which a recognition of this circle leads.

2
Awakening: The Sword of Prajna in the Visual Arts and in *Richard III*

I

The Sanskrit term *prajna* is defined as "the best of [our] intelligence" (Trungpa 1979, 62). It is imaged as the sword with which we cut through this cycle of habitual samsaric delusions. In *A Midsummer Night's Dream,* Shakespeare shows that to encourage an audience to alter its way of seeing the conventions of his art is to produce a similar effect. By changing the vantage point of the viewer, such that the art form is exposed as an object, its "subject" is also exposed as a pretense or illusion. This practice powerfully reorients the viewer's relationship to the art object; its gaps and, reciprocally, the fissures in the identity of the viewer are raised to consciousness. In this chapter I will suggest that it was natural, perhaps even inevitable, that Shakespeare in his time and place would open his plays in this way, and thus situate their audience in a Buddhist-like position of awareness.

It is useful to begin with what everybody knows: that this kind of self-conscious artistic practice is not particularly unique in the drama of his time. The play-within-the-play, the deliberately manipulative character, and the character who consciously takes on another role, usually in disguise, are all practices of the early Shakespeare, as well as of his predecessors and contemporaries in the theater. As Alvin Kernan writes, "The Elizabethan and Jacobean dramatists were in some ways the most self-conscious writers who ever worked in the theater" (Kernan 1974, 3). Self-reflexiveness in plays had become conventional. If the exploration and exposure of stage conventions in *A Midsummer Night's Dream* are unusual, it is because of their dimension: because of the degree to which they—and their effect—are insisted upon, because of the degree to which they permeate the play, and because of the skill with which they are executed.

It seems odd, therefore, that when Michel Foucault describes the mode of perception underlying the sixteenth century in which Shakespeare's play was written, he does so in a way that seems to deny the possibility of such pervasive self-reflexiveness:

> Up to the end of the sixteenth century, resemblance played a constructive role in the knowledge of Western culture. It was resemblance that largely guided exegesis and the interpretation of texts; it was resemblance that organized the play of symbols, made possible knowledge of things visible and invisible, and controlled the art of representing them. The universe was folded in upon itself: the earth echoing the sky, faces seeing themselves reflected in the stars, and plants holding within their stems the secrets that were of use to man. Painting imitated space. And representation—whether in the service of pleasure or of knowledge—was posited as a form of repetition: the theatre of life or the mirror of nature, that was the claim made by all language, its manner of declaring its existence and of formulating its right of speech. (Foucault 1973, 17)

This mode of representation, Foucault continues, is composed of a network of objects that are opaque in the sense that each signifier is a thing in itself, a thing that contains its signified within it rather than merely pointing to a meaning outside it. And because there is nothing in the universe that does not signify, all that exists is part of this network of representation:

> By positing resemblance as the link between signs and what they indicate (thus making resemblance both a third force and a sole power, since it resides in both the mark and the content in identical fashion), . . . knowledge consisted in relating one form of language to another form of language; in restoring the great, unbroken plain of words and things; in making everything speak. (Foucault 1979, 30, 40)

That is, "the function proper to knowledge" is to invest the opaque universe with voice, to make its hidden meanings plain: it "is not seeing or demonstrating; it is interpreting."[1]

However, after the sixteenth century there is a change that breaks out of this self-enclosure of resemblance and moves toward transparency:

> From the seventeenth century, on the other hand, the arrangement of signs was to become binary, since it was to be defined . . . as the connection of a

significant and a signified. . . . Discourse was still to have the task of speaking that which is, but it was no longer to be anything more than what it said. . . . Language has withdrawn from the midst of beings themselves and has entered a period of transparency and neutrality. (1979, 42, 43, 56)

Foucault uses the novel *Don Quixote* to illustrate this new use of signs:

> Cervantes's text turns back upon itself, thrusts itself back into its own density, and becomes the object of its own narrative. (1979, 48)

Self-reflexiveness is the mark of this transparent sign; it opens the new historical moment to new modes of perception and expression. Velázquez's *Las Meninas*, painted in 1656, is singled out as a prime example of this deconstruction of the older form of representation and the construction of the new:

> Perhaps there exists, in this painting by Velázquez, the representation, as it were, of Classical [seventeenth-century] representation, and the definition of the space it opens up to us. And, indeed, representation undertakes to represent itself here in all its elements, with its images, the eyes to which it is offered, the faces it makes visible, the gestures that call it into being. But there, in the midst of this dispersion which it is simultaneously grouping together and spreading out before us, indicated compellingly from every side, is an essential void: the necessary disappearance of that which is its foundation—of the person it resembles and the person in whose eyes it is only a resemblance. The very subject—which is the same—has been elided. And representation, freed finally from the relation that was impeding it, can offer itself as representation in its pure form. (1979, 16)

In other words, this is a painting about painting, about visual representation in the new historical moment, and about its ambiguous relationship to the presumed solidity of normal "reality."

Almost everyone would agree with this assessment of the painting, if not necessarily with the historical scheme it is said to embody. The painting is one of the most famous of self-reflexive artistic statements. We are shown a representation of Velázquez himself about to resume work on a painting, a painting within the painting which we cannot see but whose subject seems to be us, the viewers, since he is looking directly at us (or at the least we stand beside his model). We see a picture in which we ourselves are (or may be) inscribed; as we look into the picture, the crucial figures at whom we gaze (the artist and the princess) stare back at us. The "content" of the work, as well as the viewer's relationship to it, is problematized.

These relations that Foucault sees between the art-object *Las Meninas* and its viewers, as well as the attitude he indicates toward the art-object in itself, seem very similar to the relationships and attitudes we have been discussing with reference to *A Midsummer Night's Dream*. The painting and the play seem to be statements of the same aesthetic ideology and, we might say, of the same historical moment—what Foucault calls the classical age.[2] However, the "moment" of Velázquez's painting is 1656, that of Shakespeare's play about 1595. Therefore, when Foucault writes that the earlier system of representation that characterizes the sixteenth century had been in place "ever since the Stoics" (1979, 42), he tempts us to place the play in a formative phase of this later, classical age. In this scheme, Shakespeare and his contemporary self-reflexive playwrights seem to invent the new age that artists like Velázquez inhabit.

In evaluating this scheme, it is revealing to examine two major aspects of that mode of representation that Foucault associates with the earlier extended moment. He terms the first aspect "resemblance." It is the mode in which "painting imitated space" and in which the theater was "the theatre of life or the mirror of nature"—in whose service, as Giorgio Vasari writes again and again, the realistic imitation of nature is a primary goal.

This system of resemblances was always edging toward the problematic; it was always unstable because it was the site of its own self-contradictions. The pretense of realism (or "repetition") was never more than pretense, and this fact was always obvious in painting, as it was in the theater. Three dimensions are represented within a two-dimensional space that is framed off from the larger "reality" of the viewers, and within this framed space its maker usually inscribes himself with a signature, to say nothing of stylistic gestures. Further, Harry Berger reminds us, the single vantage point, which is implied by the artist's use of perspective to lead us to a vanishing point within the picture, falsifies "ordinary perception [which] is neither monocular nor so rigorously geometrized" (Berger 1965, 55–56). Thus, "the imaginary event is *labeled* imaginary by the very gesture which indicates its significance" (1965, 58).

It is an inescapable assumption that artists were conscious of their skillful craft, and therefore of their deceit. Indeed, their deceit was the essence of their skill. It gave them the power to represent a "clarified image of the world it replaces" (1965, 46). That is, their self-contradictory conventions allowed realistic art to represent a vision *beyond* the "real." Its "reality" is its own, but it is not ours. As Jonathan Dollimore puts it, realism "affirms the independent existence of the external world" (Dollimore 1984, 213 n. 13). To the degree that it is intended to fool the eye, it has already undercut itself by its mode of representation. What we notice, what it calls our attention to by its very skill, is its skill at *seeming,* its ability to make deceit *seem* truth. As the skill increases, as the image nears "reality," its emphasis on *seeming* also grows. In so-called nonrepresentational painting (painting that does not attempt "resemblance"), *seeming* is not an issue because it is obvious in such painting that the creation of *seeming* is not the artist's intention, not the direction in which his skill is expended. It is a paradox of art that the most "realistic" paintings are those that most powerfully call the viewer's attention to their artificiality, to the fact of their production by an artist.[3] Bottom makes this fact explicit. Because he believes completely in the "realism" of a represented lion, he composes a disclaimer that exposes the conventions of drama; he exposes the fact that the play is merely a representation. Our laughter, of course, is partly based on the wrongness of his assumption that we would mistake a representation for reality. That is, his belief reminds us of our own disbelief.

Bottom's mistake leads us to the fact that the source of artistic power lies not in its realism, not in its ability to fool its viewers, but precisely in our awareness that it *is* a representation, that it has no pretension to truth-value. We are most powerfully affected when we see the producer behind the work, when we see that he has given up both his and the work's authority to compel belief. We can then be conscious of choosing freely to be "in collusion with the artist,"[4] taking pleasure in the work's object as a Buddhist might in the world itself. We are able to play at belief as one might at any other game—precisely because we find ourselves in a situation that makes no demands on our ability to believe. The art of resemblance always implies this artificial, represented nature. Contrary to Foucault's belief, its emphasis is no more on its particular interpretation of the world than on the clarity with which it emphasizes the fact that *any* interpretation—whether the artist's or ours—is a willed and therefore more-or-less arbitrary choice. This kind of work continually undermines its apparent intentions.

Another illustration of this paradox in the art of resemblance is contained within one of "realism"'s most favored techniques, the use of implied lines of perspective to lead our eye toward a vanishing point within the picture. These same perspective lines that converge within the picture can, if extended outward, also enclose the viewer within their network of representation (just as, with a different technique, Velázquez's painter's gaze within *Las Meninas* fixes us within *that* work). Yet even as these lines hold the viewer within their grasp, they also treat him as if he were external to the painting, directing his gaze toward a particular vantage point from which to see the art-object they construct (see Kubovy 1986, 1–16). He is at the same time both the observed and the observer.

II

The second point I wish to make about this art of resemblance is that once verisimilitude became fashionable (according to Giorgio Vasari, this was not long after Giotto's time in the early fourteenth century), the inherent self-contradictions of the style became, increasingly, an artistic playground. In a great variety of ways, painters of the fifteenth and sixteenth centuries explored the limits of the conventions of realism not for the purpose of achieving greater verisimilitude, but to play tricks on their viewers in ways that made viewers conscious of being manipulated. They did, in other words, what Shakespeare did through Bottom in 1595. (In Appendix A, works ranging from the so-called Minoan civilization of Crete to Shakespeare's Italian contemporary, Annibale Carracci, are analyzed. This survey indicates something of the diversity of forms in which "realism"'s self-reflexive transparence is expressed, while the wide extension in time suggests the universality of this transparence. The main emphasis of this appendix, the fifteenth and sixteenth centuries, however, leads at the same time directly to Shakespeare. In the present chapter, then, I will focus the visual illustrations of transparence more narrowly still, concentrating on two sixteenth-century examples that are closely associated with the English court—first Henry's, then Elizabeth's.)

The first, Hans Holbein the Younger's painting *The Ambassadors*, executed in 1533, is useful in part because it is so well known. As Ernest Gilman observes, it fits the idea of art as resemblance, or as imitation. It seems to be

> an affirmation of the solidity and power of human achievement—of the instruments of policy, measurement, and exploration displayed before us, of the men who use them, and of the artist's power to image both. (Gilman 1978, 101)

Yet there are "disturbing details": one broken lute string and, more prominently, the human skull in the foreground which can be seen only when the viewer changes her vantage point, "creating the second point of view" from which "the rest of the painting becomes as blurry and indistinct as was the skull from the first vantage point" (1978, 101). This skull may be a "clever signature" of the artist's name, which means "hollow bone"; it is also "a *momento mori* and an emblem of *vanitas* posed against a vital image of worldly prowess." The result, Gilman argues, is two "wittily superimposed images":

> As Holbein celebrates and negates the two ambassadors, so the same ambiguity extends to the painting itself, which asserts both the power of perspective to create an illusion of reality and the emptiness, the vanitas, of that illusion. . . . [It] also undercuts his [the viewer's] authority as the ideal observer, but substitutes a different kind of knowledge—an awareness of the reach and limitations of his own perceptions, and a disillusioned understanding that things are and are not what they seem. (1978, 103–4)

Gilman goes on to draw an explicit parallel to Shakespeare's plays, including *A Midsummer Night's Dream:* "These double perspectives question the efficacy of the drama and expose its limitations even as they assert its power to prove mysterious after all" (1978, 116).[5] He then enlarges his web to include *Las Meninas* (1978, 209–15). From Holbein to Shakespeare to Velázquez, we are jolted from "our comfortable assumptions that we can discover and judge the truth of things unequivocally, or settle on a single interpretation in a world of doubles." All pose "the problem of seeming and being as a question rather than a conclusion" (1978, 213), a perspective that it has in common with the Buddhist view.

Yet the moment of *The Ambassadors,* 1533, is 123 years before *Las Meninas*. Remembering this fact, we might begin to wonder if this later painting (and, similarly, *Don Quixote*) is not more accurately seen as a summation of the natural tendencies of the age of resemblance than as "the representation . . . of Classical representation." Its subject is itself, its own nature. Even if, as Foucault argues, this "nature" is shown to be "an essential voice," this is a version of what we have seen in Holbein and Shakespeare also: that nothing is as it seems; that life is defined by death; that reality is dream; that the apparently fixed is unstable; and that this uncertainty is characteristic not only of the artistic subject but of the viewer's vantage point, as well as of her relationship to both that subject and the art-object itself. There is no aspect of the art of resemblance which these three works do not problematize in such a way as to make plain the artists' awareness that instability is at its heart and, at the same time, in such a way as to emphasize their deliberate placement of the viewer in a similarly unstable position.

By contrast, it is because the transparent sign of the seventeenth century has no substance in itself that it must shine its light onto its object in order to convey meaning. In the Renaissance, when "the universe was folded in upon itself" in an endless network of repetitions (resemblances), the "mirror of nature" which is "the theatre of life" must always in some sense represent the artist. In a universe of resemblances, "it" is "I," and vice versa. The essential subject of art in this age must always in some sense be a self-reflection (and *thus* artists begin to inscribe their presence in their work with signatures, of which Holbein's skull is both a spectacular and witty example). Yet the image so reflected is always false—like a mirror's. Whatever "classical" art may do, art in the Renaissance implies the effacement of its literal subject and announces itself as illusion, as a void filled by pretense, filled by the act of representation. It is at last this act that we are called upon to admire, and that patrons valued. Artistic skill at resemblance in an age of opacity always announces itself to be in some other service than it *seems*. And this tendency is clear even before the Stoics, although it becomes increasingly obvious as the age of resemblance gradually reaches the maturity of the sixteenth century.

Thus Holbein's painting destabilizes the authority of subject, meaning and perspective, just as Gilman says. Further, by forcing us to choose (or move) between two mutually exclusive vantage points, it forces us to be aware of making an interpretive choice about the relationship between the two subjects: the skull and the ambassadors. Further still, by placing the skull in the foreground of the painting, Holbein places in the foreground of our consciousness the nature of our choice, the necessity of our questioning the solidity of the ambassadors. Holbein's double system of perspective, then, not only cuts through our "normal" belief in the fixed nature of "reality," but also throws the emphasis of this operation back on us, into our own self-consciousness. In Buddhist terms, the "reality" of the ambassadors becomes relative rather than absolute. They now exist in relation to death, in relation to the illusional nature of the field in which they are represented, *and also* in relation to their destabilized perceiver (us). As we confront this painting, then, the normal reference points by which we judge "real" from "unreal" have been dissolved, and we have been forced to acknowledge this fact. We are conscious of being suspended by the artist in a situation of indeterminacy not unlike the one Trungpa says our awakening minds inhabit in the wider world when, by "using the cutting-through method of prajna," we gradually diminish our "sense of a reference or checking point" (Trungpa 1976, 121). If this dissolution does not begin, we are prey to the confusion "that man has a sense of self which seems to him to be continuous and solid" (Trungpa 1973, 5). Reciprocally, this solid "me" requires a "that" for reinforcement: "The world exists, therefore I, the perceiver of the world, exist." By contrast,

> Meditation involves seeing the transparency of concepts, so that labeling no longer serves as a way of solidifying our world and our image of self. (1973, 11)

Holbein's destabilization of his painting, its subject, and even its viewer into a situation of suspended values, then, is an act of dissolution not unlike Trungpa's description of what occurs in meditation. And like meditation, it clears the way for a new kind of affirmation. In conventional terms, because the ambassadors will die, their embassy, the importance of their human striving, becomes *more* urgent, as well as less. Their loss of absolute value becomes their *relative* gain.

If taken seriously, however, this kind of affirmation too is a delusion from the Buddhist perspective. It is an evasion of the lesson of Holbein's destabilization, not unlike the voluntary subjugation to authority that I hypothesized as a reaction to Shakespeare's *Dream*. It is simply a different way of affirming the solidity of the world, and therefore of what happens in it. It transforms the relative back into the absolute. Trungpa describes a different attitude as the appropriate one for affirming our experience of the world:

> When you begin to realize the disgusting quality of the world, you also begin to appreciate the world—because of its disgusting qualities. (1979, 59)

We are not to forget that the relative is not the absolute. We can enjoy this relative world most fully, Buddhists believe, in a spirit of renunciation:

> We must develop a confidence in our understanding, clearing out all preconceptions; nihilism, eternalism, all beliefs have to be cut through, transcended. And when a person is completely exposed, fully unclothed, fully unmasked, completely naked, completely opened . . . then one really begins to see the jewel shining in its brightness: the energetic, living quality of openness, the living quality of surrender, the living quality of renunciation. (1973, 198)

Holbein's skillful psychological manipulation has caught our consciousness. He has given us a sword of perception with which we can awake and affirm our world anew by renouncing our attachment to it—or, frightened, from which we can retreat into renewed admiration of the ambassadors, into what Thomas More calls "king's games," most valued by the ruler when those choosing to play are most aware of their collusion in it (Greenblatt 1980, 14).

Because these games must transparently *be* games if they are to serve their political purpose, the player has more than one kind of consciousness available to him. He may see no alternative to submission, on the order of the pessimistic model of Foucault and Greenblatt in which our consciousness is formed by our society's dominant culture (no matter with what complexity or even dynamism this culture is imagined), such that the self-aware player chooses subservience out of desperation. However, I have argued that Foucault is wrong about the art of resemblance, and for the same reasons I believe he (and many new historicists and Marxists) is wrong in seeing very limited possibilities for individual freedom. Because the value of the artist's (and courtier's) game depends on its transparence, we players know its nature, we know the terms on which we play. We are encouraged to be aware of the ways in which our culture forms us. With this awareness, the seed is sown for us to develop an alternative attitude of nonattachment toward our society and its reward system which might release us from desperate servitude. It might even empower us to have the pacifying effect on our society that Bottom has on his ruler within *Dream*.

In order to emphasize this more positive point of view, it is helpful to restate the situation: a dominant culture which promotes the art of resemblance as its complimentary game of choice *necessarily* runs the risk of undermining its own hegemony. Indeed, it may be that the energy fueled by the dynamics of this risk is what gives the game its value to a ruler; she too is caught in the samsaric circle of desire, and one of the consequences of her entrapment is that the circumstances are created in which we subjects might learn to free ourselves from our own. The form of authority's fullest glorification, that is, seems to depend for its value on creating the maximum possibility of its loss.[6]

III

In Shakespeare's England, this exposure of authority in the fashionable style of the age is equally clear, although its form is different. Roland Mushat Frye was one of the first to observe that the style of aristocratic portraiture, the genre that most directly articulates the ideas of the powerful about themselves, was characterized throughout the English sixteenth century, from Henry through Elizabeth, by a strong similarity to medieval iconographic art. Its manner of glorifying its subject has as much in common with sixth-century Ravenna as with Renaissance "realism."

However, this mixture of old with new does not reduce the impact of its transparency; instead, it creates another combination of visual terms for the same self-exposure, and for the same double valence of risk.[7]

Typically, as Nicholas Hilliard's portrait of Elizabeth illustrates (c. 1575), this art sets a realistic likeness of the subject individual within shallow space. The background is usually dark, and if not actually flat, nearly so (sometimes there is a curtain or drapery, but it usually opens onto a flat wall rather than outward to a window or landscape). Symbols of rank, office, and value appear on the clothing and sometimes against the background. Its use of pictorial space, then, is reminiscent of medieval iconographic style (for example, in medieval church mosaics, and in the paintings of Duccio) in which an isolated biblical character or story is presented discretely against a flat (usually gold) background. Major differences are its dark rather than light (gold) background, and its iconography of worldly rather than religious status and power. Still, the presentation is close in spirit to what Murray Roston describes as medieval: the "presentation of events [is] *in vacuo*, suspended as it were in some sacred eternity" rather than embedded "within a palpable reality" (Roston 1987, 205). It is precisely this "palpable reality," the context in which the subject appears, which is here abandoned. Jonathan Goldberg argues that this iconography mystified James I and kept him "in state" (Goldberg 1983, 84ff.). In fact, this kind of portrait presents the subject as an icon, as a secular saint. It is a statement not merely of self-importance, but of self-sufficiency, of one's personal identity and status as an absolute value; the subject is presented within a closed system, in relationship to nothing but herself and her symbols. Like things in Foucault's vision of the Renaissance universe, everything in these paintings is folded in upon itself, everything is a reflection of the individual subject.

Yet, as the realistic art of resemblance builds into itself the implication of self-contradiction, so is there inherent self-subversion in this portrait style. By rendering the subject realistically, then setting her in a context which emphasizes iconography rather than realism, the artist creates a stylistic gap in the painting which betrays the subject's insecurity, her fear of self-effacement in the "real" world. That the subject's enclosure within a frame further subverts her icon's "reality" is to be expected. Icons are not meant to be "real," but symbolic; and frames always announce the constructed nature of the image. However, the unlocalized background reinforces the fact of the frame; it isolates the subject from any outside reference point, encapsulating her in this closed system composed entirely of herself and her symbolic reflections. In the mosaics of sixth-century

Portrait of Elizabeth I, attributed to Nicholas Hilliard, c. 1575. Courtesy of the National Portrait Gallery, London.

The Empress Theodora, San Vitale, Ravenna, sixth century. Courtesy of Alinari/Art Resource, N.Y.

Ravenna, the emperor Justinian and the empress Theodora are also stylized, but they are frozen into an empowering higher context of spiritual value. The fact of their idealized representation is therefore unproblematized; it is a direct command to admire and obey them as the worldly embodiment of religious authority. The Tudors, however, are painted in imitation of their real-life human appearance, and are defined only by their own self-assertion; they are bound, framed—one might say entrapped—within it, within their attempt to make the personal into the ideal, to render this ideal visible, and to memorialize it. So to mystify the body is to denigrate rather than enhance its private reality, to deny its drives for gratification as well as its weaknesses. Goldberg writes of James that there is "subversiveness in absolutist rhetoric" (Goldberg 1983, 113); more broadly, Greenblatt states that "any achieved identity always contains within itself the signs of its own subversion or loss" (Greenblatt 1980, 9). Both views apply to these portraits. Trapped by their desire to be thought perfect, these subjects choose an art of self-denial, an art that represents a self-inflicted psychic violence. This tendency comes full cycle in the portraits of Elizabeth executed by the Bettes studio, by Hilliard, by Gower, and by Robert Peake from the late 1580s on. Roy Strong observes of the Gower painting that the subject's image is reduced "to a formal abstract akin to the principles of a Byzantine Madonna" (Strong 1969, 44). Yet even in the portraits like Hilliard's with a more realistically rendered subject, the source of her idealization still turns in on herself.

Her idealization is transparently an assertion in these paintings, then, not earned by a rendering of "real" human attributes that might suggest actual superiority. If we are to agree with the painter's idealization, then, it will be because we choose to collude with him. And as with Holbein, our consciousness of this fact is both strength and weakness. It may be, in fact, that this similarity in spirit to contemporary Continental "realism" is what made it possible for sophisticated and knowledgeable court painters from Holbein to Peake to succeed equally in both iconographic and realistic styles. (The important issue of English awareness of the artistic changes that occurred on the Continent during and after the Renaissance is too complex to be fully discussed here. It is discussed at length in Appendix B.)

This practice in the visual art of aristocratic portraiture powerfully illustrates the tensions that were present in Shakespeare's artistic context generally. Roland Frye testifies that there was "the same way of suggesting reality at work in both the visual arts and the verbal arts of England toward the end of the sixteenth century" (Frye 1980, 324). Clark Hulse argues more broadly that "any attempt to make sense of the Renaissance must find some connections among the achievements in various fields . . . including literature and the fine arts" (Hulse 1981, 141). This is not at all an uncommon view. The problem for critics has been the lack of an acceptable methodology for drawing comparisons among the arts. After surveying the history of failed attempts, however, Ernest Gilman suggests that a principal problem has been that analogies were made too glibly, without sufficiently detailed analysis on both sides of the visual-literary comparison (Gilman 1978, 1–13). He argues that attempts to establish influence between works in different media, or to erect a system for the history of art that includes both visual and literary work, are very problematic. However, he feels that issues like the particular effects produced on an audience/viewer/reader by individual works, the way of seeing the world that individual works represent, the relationship of a common cultural background to specific works, and the concept of pattern/plan/composition/structure are areas in which close study can show some convincing similarities among works in different art media. Such work is worth the difficulty. The visual arts can provide unusually vivid illustrations of carefully selected aspects of the literary arts, and the reverse is also true.

It is interesting, then, that a version of the medievalism that serves aristocratic ends in the visual arts does the same service in Elizabethan poetry. The deliberate archaisms of Edmund Spenser in language, in allegorical narrative form, and in the choice of Arthurian subject matter, all to glorify the sitting monarch, exemplify a similar artistic spirit. The Elizabethan obsession with the ongoing Petrarchan love convention (Spenser was but one of an entire generation of practitioners) was not driven only by a Neoplatonic idealization of love, but also by Elizabeth's need to mythologize herself as the feminine icon of the state, the unattainable virgin queen (confirming the cult of Diana and Cynthia, the goddess of the moon and chastity—and England). In both these cases, earlier traditions have been reappropriated to idealize the insecure present even as it is exposed. In encouraging this kind of praise from her courtiers, Elizabeth freezes herself in the role of virgin queen, whatever the facts of her private life may be, and this is the price of her confirmation of status as the female prince. Both the poetry and the portraits made in reference to her attest to the fact that she insisted on being made into a living icon, and that this image had self-imprisonment built into it.[8]

Shakespeare's dramatic art clearly participates in this same cultural ideology. Almost from the beginning, his work has been compared to the art of resemblance: belief in his "realism" is traditional. His works' implications of transparency have only become clear more recently, since comparisons between them and the late Renaissance style called "mannerism" have increased,[9] and since study of his self-cancelling metadramatic techniques has become common. Yet by now it is clear that in openly exposing his theatrical gamesmanship, he too mirrors Tudor court practice. He too plays "king's games."

He plays, it may be, with the fuller expression that narrative form allows, as we have seen in detail with *Dream*. By making his metadramatic practice obvious, Shakespeare raises our awareness to the fact that Bottom can subvert his lord's values precisely because his sole desire is to serve, and because Theseus's view of dramatic art is precisely the one we have been describing in the realm of portraiture: the belief that its function is solely to serve him. He accepts *Pyramus and Thisby* because from his point of view it seems not to take itself seriously as "realistic," because its lead actor's and reviser's character is inscribed within it, because both play and players therefore become transparent gifts to their ruler. Yet it is this quality of transparence in service that empowers the mechanicals' art as subversion—that allows it its creative power. This play, then, is a richly detailed illustration of the basic similarities between Shakespeare's art and that of the Elizabethan portraitists, as well as that of Holbein and Velázquez (and of "realism" generally), both in the relationship they express between resemblance and transparence, and between service and the demystification of the served.

It also illustrates their common dissolution of "normal" perceptions about oneself and the world, a dissolution that is fundamental to the mind awakening to the Buddhist view. This similarity is actually less surprising than it might seem. The prince named Siddhartha who became Sakyamuni Buddha did so by personal observation, experiment, and discipline, not by divine inspiration. His teachings are based entirely on his experience as a human being living in this mundane world. Their subsequent elaborations, similarly, are based on the personal experiences of other, later practitioners. There is in Buddhism no belief in an external divinity; there is, similarly, no theology to learn, or in which to believe. The teachings are meant to be tested by one's own personal experience. Although the view of the self and the world that underlies Buddhism is not what we normally see and think, it is within our normal powers to see and think it. Indeed, Michel Foucault notwithstanding, it may be that the particular approach to art that "resemblance" seems to promote has been fertilizing the Western ground for over two thousand years, preparing the way for the incipient Buddhism we are observing here.

IV

The early play *Richard III* seems a particularly good example of the kind of growth this ground could nurture. Its surface resemblance to the Elizabethan iconic portrait style seems very close. In it, Shakespeare presents a world of characters who exist for the title figure Richard only in relationship to his own will to rise; it is a closed psychic system that enacts how an obsession for power begins and how it leads to self-entrapment. We can of course see from other points of view than Richard's, as we can view a portrait from other points of view than its subject's. But he cannot, and much of the play's emphasis is focused on that fact. The result is a depiction of significant aspects of the Buddhist view about why and how a ruler hardens his or her desire into belief, how this belief is projected onto the outside world, and how this projection confirms his or her delusion by reflecting it back as if it were objectively true. At the same time, because Richard's self-contradictions are presented in terms of the gaps within his theatrical style of enactment, this play also explores the relations between resemblance and transparence, and between art and politics, just as we have seen the work of Velázquez, Holbein, and Hilliard do.

From the very beginning of the play, Richard sees himself as displaced, unfit for the new amorous atmosphere at his brother Edward's court. Despite his family's victory, he himself is less at ease than when there were Lancastrian enemies to fight. He blames "dissembling nature" (1.1.19) for his lack of grace and "fair proportion" (1.1.18); he believes that his only successful course is "to prove a villain" (1.1.30), to oppose the court in both mood and political intent. He explicitly exchanges the truth and justice that he associates with his brother for subtlety, falseness, and treachery (1.1.36–37). He deliberately constructs a personal code that reverses the values that his brother has made dominant.

Like any Machiavellian, then, his primary goal is success in the world, and his method is to mask actual intentions with false appearances. Unlike, for example, Barrabas in *The Jew of Malta,* however, Richard's world teems with his family. His situation is so morally loaded that his villainy sets him against brothers, cousins, motherhood, even kingship. He is the Machiavellian villain exponentially enlarged into a kind of primal sinner, free not only from conventional values but also from any sense of the interdependence of human beings. He lacks all sense of obligation or duty, just as he feels that he lacks place or identity within his brother's court. He is unanchored, adrift, without reference point.

According to the Abhidharma, that aspect of Buddhist teaching that explains how and why the psyche constructs the world of individual entities in which we conventionally believe, this predicament of Richard's is the primal situation. Chögyam Trungpa describes it in this way:

> When a gap or space occurs in our experience of mind, when there is a sudden glimpse of awareness, openness, absence of self, then a suspicion arises: "Suppose I find that there is no solid me? That possibility scares me. I don't want to go into that." That abstract paranoia, the discomfort that something may be wrong, is the source of karmic chain reactions. It is the fear of ultimate confusion and despair. The fear of the absence of self, of the egoless state, is a constant threat to us. . . . we want to hold on to something. (Trungpa 1976a, 20–21)

Unable to exist in this void, Richard constructs an alternative world in which he *will* have place and identity, in which he will rule. In this new construction, his older brothers are obstacles to be cast aside, his mother an old woman to evade, Margaret an empty voice, and other women merely receptacles to exploit on the way. It is a vision of the adversarial world that he had missed when the play began. He reduces its denizens to chess pieces to be mastered and deployed; he constructs a world that is a function of his desire for power, a desire that is in its turn a function of his need for personal solidity. Trungpa explains the importance of this second phase of the creative process: "Feeling the solidity of something seemingly outside you reassures you that you are a solid entity as well" (1976a, 21).

Richard materializes his vision by working as an actor in the world he refuses to believe in, the validity of which he will try to destroy. Like any actor, he enters his roles in the awareness that they are not his true identity, that they are only pretense. He can therefore invent new roles for himself and use them to his own purposes. Because he denies validity to this conventional world, he can see its lack of solidity, the ways in which it can be undermined. He treats it as malleable, as unfixed. Thus, for example, he can seduce Anne in act 1, scene 2 against all odds, including not only her hatred but also his recently professed incompetence at seduction, because he sees through her; she is essentially humane; she will not kill him. Similarly, he can kill his brother Clarence by playing the good brother, kill his nephews while playing the good uncle, and get the public to acquiesce in his enthronement by playing at Christian humility. As long as he is consciously deconstructing the old world or constructing his new one, his imagination is fecund and his vision unobstructed. Everything falls into place for him. He is a powerful creative force. [10]

And, indeed, he is fully aware of this fact. He insists that his appearance and character are his own inventions, that he is a skilled actor who has the power to recreate the shape of the world surrounding him. He boasts of it directly to us in the audience after seducing Anne: "Was ever woman in this humor woo'd? / Was ever woman in this humor won?" His triumph is great because it demonstrates the primacy of his will: "All the world to nothing!" (1.2.227–37). That is, in this very moment of recreating reality, he has solidified his sense of himself. He fits Trungpa's description perfectly.

And yet, he protests so much that we might feel he actually has some doubt about this self. Perhaps for this reason, his need to stabilize his power cannot be confined within the world of the play. By boasting openly to us in the audience about his hypocrisy, he attempts to enlist us as his accomplices. And because he has shown us the transparence of the world he exploits, he succeeds. We can see from his point of view; we allow ourselves to be persuaded to do so. We are not threatened, but rather entertained by his energy and wit. He creates a theatrical tour de force that, for the moment, seduces us as well as Anne. In his role as a transparent actor, he need be taken only as seriously as he takes himself. And as he tells us about his roles, he *seems* not to take himself seriously at all. It seems to be his artistic skill, not his own identity, which delights him and therefore us.

Though diverting, however, this extreme self-consciousness is also merely another normal stage in the solidification of the self. In Trungpa's phrasing, there is always "the self-conscious feeling that you must officially report back to central headquarters what is happening at any given moment. Then you can manipulate each situation by organizing another strategy" (Trungpa 1976a, 21). It is a way of persuading yourself that you are in control of events. And certainly Richard is doing this; he is continually organizing another strategy.

In this process, he adopts two substrategies that, as Trungpa explains, are equally a normal stage in world- and self-creation:

> In the strategy of indifference, we numb any sensitive areas that we want to avoid, that we think might hurt us. We put on a suit of armor. The second strategy is passion—trying to grasp things and eat them up. It is a magnetizing process. (1976a, 21–22)

One chooses not to feel compassion, for example, if it will impede ambition or consumption. The world and each of its parts must be thought to be consumable, and the world's function purely to assuage appetite and thus to solidify self-belief. It must be, like the world of *Richard III,* a closed psychic system. Because the psyche gives the world its shape, this world is its projection; inevitably, it will seem to confirm its creator's self-image and self-belief. We are, in this sense, what we see (and consume). Richard's desire for kingship is an image of every individual's samsaric passion, of his need to appropriate the world for his own requirements. It is not surprising that Richard can enlist us as his accomplices.

From this point of view, it is a normal expectation as well that as Richard nears, then achieves, his goal of the crown, he loses his detachment. As king, Richard must now believe in his role, must discard the idea of his actions as merely role-playing. Now he must be "for real," for now Richard must bear the burden of giving himself place and identity by himself. The creator must now rule the thing he has constructed. As a result of his success, ironically, the loneliness that he had tried to flee in the beginning of the play returns.

As this pressure on his belief increases, he tests his power more and more. He demands of Buckingham that he murder Edward's young sons. Since he has already had this same Buckingham impugn their legitimacy, the murder might seem unnecessary, but he requires it anyway, then tries to persuade their mother Elizabeth to let him marry her daughter as a further safeguard (4.4.199ff.). His behavior begins to seem obsessive. Trungpa's account of the final aspect of world- and self-construction seems to describe it well:

> Aggression, the third strategy, is also based upon the . . . feeling that you cannot survive and therefore must ward off anything that threatens your property or food. Moreover, the more aware you are of the possibilities of being threatened, the more desperate your reaction becomes. You try to run faster and faster in order to find a way of feeding or defending yourself. (Trungpa 1976a, 22)

As Richard loses the sense of humor that had signaled his self-awareness about himself as an actor, he feels increasingly threatened; his defensive measures seem more and more desperate. He trusts almost no one. Indeed, his insecurity becomes a self-fulfilling prophecy. Even Buckingham and Stanley turn against him.

He begins to suffer a kind of paralysis, a loss of energy and strength. In giving battle commands to Catesby and Ratclife he is forgetful and confused, and finally forced to make excuses ("My mind is chang'd," 4.4.456). He has bad dreams (the ghosts in act 5, scene 3). At last he recognizes the fact that he has gained nothing, that he is alone: "I shall despair; there is no creature loves me" (5.3.200).

His final oration to his troops reflects this psychic poverty, this fearful need to hang onto whatever he can (5.3.314ff.). It is a series of insults demeaning his enemies, and reminders to his followers of how comfortably fixed in life they are. This last attempt to magnetize the world is materialist, bourgeois, prejudicial—a pathetic appeal to the least exalting values. Needing to believe in his own existence, he has entrapped himself into hardened belief in a self-created role of increasingly narrow limits. There can be no escape. Despite having three times the number of troops available to Richmond, he loses the battle. Faced with his own nonexistence, his paranoia blossoms into panic. He would give his kingdom—the chimerical projection on the construction of which he has spent his life—for a horse. He would save his life by giving up the possession that defines its value. This irony, like that of Marlowe's Faustus, gives emphasis to the emptiness of his constructed self, as well as to the emptiness of its version of the world.

The slow but consistent buildup of the moral voices in the play has prepared us to see Richard in this light. Margaret's voice is alone at first, but all the women unite in act 4, scene 3 to condemn him. Elizabeth recounts his wrongs to his face in the next scene, and these voices reach their climax with the ghosts in act 5, scene 3. Ironically, however, it is Richard himself as actor/playwright who has prepared us most powerfully. Throughout the play he has been teaching us to see not only the individual characters, but also the very world of the play itself, as manipulatable, as without fixed form or stable identity. Thus when he changes consciousness from actor to believer, we do not change with him. At the end, not only both versions of the playworld, but also Richard himself, are transparent.

Terry Eagleton has observed that

> actors are, so to speak, signifiers who strive to become one with the signifieds of their parts; yet however successfully they achieve this we know that such representation is a lie, that the actor is not the character, and the stage is other than the world. (Eagleton 1986, 13)

Richard is a metadramatic representation of this truth about the relationship between theater and life. He is a *character* who strives mightily to unify himself with his role as king in order to invest himself with meaning. He fails, and from both the linguistic and Buddhist perspectives, this failure is inevitable. However, our recognition of this inevitability that is produced by Richard's metadramatic role-playing calls more into question than his own kingship and kingdom. It also problematizes the original world of the play, the world of conventional values that reasserts itself under the banner of Richmond. It encourages us to ask, Is Richmond in fact different from Richard? Or is his more inspiring speech to his soldiers merely a role, analogous to the roles Richard played when he was scheming to be king? Is Richmond's difference from Richard a difference of style of representation rather than of substance? Is his difference primarily that he is not metadramatic, that in his public statements he strikes a pose that he does not undercut by private confession? That he does not speak directly to us in the audience, but only to others within the confines of the stage? The fact that there are no certain answers to these questions matters less than the fact of our asking them. Because, as with Holbein and Hilliard, we are left in a questioning frame of mind, Richmond is as suspect as Richard. Richard's metadramatic aspect, again ironically, begins to discredit his rival as well as himself.

The effect of such questions is not to discover the truth of the character named Richmond, then, but to remind us that he too is a character. This recognition in turn shifts our attention back to the fact of his invention, and from there back to the inventor himself—back to the playwright who, through the agency of Richard, is also inscribed within the play. Questions about the metadramatic Richard lead to questions about the play's relationship with the author and the world outside the theater: What social function can this play serve? What effect is produced by such a gift, if within its wrappings the foundation of the Tudor dynasty—more, the foundation of royalty itself—is shown to be suspect?

As in the case of *A Midsummer Night's Dream,* and in the cases of Holbein and Velázquez and the aristocratic portraits of the English sixteenth century, so here in *Richard III* we have an art of resemblance that renders itself transparent as art, and that thereby calls both itself and its rather orthodox subject into question. Perhaps we must presume that it functions in society in a similar way: that it raises audience awareness into suspicion about the solidity of all constructed things, including those things constructed by political and moral orthodoxy. It makes an alternative, nonattached position possible, one that might lead to the pacification of authority. But there is no alternative to the power game in this play, despite the fact that the play makes us conscious of its own problematic nature. As individuals, we are offered the choice of playing Richard or, let us say, Stanley. Thus to write this particular play—this particular *style* of play on this particular subject for the consumption of this particular Elizabethan society—and to expect the play to be approved and applauded, seems to be to insist on the conscious and willed self-subjugation of its audience as a model of the society's posture toward its prince. Like the playwright and his dramatic representation, we must choose to play games of the monarch's choosing. Reminded of what it already knows, the audience is also reminded of how little empowering this recognition is. The subject, no matter what suspicion he or she sees confirmed, is still bound within the theater and the court, and thus within their twinned forms of discourse. The subject, that is, is reminded not only of his or her suspicions, but also that there is no escape.

There is also perhaps some titillation involved on the monarch's side, the exhilaration that often accompanies the risk of disclosing one's vulnerability. That is, there may be a reciprocal kind of give-and-take in this theatrical relationship between queen and playwright, a kind of courtiership that resembles courtship, even in (or, perhaps, particularly in) Shakespeare's early dramatic career, and even in this overtly "historical" work. This is true in spite of the fact that Shakespeare sees through the game. Or is it this awareness that allows him to play the game so well, like his character Richard in *his* early career?[11]

3
The Merchant of Venice as Sword of Prajna

I

The power of Bottom to pacify his ruler is both inadvertent and contained within *Dream*. *Richard III* may seem more threatening to authority, for it focuses more directly on an exposure of royalty. In this play Shakespeare shows the game of kings to be just as self-entrapping as that of their subjects—indeed, more so. Although Richard the king may be no more prone to ignorance than Bottom, he is far more inclined to misery: driven by desire, as Bottom is not, his passion and aggression lead him into a desperation whose paranoia finally becomes a self-fulfilling prophecy. To harness oneself to desire, *Richard III* teaches us, to try to solidify oneself by identification with an idea of anything, or by reference to anybody, is to deceive oneself and leads to self-defeat.

Despite their differences, however, each of these plays seems rather to invite questions than to discourage them, to emphasize its own internal conflicts and inconsistencies and even its own artistic transparency. They each make us aware of them as constructions, and therefore of their need for our intervention if they are to seem coherent. Yet this awareness seems not to be freeing. These plays seem to structure their incompleteness in ways that lead us to particular, consciously chosen conclusions—conclusions with strong conservative political implications. Although they both dissolve conventional beliefs about their staged worlds, they seem to have a very limited effect on the audience's lives outside the theater. Although they dissolve the samsaric circles that they portray, they do not dissolve the circle within the viewer.

With *Merchant,* performed only a year after *Dream*, the case seems different. As this chapter's title implies, Shakespeare seems here to take a crucial first step toward breaking the samsaric vicious circle in the audience itself. *The Merchant of Venice* positions its viewers so that their reactions will be quite different from anything we have so far seen, either in the earlier plays or in the visual arts.

Norman Rabkin points toward the essence of the method of this play when he cautions Shakespearean critics against "the dominant evasion, the reduction of . . . [a] play to a theme which, when we understand it, tells us which of our responses we must suppress" (Rabkin 1981, 8). Instead, he sees in Shakespeare's work a "complementarity," "an approach to experience in which . . . radically opposed and equally total commitments to the meaning of life coexist . . ." (1981, 113). Thus, rather than aiming at the traditional goal of interpretation, we critics must

> consider the play as a dynamic interaction between artist and audience, [and must] learn to talk about the process of our involvement rather than our considered view after the aesthetic event. (1981, 27)

Rabkin's recognition of the importance of process-reading, and of the coexistence of diametrically opposed ideas, will be crucial to my discussion, as it was, for example, in my discussion of Holbein. In *The Ambassadors,* two seemingly opposed vantage points force the viewer to be aware of deciding how to interrelate them. We complete the painting's meaning not as a response to either of its subjects (the ambassadors or the skull) individually, but rather as a result of the conscious *process* of looking first from one, then from the other, then again from the first vantage point. Holbein's painting is transparently a direction to the viewer to perform a particular visual movement and a corresponding psychological movement. It gestures toward a particular *process* for the viewer to enact. And it is through this process that we may invent completeness (unity).

However, we can follow Rabkin no further. His idea about process-reading requires either a gesture toward reader-response criticism, which elsewhere he prefers not to make, or a naïve faith that if one submits to the "process" one will come out all right in the end. Rabkin in fact takes this latter course, falling back on a belief that "complementarity" will inevitably result in our discovery of "a single harmonious vision" (Rabkin 1981, 113). Although our experience of *The Ambassadors,* as well as of *Dream* and *Richard III,* may have been harmonious, however, the assumptions that this "vision" is the author's (rather than at least partially the invention of the audience), that it is unproblematized, and that we can find this "vision" throughout Shakespeare, seem to require the very suppression of response against which Rabkin means to argue. We must not allow him to close the door he has opened, for the disclosure of a play's accumulating effects suggests the way plays actually are received, and therefore the responses they evoke.

Such a disclosure seems especially fruitful for *Merchant,* for it shows with particular clarity that there is no "single harmonious vision." Although this play makes its construction as artwork transparent, and in this way heightens our consciousness of its many voices, it not only forces us to recognize that any coherent interpretation is indeed our choice, but renders any such choice virtually impossible.[1] We are in the presence of a far more complex organism than *The Ambassadors.* Its internal stresses push us toward a recognition that the world as we usually see it, as a composition of alternatives or oppositions in which we can choose to favor one thing or position over another, no longer works. Its system of oppositions leads us to expect to make choices, which it then frustrates. In it, we are lost; the very possibility of our making choices is called into question. Shakespeare here creates a play in which the strains on the players of monarchs' games—on the tightrope that Elizabethans walk—are too powerful to withstand. In watching this play, we watch its—our—fibers come apart. We are placed within "a system of contradictions" (a phrase I used in the Introduction to describe the Buddhist refusal of interpretation), and forced to relate it to ourselves.

From the Buddhist perspective, this is a hopeful situation at last. Our choice to believe one rather than another interpretation of the world is our way of appropriating that world to our own uses, our way of projecting onto it our own identity, our own way of seeing ourselves. It is a way of reassuring ourselves that we have a place in the world, that our "self" is real and secure and stable. We have been aware of doing just such acts of appropriation in response to art, to Holbein and *Dream* and *Richard III,* and we have seen Richard III himself do it within the latter play. Trungpa explains how crucial it is for us to take the next step: to act on this awareness by no longer conducting our own processes of appropriation.

> Egolessness comes more or less as a by-product of seeing the transitory, transparent nature of the world outside. Once we have dealt with the projections of ego and seen their transitory and transparent nature, then ego has no reference point, nothing to relate to. . . . When we are able to see the projections as nonsubstantial, ego becomes transparent correspondingly. (Trungpa 1978, 7–8)

In this play Shakespeare confronts us with our inability to find stable reference points for our own identity, and therefore with the possibility that our solid-seeming selves might dissolve. Such insight marks the beginning of our liberation from the self-defeating, self-perpetuating circle of desire.

II

In several ways *Merchant* seems reassuringly conventional. It seems to present a dualistic opposition between good and evil, with the "good" represented by a male dominant capitalist society that is underwritten by Christianity. The power of the main female character, Portia, seems safely positioned as a function of patriarchal social conventions—as a function of her relationship with men. Her status is defined first by her dead father (with the caskets), then by her ability to impersonate a man (in the trial), and finally by her ability to manipulate a husband (with the ring). Further, because she is not in direct conflict with her father or his society, unlike the heroines of many of Shakespeare's early comedies, her father's entrapment of her is subtle; there is no physical threat. Indeed, she may seem to be a free agent, the rare empowered woman. This play appears at first to threaten neither Elizabethan authority nor its women.

Indeed, it may be the apparently unthreatening nature of this situation which, by pacifying its audience, prepares it to notice that Portia is nonetheless in distress, "a-weary of this great world" (*MV* 1.2.2). She is also nonetheless enclosed within a patriarchal cage, one *more* arbitrary than usual because it comes from the grave. The dead father has bequeathed the beloved daughter a double-bind situation. She has no satisfactory options. If she is true to him, she risks marrying a man she does not love, and risks losing the man (Bassanio) on whom she has settled her affections. If she is untrue to her father, she is "forsworn" (3.2.11).

However, Nerissa's idealist assumption about the caskets seems to minimize this double-bind situation, just as the ideology of platonic love will seem to mystify love relations in the play generally. The love choice and the integrity/virtue issue, she believes, can be unified:

> Your father was ever virtuous, and holy men at their death have good inspirations; therefore the lott'ry that he hath devis'd in these three chests of gold, silver, and lead, whereof who chooses his meaning chooses you, will no doubt never be chosen by any rightly but one who you shall rightly love.
> (1.2.27–33)

Yet if the caskets "speak" as truly as Nerissa assumes, then appearances deceive and nothing, no "meaning" in this physical world, can be certain. What idealism clarifies in this play, it also confuses. Portia's interest in Bassanio is simultaneously encouraged and discouraged. When she seems to make her choice for integrity, therefore, she is "upon the rack" with anxiety (3.2.25).

Although it is true that her integrity seems to be paid off with love (Bassanio does choose rightly), and although the paternally imposed impasse seems resolved by Nerissa's "correct" idealist assumption, there are several uncertainties about this choice and its payoff. First, Bassanio's credentials as the "right" man seem to be based on Portia's agreement with Nerissa that "of all the men that ever [her] foolish eyes look'd upon, [he] was the best deserving a fair lady" (1.2.117–19). Because he has been judged by the eye, the certainty of his "rightness" seems to be in contradiction to the message of the caskets: "All that glisters is not gold" (2.7.65).

Second, the man himself is suspect. In the first scene, his plan for wooing Portia is cast in the circulatory economic terms of venture capitalism. Bassanio borrows money from Antonio in order to finance his pursuit of Portia and her fortune; and he pursues her fortune to pay off his original debt to Antonio. Although we can give the appearance of an idealist justification to this risk-taking venture by the lead casket's injunction that "who chooseth [it] must give and hazard all he hath" (2.7.16), in fact he risks *Antonio*'s money and life, but nothing of his own. The venture itself, even when "justified," nonetheless smacks of self-interested capitalist investment strategies. Portia's appeal to him, he says, is that she

> is a lady richly left,
> And she is fair, and fairer than that word,
> Of wondrous virtues. Sometimes from her eyes
> I did receive fair speechless messages.
>
> (1.1.161–64)

Again, the Neoplatonic idealism associated with the caskets may allow the spendthrift Bassanio to seem unmiserly in contrast to Shylock, and Portia's wealth and beauty to seem manifestations of her inward beauty.[2] However, if the eye is not to be trusted, as the caskets remind us, how can this inward beauty be recognized? If these "fair speechless messages" from her eyes are reminiscent of the eyes as windows of the soul in platonic love, it must also be remembered that the caskets specifically question their truthfulness: "You that choose not by the view, / Chance as fair, and choose as true" (3.2.132–33). The young woman herself clearly judges by visual appearance, cheering when Morocco chooses badly: "Let all of his complexion choose me so" (2.7.79). It is clear that this idealism that the caskets seem to foreground as the dominant value-system of the play—and as the system to which Portia subscribes—points in two opposed directions at the same time.[3]

The problematization of this romantic couple's love is again increased by the question of Portia's integrity. Even should we believe that Bassanio is the "right" man, chosen in a trustworthy way by Portia and shown trustworthy himself, the actual choice of the caskets is also uncertain. Although choosing to subject herself to paternal authority, at the critical juncture when Bassanio is choosing the right casket she causes a song to be sung (3.2.63ff.). This song tells him nothing that Aragon did not know and not enough in itself for Bassanio to choose rightly, but it nonetheless gives him a clear hint to which he does rightly react. Thus the fact that Portia chooses to preside over the caskets may seem to empower her, but it does not erase the ambiguity of her social and moral position.

Portia's ambiguity in the caskets scenes is mirrored by her suitors. Their willingness to hazard is associated not only with love, but also with economics; it therefore cuts two ways, as giving oneself up for love and as venturing in courtship for self-interest. From this perspective, the bond plot's threat to Antonio is simply an intense representation of this same risk factor on which Venice and Belmont, economics and love, male and female values seem to agree. Lawrence Danson has argued that golden circles (ringlets, ducats, rings) help to bind the different aspects of the play together, forming harmony out of a series of paradoxes. Obviously, this implies the possibility of an idealist resolution of its contradictions. But since the value of idealism itself is uncertain, the possibility of resolution seems irreparably compromised. Where Danson sees harmony, I see interpretive impasse.

Indeed, such double-edged dilemmas, in which choices are made but issues are left unresolved, occur throughout the play. Even the clown Launcelot Gobbo is in a double bind that parallels Portia's:

> To be rul'd by my conscience, I should stay with the Jew my master, who (God bless the mark) is a kind of devil; and to run away from the Jew, I should be rul'd by the fiend, who, saving your reverence, is the devil himself. (2.2.22–27)

He is caught in an impasse from which he chooses to run away, knowing however that in doing so he follows the "fiend."

Portia and Launcelot present their impasses, then choose to evade or ignore them. Yet because they are posed in moral terms, the ubiquity of these dilemmas seems to suggest that such values, although deceptive to the uninformed (like Morocco and Aragon), will be clear to those who "see" rightly. Given Portia's and Launcelot's convictions, their problem is not that their positions give them no certain way to win. Winning—getting what they want—is easy for both of them. Their problem is that they have no certain way of being "right" and *also* winning. *Our* problem is that they consistently choose to win, and we cannot be sure how to feel about their morality.

Another of our problems as an audience is that, because of these dilemmas' emergence in several interrelated forms, we cannot easily ignore the characters' evasions. Jessica's example makes our problem particularly obvious. Her dilemma is that she is a Jew's daughter, but she loves a Christian; if she would stay "honest" and marry, she must disobey her father. The patriarchy must therefore shudder as it approves Lorenzo's assertion in the next scene:

> If e'er the Jew her father come to heaven,
> It will be for his gentle daughter's sake,
> And never dare misfortune cross her foot,
> Unless she do it under this excuse,
> That she is issue to a faithless Jew.
>
> (2.4.33–37)

However, approval is crucial here, for this speech also anticipates the Christian/idealist justification for the trial scene's conclusion. In addition, it prepares the way for Jessica's actual leave-taking in act 2, scene 6, when (as in act 2, scene 3) she voices, then erases, her shame:

> For I am much asham'd of my exchange.
> But love is blind, and lovers cannot see
> The pretty follies that themselves commit,
> For if they could, Cupid himself would blush
> To see me thus transformed to a boy.
>
> (2.6.35–39)

She too anticipates the trial scene by calling into question the appropriateness of her sex change from woman into boy, at the same time legitimatizing herself (from the point of view of the caskets) by her evasion of her shame: love is blind. Ten lines later she extends our puzzlement by extending her greed: "I will make fast the doors, and gild myself / With some more ducats." Gratiano's applause of this "gilding" is in specifically religious terms: "Now by my hood, a gentle, and no Jew" (2.6.51). Lorenzo pronounces her "wise, free, and true," presumably on the basis of her golden exterior; she is worthy "to be placed in [his] constant soul" (2.6.56–57).

We might merely think all this to be another example of Christian bigotry, with which the play is gratuitously replete, were it not for the next scene, to which it is juxtaposed. In act 2, scene 7, the prince of Morocco, with the "complexion" which Portia finds objectionable, chooses (like Jessica) gold, yet discovers a death's-head behind it. If his choice is condemned, must not Jessica's be? Portia has connected his complexion to that "of a devil" earlier (1.2.130), and both Launcelot Gobbo (in act 2, scene 2) and Jessica (at the start of act 2, scene 3) have equated the Jewish Shylock with (presumably) this same devil. In addition, his miserliness is related to Morocco's unwillingness to risk. He avoids the lead casket because it "threatens" (2.7.18).[4]

The connection to cautious Shylock is obvious. But in her choice of gold, does not Jessica show herself to be her father's daughter truly? Yet the choice is seconded by the Christians Gratiano and Lorenzo. The caskets are not only problematic in themselves, then, but they also make a negative judgment on Jessica inescapable—and thus not only on Shylock, but on Gratiano and Lorenzo as well.[5] That is, our modern problem with the anti-Semitism of the play is clearly set up as a problem in the text itself, although posed in different terms.

Leonard Tennenhouse attempts to clarify the difficulty of "reading" this text by arguing, "While the theology of the play may be correct and the morality just, the economics are suspect" (Tennenhouse 1980, 66). However, I think we have just seen that the situation is more complex than that. Theology, morality, and economics are not in these scenes independent of one another. On the contrary, they seem completely interwoven, inextricable one from the other, so that the self-cancellation of "approved" values in Jessica's case seems typical rather than unusual. Yet the play's main events are constructed in terms of rivalries and oppositions that lead us to expect to be able to choose white over black, love over revenge, giving over taking, Christian over Jew. The play sets us up to make judgments that it renders impossible to make. Like Portia, Jessica and Launcelot, we too are at an impasse. There are no "right" answers to the dilemmas the play poses, even in its own terms.

III

The treatment of Shylock makes this type of impasse particularly disturbing, but not, as modern viewers might expect, because the play seems to be prejudiced against him. He is, it is true, the "blackest" of the characters from the play's apparent point of view. Associated by both servant and daughter (as well as by his Christian opponent) with the devil, he stands for revenge rather than love, taking rather than giving, miserliness rather than hazard or generosity, Jewishness rather than Christianity. There are even times when he and his values are caricatured. Solanio quotes him as lamenting,

> My daughter! O my ducats! O my daughter!
> Fled with a Christian! O my Christian ducats!
>
> (2.8.15–16)

And at the end of act 3, scene 3, the scene with the famous humanizing "Hath not a Jew eyes?" speech, he becomes a puppet, moving from extreme grief to extreme hatred as Tubal shifts the subject from Jessica's spending her stolen money to Antonio's failed ships.[6]

Yet the real problem for us in the audience is that at the same time that he is represented as "black," Shylock is also presented sympathetically. In act 1, scene 3, the justice of his hatred is clear when Antonio stands up to him to declare that he is ready to spit upon him and kick him again (1.3.130–31). In act 2 Jessica's treatment of her father is clearly just as unfair. And particularly in asserting his common humanity with Christians (3.1.59–73) he does not ask for pity, but asserts that his desire for revenge is taught him by Christian example. He does not render himself pitiable, but strong; he justifies himself by implicating the Christians in his plan for revenge. His moral character is so firm that he threatens the righteousness of the Christian audience. It cannot judge him without judging itself.

This is our problem in the trial scene as well. From the idealist perspective, it may seem that Portia's task here is, by rescuing Antonio from Shylock, to spread into Venice the values taught by the caskets. The appearance-reality issue now takes the form of the opposition between the letter and the spirit of the law, or between justice and mercy. The hazard motif is transplanted in the form of the bond itself, with the trial as the final stage of its playing out. Yet once again the economic and power issues that injected self-interest into an unselfish, giving, loving ideology in the first three acts are present, but now even more explicitly. Indeed, both sides believe in the importance of these issues. Antonio the anti-Semite victim and Shylock the anti-Christian aggressor agree that the letter of the law must at all costs be upheld for the sake of Venetian "trade and profit" (Antonio, 3.3.30). The fate of individuals does not signify when business is at stake, for it is business on which everything—idealism and love and even the very stability of the society itself—depends.

As the scene begins, we seem to be in a comfortably dualistic situation: we are confronted by a powerful and vengeful figure, a "black" Shylock we can hate. He threatens Antonio's life. When the duke asks him to forgive the bond, and equally when Bassanio offers double the bond in payment, Shylock is given a chance to change to "correct" values. Instead, he repeats his belief that he is justified by his resemblance to these same Venetians, both in their reliance on the letter of their law and in their inhumanity (see 4.1.89–103). He is then presented as a caricature of revenge, whetting his knife on the sole of his shoe. Here, just before Portia's entrance as the young lawyer Balthazar, he is most powerfully a stock villain, most appallingly a threat to Antonio and our sense of humanity. We are helpless before him. He has appropriated our belief in law for his own terrible purpose.

Yet in using Venetian laws to oppose the Venetians' desires, he threatens them with self-discovery: with the recognition that their Christian doctrine of humanity (Portia's "mercy") and their law (protecting their "trade and profit") are inconsistent with each other, and that the rules of profit and loss have nothing to do with humaneness. Shylock applies the laws that underwrite capitalism in a direction, and with a rigor, that the Venetians are not used to seeing. They are themselves writ large in Shylock. He is their alien, their true monstrosity externalized.[7] He shows us, in fact, a monstrous image of ourselves, but we are no more ready to accept this fact than are the Venetians in the play. We are in deadly conflict with him here. We want Antonio saved.

It is the heroine Portia, in fact, who makes our spiritual kinship with the Venetians—and with Shylock—visible. She gradually discloses this kinship through a special form of play.[8] In act 3, scene 4, when she explains the role she plans, she describes the techniques by which a girl may play a boy. She refers to speaking "between the change of man and boy / With a reed voice" (3.4.66–67). This is also a description of what the boy actor is in fact doing onstage at precisely this moment by playing Portia (3.4.60–78), except that in her description the transformation is reversed. Such transvestism may appeal to the prurient interest of the audience, but it is also very clearly an analogue to the acting situation in this theater at this moment.[9] It is a metadramatic speech that reminds us that we watch a fiction enacted by a group of impersonators, and that there is a difference between the boy impersonating her, Portia, and the full-grown men who impersonate the male characters like Shylock and Antonio. Part of the "play" element in this scene is to be the contrast between her voice as a male impersonator and the deeper tones of the "truly" male characters.

As a transvestite, she will parody men. She will, she says,

> ... speak of frays
> Like a fine bragging youth, and tell quaint lies,
> How honorable ladies sought my love,
> Which I denying, they fell sick and died.
> I could not do withal. Then I'll repent,
> And wish, for all that, that I had not kill'd them;
> And twenty of these puny lies I'll tell,
> That men shall swear I have discontinued school
> Above a twelvemonth. I have within my mind
> A thousand raw tricks of these bragging Jacks,
> Which I will practice.
>
> (3.4.68–78)

This parodic spirit is crucial for our understanding of the trial scene, for it is by seeming to join her male opponent, Shylock, that her parody defeats him. By playing, she empowers herself to use his own weapon, the letter of the law, and to carry it further than anyone can imagine—to parody Shylock's inhumanity.[10] She shows us what he is by doing it better herself.

When Portia-Balthazar enters this polarized, threatening situation, we receive her as our champion against the Jew. She knows this—has engineered this—and so begins reassuringly with the pieties we approve: a repetition of the duke's request for mercy, and an increase in Bassanio's generosity to "thrice" the bond (4.1.234). However, because Shylock is stubborn, Portia must then insist on the letter of the law, even to commanding Antonio to "prepare your bosom for his knife" (4.1.245). To our dismay, she seems no cleverer than the others. Rather, she allows the tension to increase; for 138 lines we move inexorably nearer the actual deed. The noose of the letter of the law is drawn tighter and tighter. Portia is "a Daniel" (4.1.223), a "noble judge" (4.1.246), a "wise and upright," "most rightful" and "most learned judge" (4.1.250, 301, 304).

When the tables are turned, our tension is released, the threat destroyed. The tables are turned in a surprisingly comic reversal. Shylock is beaten by the letter of the very Venetian law he had championed.

Gratiano emphasizes this reversal again and again by throwing Shylock's former words of praise for Portia back in his face (4.1.312–13, 323, 333–34, 340–41).[11] The manifest irony of the fact that he is beaten on his own terms underscores the justice of his defeat, for he has, in a sense, defeated himself. Portia's victory is a *coup de théâtre*.[12]

The struggle is now over. Not only can Shylock have no blood (4.1.309–12), nor a hair's weight too much or too little flesh (4.1.324–31), but the penalty he must risk is confiscation of all property, and death. Shylock gives up the suit, Antonio is free, and we relax, no longer threatened by him.

Portia, however, does not stop. She continues inexorably to press the letter of the law against Shylock, now using it as an offensive rather than a defensive weapon. Her resemblance to him therefore becomes more and more clear, and more and more alarming. His own weapon is not only used against him but is used *in the same way,* and by our champion, our proxy onstage.[13] She plays it out as far as it can be played. Because he is an alien who has sought the life of a Venetian citizen, all his possessions and his life are at hazard *even though he has renounced the suit* and the use of the law (4.1.346–62). Gradually, our delight in Portia's victory wanes. Gradually, the weight of the law comes to press as inexorably upon Shylock as it had upon Antonio. Not only must he give up all his possessions, but Antonio's "mercy" is that he must change religions as well (4.1.387). Portia's parody begins to seem indistinguishable from Shylock's inhumanity.

By the time he leaves the stage, Shylock might seem pitiable, despite the fact that he would have been as bad or worse to Antonio. However, his defeat is precisely what we ourselves, as well as Portia and her Christian friends, wished. Yet now that we have it, it feels very uncomfortable. This legal system which Portia, by our proxy, has administered now stands exposed as political, as an exercise of power rather than justice, as a defense of the privileged status quo. We are *not* morally better than Shylock, nor is Portia, nor are the Venetians. Our difference from him consists only in privilege and therefore power.

While we watch Portia slowly play out our own profound resemblance to Shylock, twisting the same noose of law on which he relied tighter and tighter, her "reed voice" constantly reminds us that she plays a role, that she *acts* at doing what Shylock truly believed in and did singlemindedly, that she mocks Shylock as she destroys him. And because she has shown us that we are like them all—Portia, Shylock, the Venetians—this process becomes progressively more painful. The "play" that induced us to see ourselves in relation to Portia now shows the hideousness of that self. By fully playing out our unrecognized feelings of self-confidence and self-righteousness and even vengeance, she has exposed them, has shown us a reflection of ourselves that is unpalatable.[14] Our wish-fulfillment has become our nightmare. Our proxy has become our demon.

In laughing at Shylock, then recognizing ourselves in him, we may go further still: we may see that we too must give ourselves up if we are to be true to our ideas of Christian virtue, and if we are to avoid the painful emotional conflict with which Portia has caused us to respond to her "play." Does this perception lead us to long for God to batter our hearts—for some forcible conversion to turn us wholly to virtue, some such thing as Shylock receives against his will? Can we justify Shylock's end by saying that he gets what he needs and what we hope for ourselves?[15] Or, recognizing the political nature of the law, can we justify it anyway in the name not of justice but, like Shylock and Antonio, of the state and its economic foundation? If we can do either of these things, this consciously willed self-subjugation will seem very like the one promoted by *Richard III* and *Dream,* as well as by Holbein and Hilliard.

A Portia no more compromised than Theseus or Oberon, a Portia representing a benevolent though arbitrary status quo, might indeed achieve this conclusion. But it is difficult to escape our image of Portia as the cruel tightener of the noose of a law whose political roots she has exposed. And it is difficult to separate her from her earlier context, a context which she seems here to have denied; it is difficult to forget the contrast between this image of inhumanity exposed and the idealism of true love, religion, and mercy that she has professed. Shylock is finished in this play, banished in the interests of constructing for the conclusion an apparently carefree Belmont that can seem to harmonize finance and religion and love. Yet if this play is about anything, it is—transparently, we have seen—about *not* trusting appearances. Ironically, Portia herself is inextricably included in our pervasive distrust. Indeed, the image she has shown us of ourselves must make us wish to distance ourselves from her. She therefore prejudices the final movement of the play.

IV

This final movement opens with Bassanio's offer to repay Balthazar/Portia for the trial with her own money, money which also happens to be the "three thousand ducats due unto the Jew" (4.1.411). As usual, he offers nothing of his own. Portia, who is not represented as stupid, refuses this payment, pronouncing herself "well paid" by the trial's satisfactory conclusion (4.1.415). We may well shudder at her satisfaction. The man whom she has broken has left the stage only fifteen lines before. Just as discomforting, economic terms continue to dominate the play's noblest sentiments. Bassanio maintains this pattern by repeating his offer to repay kindness with money, though this time considered "as a tribute, / Not as fee" (4.1.422-23); he shows no thought that a different kind of payment might be more appropriate. Generous and courtly, Bassanio is naïve about values; he is a young aristocrat whom the world has never much tested. There has always been a patron like Antonio, or a lover like Portia, to smooth his passages and pay his debts. Portia will now educate him about the costs of privilege.[16]

She does so by inventing and taking charge of the play's third bond plot, the game of the rings.[17] In effect, she replies to Bassanio's plea, "Let me give you something," with "Give me everything. Give me the symbol of your love and marriage, the source of your wealth." She puts him in a double bind not unlike the one her father had created for her. For Bassanio to be true to his love for and gratitude to Antonio, he must betray his wife by giving the ring. To be true to his wife, he must deny "tribute" to Balthazar, thus denying his ties to Antonio. Like her father, Portia constructs an impasse from which there is no apparent escape. This world of love, at least as Portia administers it, is indeed "the real world" of hard choices. Previously, Bassanio witnessed an adversarial trial situation which Portia then apparently resolved to his satisfaction. Now the disguised lawyer manipulates her naïve young husband into a fuller participation in this adversarial way of seeing the world. She does not allow Bassanio to avoid choosing (though she herself may have).

At the same time, her ironic remarks make it clear to us in the audience that all of this is merely another of her games:

> And if your wife be not a mad woman,
> And know how well I have deserv'd his ring,
> She would not hold out enemy for ever
> For giving it to me.
>
> (4.1.445-48)

We see her skill as she secures Antonio's gloves (4.1.426) and Bassanio's ring. We see her take into her own hands the loving pledges of her husband and his friend (her rival?), so that they are huddled together within her power. As master of this game, she extends the power role she gradually created (or unfolded) as she played the trial out to its successive stages. It is the same scene, without change of place or disguise: her parodic "reed voice" has merely turned from Shylock toward Bassanio. As we have learned by our own experience, no one is safe from Portia.

The play's tone seems to change at the beginning of act 5 when the ring game is interrupted by Lorenzo and Jessica. They seem to create an idealist context in which we might see Portia when she returns to the game, undisguised, for the play's conclusion. However, although their self-teasing love duet continues the game motif, it too compromises the play's idealism. Their song is of famously unhappy lovers, culminating in Lorenzo's

> In such a night
> Did Jessica steal from the wealthy Jew
> And with an unthrift love did run from Venice,
> As far as Belmont.
>
> (5.1.14–17)

And in Jessica's response:

> In such a night
> Did young Lorenzo swear he lov'd her well,
> Stealing her soul with many vows of faith,
> And ne'er a true one.
>
> (5.1.17–20)

According to idealist (casket) ideology, love *should* be "unthrift," and we know that Lorenzo encouraged the theft. Lorenzo's speech seems merely a mock accusation, part of the lovers' game. Yet at the same time he reminds us that she enthusiastically gilded herself with money stolen from her own father at her lover's urging. We are therefore also reminded that love and money are inseparable in this play, and that the idealist caskets are made to mystify this equation, to make a contradiction seem a paradox. Lorenzo makes transparent the bigotry and greed on which their ideal love is based. Pretending not to believe Lorenzo's professions of love, Jessica continues their love-game—and its exposure of idealism—by appropriating his economic vocabulary for her own counteraccusation: by "stealing," he has compromised both her "soul" and his own vows of love. The caskets' contradictions between economy and love, bigotry and idealism, are powerfully recalled and brought forward to create the context in which Portia makes her final appearance.

The theme of law and forgiveness so compromised in the trial just past is also brought forward in a diminished form with Lorenzo's conclusion:

> In such a night
> Did pretty Jessica (like a little shrow)
> Slander her love, and he forgave it her.
>
> (5.1.20–22)[18]

In connecting several major motifs of the first four acts to Portia's game-playing mock trial of Bassanio in act 5, then, the duet actually strengthens the impact of the main problematizing issues on the conclusion.

Lorenzo's Neoplatonizing (5.1.54–88) is equally problematic.[19] His clear implication that on this night, in this place, the most ideal love possible exists within "this muddy vesture of decay" (5.1.64) seems perhaps too obviously the kind of preparation which the mistress of Belmont herself would wish designed for her entrance, and too much a contrast to the way we have learned to see her. As the musicians start to play, then, and Portia and Nerissa enter disguised as "a holy hermit and her maid" (5.1.33), speaking about good deeds (5.1.91) and philosophy and music (5.1.93–110) somewhat in the vein of Lorenzo, we might see this too as a carefully staged situation. Indeed, once they are recognized and the disguise is of no further use, both the philosophy and the music abruptly cease.

This continued undercutting of idealism and of Portia maintains our distrust. Her lover's game with her husband sustains it. First she makes him squirm by repeating Nerissa's complaint about the lost ring, then promises to be a loving wife in terms calculated to deliver a threat of adultery:

> Let not that doctor e'er come near my house
> Since he hath got the jewel that I loved,
> And that which you did swear to keep for me,
> I will become as liberal as you,
> I'll not deny him any thing I have,
> No, not my body nor my husband's bed.
> Lie not a night from home. Watch me like Argus;
> If you do not, if I be left alone,
> Now by mine honor, which is yet mine own,
> I'll have that doctor for [my] bedfellow.
>
> (5.1.223–33)

This threat is not only to the husband's honor, his right to his wife as exclusive property, but also to the very foundation of patrilineal society. Portia underscores the subversive power of women and the fragility of the male position which requires dominance. She shows that the key to this dominance is, as with the caskets' love and the trial, to "hazard," to give up control of one's destiny. Both Bassanio and Antonio do this. Bassanio is sufficiently chastened into awareness of his wrong choice that he begs forgiveness (5.1.240) and pardon (5.1.247). Antonio "dare[s] be bound again" (5.1.251), subordinating himself once more to the desire of his friend, this time in the full awareness that Bassanio has chosen again and will be Portia's. For each, the cost of male privilege within Venetian society is surrender. Only when her lesson has been learned does the victor reward the principal players—Antonio with his ships (with "life and living," 5.1.286), Bassanio with her ring and an explanation of the truth.

However, it is not clear what Bassanio need be forgiven for. It is not clear that his choice to give the ring to Balthazar was the wrong choice—indeed, Portia's ironic ending to act 4, scene 1 shows that even she does not see his choice as wrong. Her ring game, then, is arbitrary and unfair. Nor, in her lengthy disclosure of the "truth" at the end of the play, does she ever explicitly give herself back to Bassanio. This act is implicit in the return of the ring, but she lacks the grace to say it. Instead she mystifies the situation. Previously Antonio had been bound to Shylock by his body; now he is bound to Portia by his soul (5.1.249–53). Portia combines the three thematic strands of love, religion, and economics by accepting Antonio's soul as "surety" (5.1.255) for Bassanio's faithfulness, but she herself is still in the power position, dispensing favors on her terms, at her pace.

In fact, by bringing the economic theme forward into Belmont she reminds us that she, even more than Shylock, has manipulated the idea of obligation in this play, has demanded others to hazard, has placed them under bond. If she gets away with it, it is because she mystifies these bonds with religion and love. Because of her superior manipulative ability, she has beaten Shylock at his own game, and transformed his bond into her ring.[20] But it is still a bond of power in which wealth and love and religion are all subsumed, as the compression of terms from all these modes of discourse here makes clear.

V

The two men kneeling before Portia at the play's conclusion, Antonio and Bassanio, are the main debtors in this play about obligation. They are both male, they have both defaulted on their debts (Antonio cannot pay Shylock, Bassanio gives away Portia's ring), and in each case Portia nullifies the penalty. We might add to these facts the similarities between the apparent male antagonists Antonio and Shylock in the three main thematic issues of the play: their religious bigotry, their drive for profit, and their indifference (if not hostility) to heterosexual love. In this light, Portia's unconditional victories may seem positive. Her cancellation of debts might seem like mercy and, in conjunction with her defeat of the malicious creditor Shylock, might even make her seem to deny the importance of economic values in favor of religious tolerance and love.

At the same time, however, each of these victories concludes a threat by Portia to legal and economic principles (represented by Shylock's bond and Bassanio's marital rights of possession) that underlie the systematic acquisition, preservation, and patrilineal continuance of wealth, and that thus underwrite the stability of the society. In this different light Portia is not only untrustworthy in herself; she also exposes the unruly woman's ability to disguise the danger she poses to a stable patriarchy by paying lip service to virtue and love. Further, the inconsistencies between her idealism and her practice expose the similar inconsistencies of the male merchant aristocracy. By subverting the play's idealism, her exhibition of personal power subverts the state's legitimation as well as her own. Her final "victory" contains the potential destruction of both herself and her society.[21]

Gratiano's typically male anxiety at the play's conclusion might equally be ours, then:

> Well, while I live I'll fear no other thing
> So sore, as keeping safe Nerissa's ring.

Though in a different key, he echoes our own gradual loss of ideology as we have watched this play. Like him, we can no longer keep our facile assumption of personal safety, no longer distance ourselves from the disturbing implications of events in the play, no longer even believe that we understand them, that we have at least intellectual control over them. We are left without interpretive options. The comfortable responses— seeing Shylock as a villain who can be a scapegoat for our cultural disease, and seeing Portia as a heroine who makes Venice safe for business and law through love and mercy, then safely subsides into wifely subservience—are cut off. Not only are both sides of the opposition (represented by these two characters) problematized, but they have also been represented as profoundly similar. More difficult still, we in the audience have been forced to internalize them, to see ourselves in them both, and in both positive and negative terms. We have thus been taught to distrust and even to fear what most we want: love, money, the self-justification of religion. And we have been taught to distrust not only Shylock and Portia, but ourselves.

Nor does this play efface itself and the discomfort it causes, in the manner of the earlier plays. Portia's role-playing is transparent, and thus exposes the play as the playwright's construction. However, unlike *Dream* and *Richard III, Merchant* does not use this self-referentiality to disclaim its own significance. It is, in fact, no more self-effacing than the female character who is its agent. As we have seen, the contrary is true: the play's "alterity" actually emphasizes the contradictions among its voices, facilitates our internalization of them, and thus heightens our own experiential validation of the impasse. We are not at last pacified into self-subjugation, as we may be in the earlier plays. We are not offered that, or any other, option. Antonio's and Bassanio's final virtue is not only coerced, but coerced by a force inimical to social stability as we "normally" understand it, and certainly as Elizabethan society understood and practiced it. Or, from the opposite point of view, the cost of Venetian stability —of law and business as well as love and marriage—has been the defeat of its practitioners: first of all Shylock, then of Antonio and Bassanio. The cost of male privilege is male subjugation.

Shakespeare, then, seems in this play to challenge the status quo at every level. How could this be?

One possibility is that the inclusion of apparently villainous Shylock and apparently ideal Portia gives his audience a chance to shape his play into terms it wishes to believe. Perhaps Shakespeare, through his experiences with audiences, knew that most people subscribe to a version of "reality" that is, on one level or another, a product of wishful thinking. Perhaps he knew that every reading of this play, like every version of the world, is largely produced by the reader's desire so to read—indeed, by his *need* to project his wishful thoughts onto a screen so that he can believe in them. *Merchant*'s impasse quality, its process of foreclosing on interpretive options, makes the fact clear that its dramatic form is essentially empty of meaning—like the world itself, including the Elizabethan world, on which we write our own projections. It highlights the nature of all our "readings." It throws the play's emphasis back on ourselves, just as Portia and Shylock do.

Interestingly, the conventional desire to interpret against the villain and in favor of the heroine seems in this play to be in conflict with another conventional desire: to justify the present form of social order on which our security in the world seems to rest. It may be that Portia enacts one of patrilineal society's greatest fears, the nightmare that Queen Elizabeth might assert her royal power in her own person, as a woman, rather than by playing self-effacing roles. Portia erases neither her female sexuality nor her gender, unlike the historical Elizabeth, who played the roles of virgin queen and prince.[22] Our internalized demonic vision of Portia at the end of Shylock's trial is also imaged as an objective power loosed within society to destroy (change) it, to subjugate us (males) with Bassanio. This image cannot be embraced; once seen, however, it cannot be rejected as untrue to the play, nor domesticated as unfearful. Our composure therefore requires a reading of the play and society in which this vision is rendered invisible.

But we have been led to see it. In Shakespeare's dramatic situation both its impasse and the emphasis it throws back on the projected nature of our interpretation seem inescapably visible. Confused and threatened from both within and without, we in its audience now find ourselves in free fall without net or parachute.

As we have seen, however, our frightening recognition of this confusion can be fortunate:

> According to the Buddhist tradition, the spiritual path is the process of cutting through our confusion, of uncovering the awakened state of mind.

In our confusion,

> we adopt sets of categories which serve as handles, as ways of managing phenomena. The most fully developed products of this tendency are ideologies, the systems of ideas that rationalize, justify and sanctify our lives. Nationalism, communism, existentialism, Christianity, Buddhism —all provide us with identities, rules of action, and interpretations of how and why things happen as they do. . . . [Such concepts] are used as tools to solidify our world and ourselves. If a world of nameable things exists, then "I" as one of the nameable things exists as well. (Trungpa 1973, 4–7)

But as we saw in *Richard III,* this reciprocal belief in our own and our world's solidity creates the vicious cycle of samsara that is, in the Buddhist view, "the root of our suffering" (Trungpa 1973, 8–9). In this confusion,

> If we enjoy pleasure, we are afraid to lose it; we strive for more and more pleasure or try to contain it. If we suffer in pain, we want to escape it. We experience dissatisfaction all the time. All activities contain dissatisfaction or

> pain, continuously.... We are continually struggling to maintain and enhance ourselves. (Trungpa 1973, 152–53)

Trungpa brings this view of human confusion closer to our study of Shakespeare by comparing it to a theatrical situation:

> In order to operate as an individual, we have a portable stage set that we carry around with us. We constantly make ourselves into a little theatre display piece. We do that all the time in our life situation: we have our appropriate backdrop and we have our appropriate lighting and we have our appropriate actor, namely us, "me"—all this that comes on the stage could be included. We do that constantly, always. So here's a game, or play, that's taking place constantly.

The key to ending the suffering that confusion brings is not necessarily to change these roles. In themselves, the natures of the roles are not particularly significant. Rather, it is simply necessary to see that they *are* roles, and to adopt the same attitude toward them that we have already taken toward stage plays:

> ... we [Buddhists] are working on the area where our attitude could be changed much more than the set of the theatre: looking at how you do it and why you do it, if you have to do so or if you don't. (Trungpa 1974, 20–21)

In *Merchant,* Shakespeare forces us to see that no matter which way we turn, our ideologies dissolve, our attempts to categorize experience end in impasse. He forces us, that is, to see our confusion for the theatrical delusion it is. This is the basic recognition from which the Buddhist path begins.

Although, as we have seen Terry Eagleton remark, the world is "other" than the theater (1986, 13), the Buddhist view sees this "other" to be a mimic of the stage. It sees that both the stage and "the world" (as conventionally conceived) "lie." Eagleton too knows that our conception of the world is as much a text of our own creation as is our version of a playscript, for he asks a corollary question that applies equally to the stage and "life": "If everyone is defined by what they are not, fashioned in relation to some other," can there be any absolute identity (Eagleton 1986, 23)? This question loosed by contemporary linguistic theory is easily rephrased in Buddhist terms: Can there be a solid self?

The Merchant of Venice has cast us off into this midair intersection of Derrida and Buddhism. The question is enabled by an attitude toward experience that allows us to see through our social envelope. It allows us to escape that formative power of society over our consciousness that is alleged by Marx and many new historicists, and that is generally assumed by Foucault in his interrogation of social structures. This radical shift in awareness is the prerequisite to all change that is to be truly surprising, that is unconditioned by prior assumptions, even those we have held about particular versions of society. This awareness that *Merchant* teaches is truly revolutionary in its possibilities.

In the following chapters, we shall see Shakespeare exploring in detail the difficulties and the possibilities to which this awareness opens us.

4
The Cause of Suffering and the Birth of Compassion in *Julius Caesar*

In several subsequent plays, Shakespeare enlarged his exploration of both the frightening and the fortunate implications of this awareness of our confusion about the self and the world. Indeed, as he began more and more to emphasize the tragic mode of perception, his shift may seem natural. Tragedy (and history, as we have seen with *Richard III*) is specifically the discourse of the empowered. Linking themselves to the inexorable turning of the wheel of fortune, its principal characters place the ebb and flow of political power in the foreground. As a result, from the Buddhist point of view, they also enact in this foreground the first two of the Buddha's Four Noble Truths, perceptions that by now may seem familiar: first, that suffering is a constant in human life; and second, that the cause of this suffering is our mistaken belief in a solid self and our consequent endless self-entrapment in the vicious cycle of hope and fear—our constant striving to achieve happiness by satisfying our desires and, once they are satisfied, our fear of losing this needed self-confirmation.[1]

The play *Julius Caesar* presents this confusion differently than *Merchant*. Instead of closing interpretive options down, it opens its major events and characters to ambiguous, even contradictory, possibilities. At the same time, it presents one character of extremely noble intentions who is driven to face his impasse-situation more directly than any character we have so far examined.Thus this play dramatizes an alternative version of confusion, as well as a fuller representation of how it works within us to create an impasse situation, and of how impossible such situations are to escape. Awareness of the cycle of samsara is in this way shown to be the frightening yet necessary ground of nirvana.

The play's political foreground introduces us to the openness of our interpretive options at once, with the ambiguous phenomenon of the rising

Caesar. The humor of his supporters the plebeians, their plays on "sole" and "soul," on "with awl" and "withal," their ambiguous use of "conscience," "mend," and "out" (1.1.13–26), are too obvious to seem clever. This wit has a further political agenda, however, for it shows the plebeians' deliberate defiance of the tribunes' authority. When with greater eloquence and, apparently, reason, these tribunes chastise them as a changeable mob (1.1.32–62), the criticism therefore seems just and Caesar's cause suspect. However, we might also hear self-righteousness in the tribunes' rebukes, and we might remember that the discourse of authority often cloaks itself in the language of reason. When in addition we remember that these tribunes are elected to represent the interests of these very plebeians, it becomes clear that they have a vested interest in opposing their own constituency's support of Caesar: if he becomes emperor, the tribunes will be out of a job. Further, it is the tribune Murellus's unaccountable failure to understand the cobbler's trade (1.1.12) which makes the circumstances of the plebeians' puns seem contrived, and this in turn undercuts what cleverness they may have. The first scene, then, introduces the fact of social discord in Rome, torn by two antagonistic political attitudes between which we cannot choose.[2] This political ambiguity intensifies in the second scene. Despite Cassius's egoism and his admission that he is trying to manipulate Brutus (1.1.308–15), his cause has great appeal. His distrust of unnatural ambition; his idea of the republic's senate as a group of noble equals; and, in general, his appeal to the idea of freedom—all have power. On the other hand, in act 2 we see the private side of things more fully, and this does not give us confidence in the conspirators. At 2.1.10–34, Brutus makes it clear that he will kill Caesar because Caesar "may" forget his human limitations and the general good. Brutus concedes that he has never known Caesar's "affections sway'd / More than his reason," but because he "might change" he must die. Under such reasoning, which of us is safe?

This discomfort with the conspirators is shortly generalized. Act 2, scene 2 fills us to satiation with their deceit. The plotters crowd into Caesar's house, permeating his private world with manipulative deceivers so that his death seems inescapable. At the same time, Calphurnia's concern for Caesar, and his for her, humanizes him. This domestic scene that precedes the murder makes it difficult to see Caesar as the monster pictured in the conspirators' rhetoric. By the end of this second act, we are watching the inexorable progression of events with a kind of helpless horror.

The larger dimensions of existence that stand behind the political foreground and occasionally penetrate it (the dimensions of prodigy, prophecy, dream, and ghost) are even more intensely mysterious, both to the characters and to us, though in different ways. Casca summarizes the characters' general insecurity in an inscrutable universe with a literal description of its behavior: "all the sway of earth / Shakes like a thing unfirm" (1.1.3–4). However, to us in the audience there is another level of uncertainty. The unnatural events described at 1.3.3–28 and 63–68 (and again at 2.2.17–24), as well as Calphurnia's dream in act 2, scene 2, each have equally plausible yet contradictory interpretations, and in each case both of these interpretations are "true." In the case of the prodigies and unnatural events, only one interpretation is given onstage, by Cassius: that Caesar has grown larger than any man should, and is about to create an imbalance in the universe by becoming emperor. The prodigies of nature reflect the unnaturally "prodigious" growth of Caesar (1.3.77–78), such

> that heaven hath infus'd them with these spirits,
> To make them instruments of fear and warning
> Unto some monstrous state.
>
> (1.3.69–71)

From this perspective, the prodigies are signs that Caesar should not be crowned. However, there is an unspoken but well-known Elizabethan alternative. These prodigies come immediately after the scene in which the conspiracy plan is broached to Brutus. They can therefore be "read" as a cosmic reflection of the horror of the thing planned (and to be accomplished, as we in the audience know from our history books): the murder of Caesar. If he is not in fact crowned, he is certainly viewed by the general populace as their leader; he is all but emperor; he is certainly the order-figure.[3] One conventional response for an Elizabethan audience would be to see the prodigies as reflections of the chaos that will inevitably attend the murder of authority. *Both these possibilities are proven "true" in the play.* In act 3, scene 1, we will see that Caesar is indeed ripe for dying, yet the rest of the play will present the universal chaos that results from his death.

The same contradiction applies to Calphurnia's dream of Caesar's bleeding statue (2.2.76–79). She herself interprets the dream as a portent that Caesar will die if he goes to the senate on the Ides of March. Decius deliberately tries to mislead Caesar into the opposite interpretation, that "great Rome shall suck / Reviving blood" from Caesar's leadership (2.2.87–88). Despite Decius's deceitful motive, it is again clear that *both* interpretations are "true." Caesar *does* die, as Calphurnia fears. But also, his spirit lives and nourishes the empire. Antony's swearing vengeance is accomplished in Caesar's name, and Cassius and Brutus both die with his name on their lips.[4]

This is a universe, then, all of whose dimensions—the individual, the political, and the cosmic; the human, the animal, and the heavenly; the dead and the living—are ambiguous and yet interpenetrate one another. This is a play world which is not only opaque and unreadable, but inescapable as well. Brutus is placed at the center of this pressurized world's gravity, its microcosm. The division within his mind that he vents in 2.1.10–34 parallels the political division in society and is a microcosm of the uncertain cosmos. The shift from the public places of act 1 to the private homes of act 2, which are then themselves penetrated by the group of conspirators, suggests a similar interpenetration of public and private life. Jonathan Goldberg, in a different context, and focusing on act 1 alone, has made a similar observation about the "continuity of inner life and outer life, private and public" (Goldberg 1983, 168).

The claustrophobic nature of this situation for Brutus is intensified by our awareness in the audience that he is trapped in a double-bind situation, partly self-created. On the one hand, his soliloquy opening act 2, scene 1, shows Brutus to have the noblest and most unselfish of motives: he will be his nation's savior, even though it means sacrificing the man he loves. He creates for himself an imperative for action even though certainty is impossible. Given his public conscience and his personal identification with his own integrity, he has no choice but to kill Caesar. However, things are never so simple. The Elizabethan audience might recognize a second moral imperative: to avoid the risk of civil war, general misery, and universal discord.[5] Although Brutus himself does not state this view, we cannot miss it. Calphurnia reminds us of it at 2.2.30–31:

> When beggars die there are no comets seen;
> The heavens themselves blaze forth the death of princes.

If there were further doubt, of course the events subsequent to the assassination would be enough to resolve them. Caesar must not be killed.

Nor are we merely passive observers of Brutus's no-win situation. We too have seen Caesar's blind pride. We have heard him say, in assessing Cassius,

> I rather tell thee what is to be fear'd
> Than what I fear; for always I am Caesar.
>
> (1.2.211–12)

And we have watched him find a way to keep his image of greatness while justifying his decision not to go to the Capitol:

> Cannot, is false; and that I dare not, falser:
> I will not come today.
>
> (2.2.63–64)

Although we may see the weakness in Brutus's argument, we have information of our own. We too are pulled in two directions at once about Caesar, and this uncertainty allows us to appreciate the double-sidedness of Brutus's position. Yet it is his position, not ours; it is his insistence on nobility, on taking action and making things right when he cannot know what "right" is, that most fully entraps him.

Caesar, though ambiguous, seems less complicated. He is ignorant from the start. Uniquely, he thinks he knows who he is and what he wants. Like Richard of Gloucester, he resorts to the stage to get the crown, opening the play with a formal procession, a show of power and majesty for the city ("Set on, and leave no ceremony out," 1.2.11). As part of this show, he enacts "appropriate" humility (offstage) by refusing the offer of the crown three times (1.2.221–47). But although Caesar knows the pageant he performs to be a pretense, the role he plays in it is of the great man he actually believes himself to be. It is because of this belief in the role he plays (in defiance of his knowledge that it is a role) that the script he writes for himself is so easily incorporated into that written by the conspirators. He, not the soothsayer, is a dreamer.

Despite his inner conflict, Brutus is not radically different. It is his belief in his own nobility that shows his blindness. His discomfort with the secrecy and deceit needed to kill a great leader (2.1.77–85), and his discomfort in general with widespread killing, not to mention chaos, indicates not only his moral values, but his naïveté. He still believes in the world's stability and clarity. He believes in himself and his ability to save Rome, and so he joins the conspiracy. It is, ironically, these naïvely self-serving beliefs that make him the prime architect of just that instability and chaos from which he meant to save his beloved country.

It is also this naïveté that moves him to ritualize the murder.[6] Brutus wishes to transform the assassination into a pure and cleansing act: "Let's be sacrificers, but not butchers," "purgers, not murderers" (2.1.166, 180). He wishes to enact a tragedy with Aristotelian effects. The audience, Rome, will be purged of its impurity. He is therefore scrupulous about the form of the act. Every move must reflect those high principles that alone can justify the deed. Thus he refuses to swear an oath:

>   ... unto bad causes swear
>   Such creatures as men doubt; but do not stain
>   The even virtue of our enterprise,
>   Nor th' insuppressive mettle of our spirits.
>
>   (2.1.131–32)

And thus he leads a carefully selected cast of Roman aristocrats to Caesar, that they may first display the nature of the victim to be sacrificed, then perform the ritual murder itself. They begin by asking him to be "moved," to change his mind in human sympathy for another, and his reaction shows that Brutus's guess was right. Caesar delivers a showpiece of tragic *hybris* (3.1.58–73). He compares himself to the one star perfect enough to be constant—the "northern star," the pole star about whose central position the heavens revolve. He cannot even "pray to move" (3.1.59). He believes in his role of righteous power, a role that the circling conspirators provide him the occasion to play out to its ultimate self-apotheosis when Cinna renews the request for mercy, and Caesar again refuses: "Hence! wilt thou lift up Olympus?" (3.1.74). Caesar is revealed as the appropriate victim. He deserves to be sacrificed.

Caesar has risen to great heights, and is on the brink of being crowned emperor. The wheel of fortune turns. From the tragic perspective—from the perspective of Brutus's ritual pattern of action—Caesar *should fall now*. We cannot fail to see this. When, in his funeral oration, Brutus emphasizes that he killed Caesar "as he was / ambitious" (3.2.26–27), that he gave him "death for his / ambition" (28–29), Brutus explains not only his own motives, but also the relationship between the wheel of fortune, *hybris,* and the fall of the tragic hero. He appeals, that is, to our sense of theatrical genre as well as to our political understanding. If there is uncertainty about the political efficacy of killing an order-figure, the act is further justified by appealing to the rules of tragedy. It is mystified by its ritual/aesthetic form.

As part of this ritual, each conspirator stabs the victim. Then, the sacrifice done, the circle opens again to show the victim's corpse to the populace, and to complete the ritual:

>   Stoop, Romans, stoop,
>   And let us bathe our hands in Caesar's blood
>   Up to the elbows, and besmear our swords;
>   Then walk we forth, even to the market-place,
>   And waving our red weapons o'er our heads,
>   Let's all cry, "Peace, freedom, and liberty!"
>
>   (3.1.105–10)

With their arms and swords splashed with blood, Brutus's cry of "Peace" may seem too obvious a mystification to succeed. Yet we do not question Brutus's noble sincerity about Rome. Rather, we question his wisdom, for it is this very sincerity that empowers his belief in the righteousness of his ritual, and in the truthfulness to himself of his role in it. Ironically, the sacrificer at last seems as naïve, as blind, as ignorant, as does his victim. They both believe equally in their self-created and grandiose roles: Caesar as emperor, Brutus as savior.

This grandiose view and its exposure is made virtually explicit in the next exchange:

> *Cas.* ... How many ages hence
> Shall this our lofty scene be acted over
> In states unborn and accents yet unknown!
> *Bru.* How many times shall Caesar bleed in sport,
> That now on Pompey's basis lies along
> No worthier than the dust!
> *Cas.* ... So oft as that shall be,
> So often shall the knot of us be call'd
> The men that gave their country liberty.
>
> (3.1.111–18)

From the self-glorifying point of view of the conspirators, this is such a great deed that it will be remembered through reenactment in "many ages hence," "in states unborn and accents yet unknown." From the point of view of the theater audience, however, the speech is self-referential: this present representation of *Julius Caesar* is obviously the ready example of such a reenactment, of such a remystification of the murder. And, this metadramatic dimension of the play opened, we may see that Caesar played to the cue that the conspirators offered him because it was perfectly designed for his own script; he was perfectly prepared to glorify himself. He fits himself precisely into the tragic script prepared for him by Brutus by playing his own role, his own self-image. Caesar, that is, is perfectly cast in two plays at once, the second (Brutus's) enclosing the first (his own). He is self-entrapped. Shakespeare makes this fact evident by representing it in transparently theatrical form.

Seen from Brutus's perspective, this tragic play within the play has a different effect, one very like that of illusionism in the visual arts. (For a fuller discussion of this issue, see the analyses of Masaccio, Mantegna, Romano, and Carracci in Appendix A.) It enacts a "real" event, the murder of Caesar, the effect of which depends on viewer recognition that it is not what it seems to be (not a murder). Thus the artist, Brutus, gives it a ritualized tragic form, and it is this form of ritual sacifice, this artwork, which is in fact the "reality" Brutus intends. He makes the manufactured nature of its form transparent so that he himself will be seen to be inscribed within it, so that his motives will become more important to the viewer than the deed itself, so that his motives will determine how the deed is received. Brutus gives a carefully crafted construction that contains himself as gift to the people of Rome. In both self-glorification and selfless idealism, he tries to make himself rather than Caesar the central issue of his tragedy.

This self-ennoblement may work briefly: we see the murder from the tragic (rather than the political) perspective that Brutus gives it, and see that from this perspective blind Caesar needed to die. However, like Caesar, Brutus plays his role out to its ultimate extension, insisting on enacting a conclusion to his tragedy, a funeral ritual in which he will explain the meaning of his tragic act, will spell out his motive. Like Caesar too, Brutus plays his role perfectly. And, as in the case of Caesar, this perfectly played role destroys him; he is blind to its danger because he believes in its "truth"—that he is indeed his country's savior and that this will be evident to everyone, once explained. He has the naïveté of the idealist: his motives are pure, and so his acts must be efficacious.

Therefore he lets Antony live, he lets Antony speak, and he lets Antony speak last. Brutus is scrupulously fair, and thereby he plays into Antony's still more all-enclosing script.[7]

A funeral ceremony seems a fitting conclusion to a tragedy. The deceased will be memorialized and mourned. His death will somehow be rationalized. The participants will be emotionally purged. The whole community will come together to contemplate their common mortality, exemplified by Caesar, the great man who fell. The *memento mori* theme is implicit: along with personal feeling there is a distancing, philosophical view of human life and its transience. Human life is filtered through an aesthetic lens.

Brutus plans to shape the image this lens projects, but so does Antony. We see him commit himself to avenge Caesar's death almost as soon as he learns of it (3.1.259–75). There is therefore dramatic irony in our recognition of the difference between what the Romans hear and what we hear. This irony seems to distance us comfortably from the mob, his audience onstage. We are uniquely in a position to appreciate his cleverness in manipulation, without ourselves being manipulated. This cleverness extends even to Antony's ability to seem to follow Brutus's rules not to say anything against the murderers (3.1.245), yet get the opposite of the effect Brutus intends. He insinuates suspicion; his art defamiliarizes the tragedy made by Brutus. Caesar's death is demystified.

Once Antony crystalizes our uncertainties about the assassination, he establishes our common ground: "Then I, and you, and all of us fell down" (3.2.191). This is true for us in the theater as well as for the mob onstage. Brutus's tragedy has raised us from the political to the philosophical view of Caesar. As Antony returns us again and again to the fact of Caesar's death, we are reminded again and again of human frailty, of our own mortality. Pacified by our conviction of our own superiority to the mob, we too allow ourselves to be leveled. We too will die. Our distance from the Roman funeral audience diminishes in spite of the dramatic irony of the situation. Despite our awareness that Antony is deliberately being manipulative, he engages us in the theater audience as directly as he does the audience onstage. Not only does the so-called "mob" change its sympathies from Brutus to Caesar, but so do we.

Then he lifts the mantle from Caesar's corpse and shows "us all" the naked, bleeding body covered with wounds, Caesar's "dumb mouths" (3.2.225). The illusionist Antony displays the truth behind his funereal enactment, which is also the truth behind the ritual of purification staged by Brutus, as well as the implication of Caesar's own pursuit of power. This revelation affects us as do the changed vantage points we take when faced with Holbein's *Ambassadors*. Never again will we see Brutus, or the action of the play generally, outside of the context of death, outside of our sense of both their and our mortality. The funeral is not merely a turning point for the plot and for our feelings about the characters. It is also a turning point for our consciousness of ourselves. What we have been led to know, we cannot unknow. Whether we think by analogy of illusionist art, or of Holbein's forcing us to change our vantage point, the effect is the same. We are now, by the very things we see, in collusion with the artist whose artistry caused these shifts. We are aware of seeing as Antony would have us see.[8] Brutus for a moment caused us to suspend judgment about his murder of Caesar by concentrating our attention on its aesthetic form, on the murder as tragedy. Antony's ceremony has carried us a step further. We see the transparently constructed form of the funeral; we also see the gap between this perception and the mob's blindness to it. This second level of awareness shifts our attention from the form of the funeral to the more elemental fact of its transparency. Antony, that is, deepens the illusionism begun by Brutus. Seeing through the funeral, we are consumed (as the mob is) by the "reality" underlying it. The political influence desired by Brutus is exposed as essentially theatrical, just as Caesar's was.[9] In its expression of universal uncertainty, of death, and of actual personal loss, Antony's art opens to the full dimensions of the terrifying world in which we now find ourselves implicated. There is no welcoming refuge, no orderly status quo, either with an emperor or with a republic.

It is as if during the funeral we gradually become aware of a deepening vanishing point in this play, and even of multiple systems of perspective. Its ironies and contradictions begin to cluster together. The second play within the play, Brutus's, ends the tragedy of Caesar while at the same time being the act of self-assertion that begins his own. It is the culmination of the anti-Caesar side of the meanings of the prodigies and of Calphurnia's dream, and at the same time the beginning of a chain reaction that will fulfill their second meanings: that Caesar should not be killed and that Rome will be nourished by his blood. The full implications of Brutus's double bind will now be enacted.

This second movement is underlined in subsequent scenes by the aftermath to Caesar's now-demystified assassination. The many-leveled uncertainty of the first two acts intensifies into human chaos: Cinna the poet's dismemberment, the senatorial bloodbath, civil war. Smaller reflections of this discord make it seem directionless, as if in a moral and political void, yet nonetheless universal and inescapable. The avengers decide whom to purge, even to trading off their own relatives with one another (4.1.1–6). Antony schemes to reduce Caesar's legacy to Rome, even though it was one of the foundations of his funeral eloquence (7–9); and he turns against Lepidus in the rest of act 4, scene 1, without any clear need to do so. In this scene, indeed, Shakespeare seems to demystify an Antony who has himself been the agent of Brutus's demystification. Antony's image as agent of justified chaos is balanced against an image of Antony as self-seeking gangster/terrorist.[10] As the disagreements between Antony and Octavius are renewed (5.1.16–20), and as the more prolonged one between Cassius and Brutus is added to it (scenes 2 and 3 in act 4), there seems to be no corner of the play's world which is free of blind destructiveness. There is savagery and chaos and betrayal on all sides.

The full irony of Brutus's predicament is now clear. The man who would be noble must follow the implications of his noble convictions to their end. He does so, and achieves the opposite of his intentions. Because of his nobility he, more than any of the other characters, must face the world's ambiguity and mystery at their most intense.

At the same time that our vantage point is distanced from the play to see this large context, however, we are also drawn into the depths of its mystery, as the lines of perspective that issue from a painting's vanishing point enclose its viewers. Our distance allows a panoramic awareness of the play's full chaotic canvas; in this awareness, Antony and Brutus and Julius Caesar are merely the figures it contains. This awareness, in turn, intensifies our sympathy for these figures as they become victims. Antony's funeral teaches us to see far more than he, and thus even to feel sympathetic toward his enemy Brutus.

This mystery, and the split awareness with which we experience it, is well illustrated in the second half of the play by Caesar's ghost (in act 4, scene 3). From one point of view this ghost, whether hallucinatory or "real," seems a penetration into the mundane from another dimension. We have already seen the prophetic truth of dreams, as well as the prophetic prodigies of nature. Whether objective or subjective, the ghost exists as a similar mystery in Brutus's consciousness. This mystery is further deepened, and made to seem inescapable, however, by the fact that we experience it as both objective and subjective at the same time.

It comes to Brutus when he is restless from his long wrangle with Cassius; he has called for music, a book, anything to distract him. We know that he killed Caesar in spite of loving him, and that Brutus's sense of morality is meticulous. One natural assumption, therefore, is that the ghost is a hallucination, a representation of his divided, perhaps guilty, mind. He alone sees it, and he alone hears those nearby crying out in their sleep.[11]

However, we have also heard Antony invoke "Caesar's spirit" in alliance with the goddess of discord (3.1.270), and we have seen the objectively real chaos which has become ubiquitous, in private as well as in Rome generally, and in the animal and human as well as the heavenly dimensions. In this play's world, Caesar's spirit can with equal plausibility be seen as an objective presence, as another "real" representation of discord, just as indeed can Antony himself. Even the play's title seems to suggest this continuing presence.

The discussion by Leonard Tennenhouse of the queen's two bodies is suggestive of this duality (although Tennenhouse argues with reference to the history plays and, at greater length, to *Hamlet;* see Tennenhouse 1986, 79–93). He points out the distinction between the natural body of Elizabeth the individual person and the symbolic body of Elizabeth the icon of the state. This double dimension applies equally to Caesar, and therefore to his ghost. On the one hand it exists objectively as the spirit of Caesar and of the empire that Caesar would have brought about. On the other hand, it represents Brutus's personal feelings of loss and guilt from the killing of the individual who was his friend.

Here, then, Brutus begins the process of facing the full horror of the double bind in which his own nobility placed him. Since the first act he has been "with himself at war" (1.2.46). Now he begins to feel the pain of the vicious cycle of samsara, of the self-destructive nature of desire, even more acutely. He has tried to break out of this cycle by denying the fact of Caesar's natural body, obscuring the fact that he murdered a private person whom he loved. He tried to kill the spirit of Caesar, to divorce his iconic boy from his personal one, to transform Caesar's body and blood into ceremonial symbols. The ghost's integration of its objective and subjective existence represents the impossibility of Brutus divorcing the two. In seeing Brutus with this ghost, we see him exposed to the inevitability of his failure.

From this point of view, then, it is also inevitable that he will kill himself, for there seem no other options so long as he clings to his sense of honor and nobility. With Cassius dead, Brutus seems accurate in his assessment that he has lost the war. He will therefore kill himself not "to prevent / The time of life" (5.1.104–5), but because he believes that it is all but over anyway. He will do it himself rather than have an enemy do it. He can at least keep the independent self-mastery that his noble self-image requires.

He does not do it from a failure of nerve, as Messala says Cassius did: "Mistrust of good success hath done this deed" (5.3.66). Nor does he turn his face away as Cassius did, nor have another person plunge the sword into him. In these respects Brutus seems more right, more noble. He lives up to his own high standards.

However, he does not see beyond those standards, as we have been taught to do. He seems merely to believe that he has miscalculated in political and military terms:

> Our enemies have beat us to the pit.
> It is more worthy to leap in ourselves
> Than tarry till they push us.
>
> (5.5.23–25)

He demonstrates his self-mastery by ending himself as he did Caesar, with an impeccably enacted ritual. Perhaps this self-mastery, indeed, implies an acceptance of fate that might exemplify a kind of Stoic heroism. However, just before killing himself, Brutus shows the egoism of such acceptance:

> I shall have glory by this losing day
> More than Octavius and Mark Antony
> By this vile conquest shall attain unto.
>
> (5.5.36–38)[12]

He is still wedded to his nobility; he kills himself not in wise renunciation, but for a greater reputation in the world than he could otherwise achieve. As in his ritual murder of Caesar, so in his own ritual suicide Brutus means to mystify a real death, this time in the self-interested pursuit of fame. He makes a display of his nobility for future generations to admire. In this context his final words, "Caesar, now be still, / I kill'd not thee with half so good a will" (5.5.50–51), suggests that his suicide is also an escape from guilt, an erasure of the only stain on his honor.

Thus the root issue remains untouched by Brutus. The self-destructiveness inherent in desire was clear to us in Caesar's death, but not to Brutus. Even more obviously here at the end, then, Brutus reenacts this truth, that to keep the noble identity in which he believes, he must obliterate himself. The pain of the dilemma of ego is taken to its ultimate implication, to the self's final recourse in escaping pain. At last, it is not the world, but the self, which is inescapable.[13]

Dead, Brutus is proclaimed by his enemy to be "the noblest Roman of them all," the type against which the concept of humanity is measured and defined:

> ... the elements
> So mix'd in him that Nature might stand up
> And say to all the world, "This was a man!"
>
> (5.5.68, 73–75)

There is no certain reason to doubt Antony's sincerity. Although the victor often rewrites history to his own advantage, he is not always conscious of what he does. However, we must be suspicious, for it is the kind of thing we have seen him do before, quite consciously, when in the funeral scene he rewrote Brutus's version of Caesar's death in order to open his own terrorist campaign. Having demystified Brutus's ritual in the third act, he now tries to remystify Brutus in the play's final ritual. But here too, of course, the attempt is self-serving. Antony the victor is at once glorified by beating a glorified opponent, and ennobled by his gracious show of noble magnanimity.

In fact, though, whether this closing speech is sincere or consciously self-serving does not matter. Either way, it cannot ennoble Brutus in our eyes. We already know too much. Instead, it shows that Antony too has failed to learn the lesson of Brutus's failure—failed to learn the very lesson that, by distancing us from the action, he himself has taught us to see. Antony is as blind as Brutus and Caesar.[14] Not a new stability, then, but a renewal of the flux of the endless struggle for power is placed squarely in the foreground of the play's conclusion. The Roman ideal, "glories," remains on Octavius's lips in the final line.

We can now see, thanks to Antony, the blindness that always motivates this struggle—that of Antony and Octavius, that of Brutus, that of Caesar. Antony implicated us in the play's action during the funeral by swaying us with the mob, defamiliarizing tragedy, exposing Brutus, and reminding us that we, like the characters in the play, will die. We can see our common humanity with Julius Caesar. We can see that it is Brutus's noble self-image that blinds him and that makes his fall inevitable. Yet by the end we can also sympathize with Brutus, for he sees at last what we have seen since the funeral, that there is no escape. At the same time, because the subsequent action of this tragedy has purged us of the false view of the world held by Antony and Caesar as well as Brutus, we are distanced into a new self-awareness. Tragedy has done its work of renewal on its audience. In this awareness we see through the values taught by Roman society. We see through these values' confirmation of the solid self on which ego depends, but without losing our fellow feeling for the characters who suffer in this delusion. We find ourselves in a Derridean gap where society's conventions of meaning are dissolved—and, therefore, where the space necessary for the beginning of Buddhist wisdom has been cleared.

However, this space is very frightening. Although it is an emptiness that to the awakened mind displays itself as fullness, it is at the same time a lonely place "of desolation" (Trungpa 1976a, 151):

> The attainment of enlightenment from ego's point of view is extreme death, the death of self, the death of me and mine, the death of the watcher. It is the ultimate and final disappointment. (Trungpa 1976a, 6)

Brutus demonstrates in literal terms the truth of this assertion. Faced with the possibility that he might be less noble than he had thought, Brutus chooses to kill himself. He illustrates the startling fact that the loss of our idea of ourselves as solid beings with stable identities, the loss of the idea of what one calls "I," and the reciprocal recognition that the place we habitually think "we" fill in the world is actually a void, is in fact more frightening to us than the loss of life itself. From ego's point of view, that is, enlightenment is a threat, quite the reverse of what is "normally" desired. Therefore, Brutus retreats.

Yet as we have been taught by Brutus to see though this desire for the self, so the play leaves us with the alternative that he rejects. In this desolate landscape, it is true, we will be frighteningly alone, without the reference points of a solid world or self. "But," Trungpa encourages us,

> it is possible to make friends with the desolation and appreciate its beauty. Great sages . . . marry themselves to desolation, to the fundamental psychological aloneness . . . , the marriage of shunyata and wisdom in which your perception of aloneness suggests the needlessness of dualistic occupation. . . . We discover how samsaric occupations feed and entertain us. Once we see samsaric occupations as games, then that in itself is the absence of dualistic fixation, nirvana. Searching for nirvana becomes redundant at that point. (Trungpa 1976a, 151).

Precisely by facing the fact of our samsaric "occupations" fully, we can come to feel free in them. We need not stop our normal activities, but simply see them differently. Trungpa says that "the phenomenal world is an outfit, it is a show, a self-existing show. It is a performance, living theater" (1975, 160) in which

> you do not regard the situation outside as separate from you because you are so involved with the dance and play of life. . . . You experience no warfare of any kind, neither trying to defeat an enemy nor trying to achieve a goal. (1973, 100)

We are wrong to think that we are our egos. They are merely our *idea* of what we are, an idea that Shakespeare teaches us through *Julius Caesar* to unlearn. We must get used to the idea of going to our own funeral every moment, rather than, like Brutus in *Julius Caesar,* staging someone else's. Thus this play positions us on the brink of a void which, when fully realized, becomes the ground of our fulfillment. It pushes us toward the perception that "we are just a speck of dust in the midst of the universe." With such a recognition we can see that

> at the same time our situation is very spacious, very beautiful and workable. In fact, it is very inviting, inspiring. If you are a grain of sand, the rest of the universe, all the space, all the room is yours, because you obstruct nothing, overcrowd nothing, possess nothing. There is tremendous openness. You are the emperor of the universe because you are a grain of sand. (1976a, 6–7)

In this state we come to realize

> that space contains matter, that matter makes no demands on space and that space makes no demands on matter. It is a reciprocal and open situation. . . . The Buddha had no ground, no sense of territory. (1976a, 58–59)

And in such spaciousness we approach the Buddha's Third Noble Truth: that the constant pain created by hope and fear and desire is not to be evaded, as Brutus tried to do in his suicide; rather, it ends when it is so fully experienced that a state of nonstriving and nonopposition is achieved. For indeed it is this samsara that is in fact "the origin of the path" (1975, 56), the very basis of our liberation:

> Generally, when the idea of ego is presented, the immediate reaction on the part of the audience is to regard it as a villain, an enemy. . . . But having seen the emotions as they are, we have more material with which to work creatively. This makes it quite clear that the notion of samsara is dependent upon the notion of nirvana, and the notion of nirvana is dependent upon the notion of samsara; they are interdependent. If there were no confusion, there would be no wisdom. (1976a, 68)

This open situation, without a sense of territory, is not only personal in its implications, however. Like Shakespeare's play, it can radiate outward; its emptiness provides the space where Buddhist compassion can arise, a state of being quite different from normal pity. Trungpa explains the Buddhist stance toward ending the suffering of others:

> . . . true compassion is ruthless, from ego's point of view, because it does not consider ego's drive to maintain itself. It is "crazy wisdom." It is totally wise, but it is crazy as well, because it does not relate to ego's literal and simple-minded attempts to secure its own comfort. (1973, 210)

In this state, we do not assume that what the sufferer thinks he wants is necessarily what is best for him. However, because we do not need to maintain "our territory," we do not impose our own sense of what is right or good or helpful on him, either. Instead, we try to provide a situation in which there are no externally imposed demands or even expectations, in which the sufferer can be free from striving for a moment, become still, see himself more clearly than usual, perhaps experience his own emptiness and see for himself what is truly needed—whatever that may be for the particular individual. Thus,

> ... compassion is environmental generosity, without direction, without "for me" and without "for them." ... It implies larger scale thinking, a freer and more expansive way of relating to yourself and the world. ... [It] is ... not a matter of giving something to someone else, but it means giving up your demand and the basic criteria of the demand. (1973, 99)

If we now look back at *Julius Caesar* from this large perspective which it has opened for us, Antony's tragedy in a later play may already seem implicit in his failure to learn the lesson Brutus teaches us here. And that of Brutus himself seems merely a more detailed reenactment of Caesar's; Brutus's tragedy clarifies—is *about*—Caesar's.

Indeed, from this view the two character's tragedies are reciprocal. As we see the tragic form of the death of Julius Caesar defamiliarized, and as we see Caesar's essential similarity to Brutus, the tragic form of Brutus's death is also defamiliarized. The action of the play as a whole becomes self-reflexive. Antony's exposure of Brutus's ritual, the killing of Julius Caesar, becomes the exposure of the full play's epitome. Shakespeare's tragedy is defamiliarized as well.

From this point of view, the title may refer to a specific act: Brutus's tragedy of Julius Caesar in act 3, scene 1. As Brutus's play is an attempt to mystify Caesar, so does Shakespeare's *seem* an attempt to mystify *his* Caesar, the sitting English monarch. It is a tragedy: it seems to heroicize the fallen by seeming to show the fall to be both unmerited and unfortunate. It gives full voice to the noble-sounding egalitarian rhetoric of the rebels Brutus and Cassius in order to show the chaos to which it leads. Set in Rome, the play seems at once to defend monarchy, and to posit this defense in universal rather than local terms. There seems no harm in it.

But if there *is* harm in Brutus's tragedy of Julius Caesar, there is also harm in Shakespeare's. Its self-reflexiveness subverts its seemings. Shakespeare has used an approved discourse, the tragic play, to subvert that discourse, to subvert the vehicle on which the self-justifying ideas of established social authority depend.[15] By showing us that the cause of Brutus's impasse in the world is ours, is within ourselves, Shakespeare implies that it is avoidable. One *need* not be tragic, whether one is Roman or Elizabethan. Another life, one in which we feel Buddhist-style compassion for other beings in the "real" world as well as in a play, is possible.

At the end of *The Merchant of Venice* we imagined ourselves in the process of free fall, without tenable options, all positions having been rendered both threatening and self-contradictory. By the end of *Julius Caesar* we have progressed one step farther. The cause of this destructive impasse has been shown to be the need to solidify the self in a self-image, and then to live up to that image. This desire has been given the form of ambition, the will to nobility and power. If, in our fall after the dissolution of our secure self-belief in *Merchant,* we felt tempted to look for something solid to hold onto, something to cling to for security, a tree perhaps on the edge of a cliff, in *Caesar* we learn that nothing is solid. The tree will fall away when touched. Possibly there is no tree. Certainly, hoping for such a tree has caused our fall in the first place.

We have learned the Buddha's Second Noble Truth, that this desire to cling perpetuates and intensifies our pain in the world. We have also learned the Third, its antidote: the teaching not to escape, but to allow ourselves to be in the process of falling. Our compassion for Brutus is reciprocal: it has prepared us to allow this possibility for ourselves. Unlike Brutus, we must give ourselves up, not pursue an image of ourselves, no matter what the source: the Buddha, society, even the queen. And our example may clear a space in which others can do the same.

This, it may be, is precisely the subversive act to which Shakespeare leads us at the end of this play—not by precept, to be sure (that would be impossible, from both the Derridean and the Buddhist perspectives), but by guiding us to see through the transparent artwork that he entitles *Julius Caesar.* Seeing through it, we glimpse the now unmasked artist inscribed within. His project, unlike that of his characters, is not to mystify himself, but to reveal himself, to use the power of his art to undermine his authority as artist. In doing so, he laughs at the king's game he pretends to play; in teaching us to see his laughter, he beckons us to join him.

5
The Emptiness of *Différance* and the Six Samsaric Realms in *Antony and Cleopatra*

I

In the later Roman play *Antony and Cleopatra*, similar issues are confronted even more explicitly, and on an even grander scale. The two main characters are more "glorified." The Antony who has triumphed over Brutus has now met Cleopatra. Roman honor, duty, and reason join Egyptian pleasure, imagination, art. On this enlarged canvas, the two lovers are still more obviously represented as actor and actress. They invent and act out many roles; through them, they claim to transcend politics, human nature, and even this mundane world. They are also far more aware than Brutus of the flux of things, including themselves, and of the roles they play as roles, rather than as their own true identities.

Particularly in Antony, however, there is posed against this awareness another awareness, one of impasse, of a conflict in desires which cannot be resolved. And in Cleopatra there is a recognized ulterior motive that *her* roles are fashioned to serve: her increasingly desperate need to keep Antony in her thrall. This play is therefore more searching than *Julius Caesar* in its interrogation of the relationship between "play" and ego; of the power, as well as the limits of power, in role-playing; and of the relations between world and theater. From the Buddhist point of view, it draws a fuller portrait of the Second Noble Truth, the cause of suffering. The vicious circle of samsara is described in far more psychological detail. This play, then, seems a natural sequel to its Roman predecessor, *Julius Caesar*.

The relationship between theater and transcendence is powerfully represented in Enobarbus's famous description of Cleopatra at her first meeting with Antony (2.2.191–218). She enters by water, on a barge; she lies in her pavilion, dressed in tissue-thin cloth of gold, surrounded by "pretty dimpled boys." Everything near her, inanimate (water, wind, air) and animate, is reported to have been transformed by the sentiment of love; her similarity to Venus, goddess of love, is both unmistakable and explicit (2.2.200). She represents one aspect of her real identity (as lover) in her self-apotheosis as love-goddess. This representation is spectacularly successful: Antony falls in love; Enobarbus reproduces it in words for others.

Yet the terms of this reproduction raise questions about the relationship between Cleopatra's play and its meaning. Enobarbus says that Cleopatra was "o'er-picturing that Venus where we see / The fancy outwork nature" (2.2.200–201). Sir Philip Sidney spoke for the Neoplatonism of the age in asserting that the imagination—"fancy"—can express the truth behind life's misleading appearances: because it is not bound to those appearances, it can invent forms never seen in nature, yet more true, and hence more beautiful. "Fancy" can perfect nature, and show it as it should be—as it *would* be if it could. In this spirit, Enobarbus remembers a specific painting that does seem to him to "outwork nature." His comparison is between a pure work of fancy, the painted Venus, and this living woman who has "staged" herself as Venus in the flesh. In this self-created role, Cleopatra is said to exceed even that work of art. She is not pure art, which alone might presumably express the ideal truth behind nature; rather, she is a blend of art and nature. She is nature perfected, the ideal bettered *and* made "real." In her dramatic art, the Neoplatonic world of imperfect shadows is magically transformed into a world in which the ideal can exist in the flesh. In light of her spectacular success with this dramatization, are we to believe that acting, unlike painting, can create another dimension of existence? This seems to be Enobarbus's claim.

However, these apotheosizing sentiments seem incongruous, coming from the character who earlier had satirized Cleopatra: "I have seen her die / Twenty times upon far poorer moment" (1.2.141–42). Perhaps this well-known cynicism gives unique credibility to his glorification of Cleopatra? He seems not to be the kind of character who is easily won over. Or is he once more making fun of her, this time with a heavier-handed sarcasm than before, his reproduction turning toward parody? The degree of exaggeration here seems quite different from his earlier ironic style. Or, again, is he deliberately inflating her in order to make a good soldier's tale for his old Roman comrades in arms, to whom he is newly returned? Does his reproduction merely transform a normal, human-scale self-staging into an Olympian-scale barracks story about a magical woman from the East? The form of Enobarbus's reproduction renders its meaning uncertain.[1]

This intellectual tension is typical of the play, and it is largely derived from the fact that the principal characters present themselves as actors from the very beginning onward.[2] For one thing, the form that Antony and Cleopatra give their love is mainly game-playing. In her very first line, Cleopatra calls on Antony to play the game of declaring how much he loves her ("If it be love indeed, tell me how much," 1.1.14). Antony's witty reply shows that he is fully aware of the game: "There's beggary in the love that can be reckon'd" (1.1.15). By making the rules of her game literal, he shows their limits, and his different expectations: a game in which love is said (as it is felt?) to be infinite. At one stroke, in *his* first line, he shows his awareness that this is a game, and that its rules are both arbitrary and limiting; at the same time, by the very act of protesting its rules, Antony transcends them into an implication of the infinity of his love. Cleopatra then retakes command by accepting Antony's literalist play on her "how much," and establishing it as the rule of their game: "I'll set a bourn how far to be belov'd" (1.1.16). In acquiescing to this rule, he repeats his demand for an expansion: "Then must thou needs find out new heaven, new earth" (1.1.17). The tension between the limitations of this world and the limitlessness of their love is expressed from the very start in terms of playing.

Indeed because, as Cleopatra insists, this limitlessness must be expressed in this world, their game-playing becomes the *necessary* form for their love, allowing it to be in the world, yet to seem to transcend the world. In play, they seem able to make the hyperboles of love into literal enactments. They can discuss a love without limits in finite terms, act out the stories of Mars and Venus, reverse sexual roles (2.5.22–23), even reverse the human microcosm idea so that Antony becomes the macrocosm (5.2.76f.). The normal lovers' situation, in which expansive delight in love is expressed by fun in games, seems raised to a higher power. Thus the ruler-soldier Antony can assert from the very beginning that "kingdoms are clay" (1.1.35).[3]

As this phrase suggests, the same attitude seems to extend to war as well, and thus to the whole world of the play. In Cleopatra, whose interest in the military occupation is obviously an extension of her love for her soldier, this fact is not particularly surprising. Thus, when she is reproached for fleeing from the first naval battle, she seems perfectly consistent with herself when she turns this reproach into a lover's counter-accusation. She is surprised that Antony would expect her to be serious about fighting: "I little thought / You would have followed" (3.11.55–56). When she misapplies his armor in preparation for the land battle (at the start of act 4, scene 4), they are both in high spirits. She is playing at

Venus, trying to arm her Mars without knowing how. Her ignorance does not matter to either of them.

For the great soldier, this attitude seems more surprising, but it accounts for the two decisions that are apparently his worst: the choice to fight by sea, and afterwards the challenge to Caesar to fight in single combat. The first causes the loss of a great battle that his "absolute soldiership" by land might have prevented (3.7.42, 34–38). Enobarbus's desertion, announced at the end of act 3, scene 13, underscores the blindness and perhaps the desperation of the second. Why does he make such bad decisions? There are no mitigating circumstances: he has good advice, and is operating in an arena in which he is expert.

He says that he will fight Caesar by sea for one reason only: "For he dares us to't" (3.7.29). Enobarbus warns that in this decision he gives himself up "merely to chance and hazard, / From firm security." Antony simply repeats, "I'll fight at sea" (3.7.47–48). There is honor in accepting a dare purely, without regard for its probable result. In his challenge to Caesar, he proffers a similar opportunity to another. In each case, honor takes precedence over pragmatism.[4] War seems to become for Antony a thing done less for the ulterior motive of conquest than for itself, as the self-expression of an honorable warrior. War and love become, for both Antony and Cleopatra, similar in value, events to be played as self-representations. For this purpose, they seem to feel licensed to take whatever liberty they wish with the conventional outward forms of things.

Caesar is not only their antagonist, then, but also their contrast. This is clearest in the first half of the play in his relationship with Pompey, who says, "'Tis not my profit that does lead mine honor; / Mine honor, it" (2.7.76–77). Pompey refuses to dishonor his role as host; he will not take advantage of his chance to "fall to their throats" while the Roman leaders are defenseless on his ship (2.7.72). Caesar, on the other hand, is devoted to power; honor is for him merely an instrument of this obsession. He alone does not join the revelry on Pompey's boat. Instead, he makes a show of honorable Roman comradeship to pacify the feasting Pompey into unfavorable negotiation (act 2, scenes 6 and 7). Later, in act 3, scene 5, having just made a peace with Pompey, Caesar begins a new war with him. In Eros's description, this act seems treacherous not only against Pompey but also against Lepidus, with whom he refuses to share a deserved part of the honor for Pompey's defeat. Caesar's "honor" seems as empty as his "love," in the name of which he marries off his sister. He will corrupt any values to preserve or enhance his power.[5]

The hollowness of this Roman honor, when defined as the reward for success, is represented more generally as well. Even Antony's seems to be repressive. In act 3, scene 1 his successful general Ventidius complains about the way this Roman system of honor works in the military. Having quelled the Parthian uprising, he stops at the letter of his orders rather than follow up on his advantage:

> I have done enough; a lower place, note well,
> May make too great an act. For learn this, Silius:
> Better to leave undone, than by our deed
> Acquire too high a fame when him we serve's away.
> Caesar and Antony have ever won
> More in their officer than person.
>
> (3.1.12–17)

Antony, however, often seems in himself to be more like Pompey than Caesar. In act 3, scene 7, his naval battle seems to express the idea that honor is a form of pure integrity, without ulterior motives; at the beginning of the play, similarly, kingdoms were for him but clay. Caesar is the play's strongest representation of the opposite. The idea that he does not deserve the glory he receives is reemphasized when the soothsayer warns Antony to stay away from Caesar:

> Thy demon, that thy spirit which keeps thee, is
> Noble, courageous, high unmatchable,
> Where Caesar's is not; but near him, thy angel
> Becomes a fear, as being o'erpow'r'd.
>
> (2.3.20–23)

For Caesar, in this view, victory is a matter of "natural luck" (2.3.27). It is unearned. Its consequence, honor, is therefore also suspect.

The most explicit statement of this contrast between Caesar's mental climate and that of the lovers is by Cleopatra in act 5, scene 2:

> My desolation does begin to make
> A better life. 'Tis paltry to be Caesar;
> Not being Fortune, he's but Fortune's knave,
> A minister of her will: and it is great
> To do that thing that ends all other deeds,
> Which shackles accidents and bolts up change,
> Which sleeps, and never palates more the dung,
> The beggar's nurse and Caesar's.
>
> (5.2.1–8)

Worldly success, ambition, outward things in general, all are subject to "accident" and "change." They are conditional rather than absolute, not to be trusted or valued. Caesar is an example of one who pursues position and power, the world's *apparent* gifts. But this pursuit makes him like "the beggar." He is not self-sufficient, but is dependent on the favors of a higher power, Fortune; and although the worldly stakes he plays for are larger than those that consume the dreams of beggars, he too is always longing for more; he too is never satisfied, never without an ulterior motive. He never does a thing purely for the value of the doing. Cleopatra sees this as an impoverished perspective. Regardless of wealth and empire, Caesar is "paltry," a mere "knave." He is the servant of a power that happens to side with him just now, but that is ultimately as fickle as the other powers of the world.

To the degree that Antony is as committed to gamesmanship in love *and* war as Cleopatra believes herself to be, both lovers seem to offer a contrast. They believe that they can raise themselves to an unconditioned realm of pure play that exceeds Caesar's "Fortune." They believe that they have found a way to be in this world of "accident" and "change" while avoiding its limitations.

Yet despite this belief, they both feel the threat of imminent loss throughout the play: for Cleopatra, of love; for Antony, of power and command, and of the honorable identity with which they seem associated. Their self-awareness is at a level beyond Caesar's, as their attitude toward playing often indicates. This awareness, however, is a mixed blessing, for it also leads them to recognize the tension between their vision of transcendence and their position in the world (as we have just noticed in the opening scene). This recognition leads in turn to panic and to a changing attitude toward "play." Therefore, their sense of their own and the world's conditional nature, of changeability, does not lead at last to wisdom, but instead to the blindness of despair.

Antony knows the cost of his love games from the very first: "Let Rome in Tiber melt, and the wide arch / Of the rang'd empire fall! Here is my space, / Kingdoms are clay" (1.1.33–35). He also knows what his old Roman companions think of this change. He urges a messenger from Rome,

> Speak to me home, mince not the general tongue;
> Name Cleopatra as she is call'd in Rome.
> Rail thou in Fulvia's phrase, and taunt my faults
> With such full license as both truth and malice
> Have power to utter.
>
> (1.2.105–9)

But he has trouble reconciling himself to this cost. As early as the second scene, when he learns of Fulvia's death, he says,

> I must from this enchanting queen break off;
> Ten thousand harms, more than the ills I know,
> My idleness doth hatch.
>
> (1.2.128–30)

When he fears his honor to be seriously at risk, he returns to Rome to try to resecure it. But then, having married Octavia, he returns at once to Egypt. Each turn in his fortunes renews his inner conflict. After following Cleopatra's flight from the first naval engagement, he says:

> My very hairs do mutiny; for the white
> Reprove the brown for rashness, and they them
> For fear and doting.
>
> (3.11.13–15)

Yet he will fight by sea once more. Throughout the play, Antony sees his situation clearly. He sees that he must choose, and that he cannot. Ironically, it is because he is courageous enough to face this impasse honestly that he defeats his own higher instincts.

His consciousness of this impasse reaches its climax in act 4, scene 14. He believes himself to have lost everything he values in the second naval battle: "She, Eros, has / Pack'd cards with Caesar's, and false-play'd my glory / Unto an enemy's triumph" (4.14.18–20). His recognition of the flux of things now comes to embrace not only politics, power, and war, but also honor, and even Cleopatra's love. Indeed, he applies this lesson to himself as well, comparing himself to the changing, insubstantial shapes of a cloud:

> My good knave Eros, now thy captain is
> Even such a body. Here I am Antony,
> Yet cannot hold this visible shape, my knave.
>
> (4.14.12–14)

The self-awareness that allows him to play in the world also allows him to see the script of his rival (4.14.73–77), and in this way leads him to the end of games, to the limit that he will not accept in this world: "there is left us / Ourselves to end ourselves" (4.14.21–22). His perception of the universal flux becomes at last too personal, too threatening, to accept.[6] The loss of his old self of honor and love seems more threatening to him even than death. His recent experience of pure honor and love joined together is too delicious to let go. Its contrast to the humiliation in Rome that now seems imminent is too great. The player for whom acts are signs must face a future in which he has no significance. Suicide is Antony's panicked response to the self-deconstruction that is inevitably implied by the process of playing life. If one has the courage to see, and to play, one risks this panic. The paradox of being purely honorable (and loving) is that this state implies being unanchored, insubstantial, a floating signifier. For Antony, death becomes an escape from his fear of losing his idea of himself. That is, he comes to demonstrate the endlessly self-defeating nature of desire. This view is further emphasized by the circumstances that follow.

In this desperate mood, Antony learns of Cleopatra's lie that she has killed herself for the loss of his love (4.14.29–30). It allows him to believe in love again, and he grasps at this straw; he embellishes it and constructs an afterlife "where souls do couch on flowers," where he and she can "hand in hand / And with our sprightly port make the ghosts gaze" (4.14.51–52). In this imagining, copying both Eros and, as he believes, Cleopatra, he tries to kill himself.

And botches the job. Enthralled by love, then fooled by a lover's game; unable to endure his limitations, then unable to kill himself—this hero seems greatly reduced. His brave echo of Cleopatra, as he falsely imagines her, "I am conqueror of myself" (4.14.62), seems delusional. His self-awareness has fled. When Cleopatra joins him and reaffirms her love, and hence also his sense of his own honor, this blindness is merely confirmed:

> The miserable change now at my end
> Lament nor sorrow at; but please your thoughts
> In feeding them with those my former fortunes
> Wherein I liv'd, the greatest prince o' th' world,
> The noblest; and do now not basely die,
> Not cowardly put off my helmet to
> My countryman—a Roman by a Roman
> Valiantly vanquished.
>
> (4.15.51–58)

The irony of this death—the fact that it was unnecessary, that it was provoked by yet another lover's ploy—shows not Antony's independent spirit but his abject dependency. This irony so undercuts his delusion of triumph that it demonstrates the truth of Antony's fear; he is indeed without the unconditioned identity he tries so desperately to construct. Desire is ultimately self-defeating because it falsifies reality, projecting itself into belief.

The irony of his suicide is further intensified by the fact that it is performed according to a Roman script in which one stabs oneself in a particular way. It is a little ritual in itself (though badly played), meant to endow his death with meaning, to preserve forever the values he upheld in life: honor and love, erected now as absolutes, as offerings to fame. So enlarged, they show themselves still more clearly to be merely delusions. The self-aware soldier kills himself in the service of self-image. That this suicide is performed in order to avoid another's (Caesar's) script, another version of "reality," simply reinforces the sense that Antony is trapped by belief in the solidity of his own perceptions, unready for the degree of awareness of change that he has. And so he must believe in transcendence: "I will be / A bridegroom in my death, and run into't / As to a lover's bed" (4.14.99–101).

Cleopatra is similar. Player though she is, even in the opening scene her skepticism about Antony's boundary-less "Let Rome in Tiber melt" shows her insecurity:

> Excellent falsehood!
> Why did he marry Fulvia, and not love her?
> I'll seem the fool I am not.
>
> (1.1.40–42)

Much of her subsequent playing is similarly calculated to catch him and hold him.[7] In the next scene, she plays hard to get, pretending not to see Antony at 1.2.87, and leaving before he can approach. In act 3, scene 3, she instructs Charmian to find Antony and make this report:

> I did not send you. If you find him sad,
> Say I am dancing; if in mirth, report
> That I am sudden sick.
>
> (1.3.3–5)

Upon his arrival less than ten lines later, she plays her roles directly to him: "I am sick and sullen"; "Never was there queen / So mightily betrayed"; "I see, / In Fulvia's death, how mine receiv'd shall be" (1.3.13, 24–25, 64–65). When she gets the effect she wants, she urges him too to "play," to go to Rome and

> ... play one scene
> Of excellent dissembling, and let it look
> Like perfect honor.
>
> (1.3.78–80)

But in teaching him that Roman honor can be "played," she shows her own recognition that games need not be taken seriously. As with Antony, this self-consciousness will undermine the value of her games; and as with Antony, this recognition will lead to further insecurity.

Cleopatra's split consciousness has a cyclic nature, just as Antony's does. Where he vacillates between Rome and Egypt, she keeps focused on him. Like his, however, her emotions are fueled by desire, and they frequently spiral out of control. In act 2, scene 5, when Antony is in Rome, the eunuch Mardian's deficiency at billiards (everything about Cleopatra requires sexual interpretation) reminds her of the mock-serious nature of theater: "when good will is show'd, though't come too short, / The actor may plead pardon" (2.5.8–9). She recognizes that the value of play is in the act of playing, not in its quality or result.[8] Nonetheless, she is restless, worried, insecure.[9] She requires another diversion (again, one in which she can play with a pole), fishing. It fuels her imagination: each fish will be "an Antony" who is "caught" (2.5.14–15). Through this game she imagines solving her "real" problem, Antony's absence. Charmian's reminder of the sexual possibilities in "angling" and their associations with Antony then triggers Cleopatra's memory of their cross-dressing sexual games, in which she "put [her] tires and mantles on him, whilst / [She] wore his sword Philippan" (2.5.22–23)—again, she remembers having had an extended "thing" to play with. This seems to be a memory of a game played without insecurity or ulterior motive, played as she has just described play in the theater, for the sheer delight in the playing. However, when the messenger from Rome enters at the very next line, her fears are extreme even before she hears that they have been realized, that Antony has married Octavia. She puts herself through a torturous mental cycle: delight, then striving to secure that delight, then remembering a greater delight, then fearing its loss, at last furious at its actual dispossession. This is the viciously self-perpetuating cycle of samsara, born of a desire which, like Antony's, projects itself into believed reality.

The irony of desire is further demonstrated at Antony's death, when Cleopatra's frustration is of course intensified. The irony derives from the fact that his death is an unanticipated (because unwished for) form of what is actually her ultimate wish-fulfillment: an ultimate statement of her lover's devotion, in a form that ensures that he will never again be disloyal. Unable to live with her wish so completely realized, she turns to her own suicide script, for which she has been buying time all through act 5. She too will "play," but in a peculiarly Egyptian form of her own devising, rather than in Caesar's Roman one. She will avoid her humiliating part in his triumphal pageant by creating a ritual in which she can honor her dead love, thereby reciprocally achieving honor for herself. Honor and love will be joined once more in their joined deaths. The possibilities in Enobarbus's description in act 2, scene 2, will be fulfilled.[10]

In preparing for this final act, she uses essentially the same terms that he did for her, in order to apotheosize her lover. She invents an Antony who is "past the size of dreaming," who is the Neoplatonic ideal made flesh:

> Nature wants stuff
> To vie strange forms with fancy; yet t'imagine
> An Antony were nature's piece 'gainst fancy,
> Condemning shadows quite.
>
> (5.2.97–100)

At least implicitly, the magical power of their "play" at love and war is affirmed; it has allowed a human being, Antony, to transcend normal human limits. Implicitly too, then, the woman with whom he played and for whom he died, the woman whose imagination can create this grand transcendent vision, is here created as a being who is his equal. And although her terms are those of Enobarbus, her tone is unambiguous.

Indeed, she also invents her own terms. She visualizes him not as the conventional microcosm, but as the macrocosm itself:

> His face was as the heav'ns, and therein stuck
> A sun and moon, which kept their courses, and lighted
> The little O, th' earth.
>
> (5.2.79–81)

She recreates him as the exemplar of a limitless human potentiality, a belief sufficiently glorious and aggrandizing to die for.

In her death, she constructs a deliberately staged performance:

> Show me, my women, like a queen; go fetch
> My best attires. I am again for Cydnus
> To meet Mark Antony.
>
> (5.2.227–29)

This staged quality is reemphasized after she has died and her corpse laid out before us. Charmian tends her queen's costume: "Your crown's awry, / I'll mend it" (5.2.318–19). She then turns to her own suicide as she finishes the line "and then play," echoing Cleopatra's earlier wish that, once she is well costumed and her death enacted, her followers will take "leave / To play till doomsday" (5.2.231–32). In dying as in life for Cleopatra, there is nothing else.

Like Antony, then, it is in "play" that she gives up the world in loyalty to her love. In doing so, again like Antony, she exalts her honor with her love. This intention is clear from her first thought of suicide, just after Antony's death: "Let's do't after the high Roman fashion, / And make death proud to take us" (4.15.87–88). Her dying speech is similar:

> Methinks I hear
> Antony call; I see him rouse himself
> To praise my noble act. I hear him mock
> The luck of Caesar, which the gods give men
> To excuse their after wrath. Husband, I come!
>
> (5.2.283–87)

She recreates herself. If earlier she has been caught in a circle, whirling around an axis that connects the poles of delight and insecurity, now she seems to have raised herself beyond this pattern, to have found a stable place without self-doubt where desire and fulfillment are perpetually in balance. She believes in her final role. To her as to Antony, this final "play" *is* "reality."[11]

The expectation which informs this final enactment is also similar for both lovers. It is to lead to an eternally transcendent sexual existence. Antony envisioned a place "where souls do couch on flowers," and entered it like "a bridegroom" running "as to a lover's bed" (4.14.51, 100–101). Cleopatra also puts primary emphasis on the sexual aspect of his prowess:

> Noblest of man, woo't die?
> Hast thou no care of me? Shall I abide
> In this dull world, which in thy absence is
> No better than a sty?
>
> (4.15.59–62)

She is overcome by her anticipation of utter boredom in a world made "dull" by the loss of its best hunk of male flesh:

> O, wither'd is the garland of the war,
> The soldier's pole is fall'n! Young boys and girls
> Are level now with men; the odds is gone,
> And there is nothing left remarkable
> Beneath the visiting moon.
>
> (4.15.64–68)

In her own death scene she enacts these same sensual values. She takes the asp to her breast as if in love-play, speaking to it as if to a diminutive lover, "Poor . . . fool" (5.2.305). When it is actually "feeding" on her breast, Cleopatra responds as a mother would to her suckling child:

> Peace, peace!
> Dost thou not see my baby at my breast
> That sucks the nurse asleep?
>
> (5.2.308–10)

This sensation is as sweet as a lover's caress ("as sweet as balm, as soft as air, as gentle—," 5.2.311), so that she forgets the child and imagines the lover ("O Antony!—"), then becomes greedy, as lust takes her ("Nay, I will take thee too," 5.2.312). She takes the second asp to herself as well, and dies. In taking that second asp, she is increasing the pleasure of her anticipation even as she hastens her death. She is still focusing on sensual experience, as Caesar himself sees when viewing her corpse:

> . . . she looks like sleep,
> As she would catch another Antony
> In her strong toil of grace.
>
> (5.2.346–48)

Just before her death, Cleopatra makes the nature of this anticipation explicit. She imagines that if Iras, who has died before her,

> first meet the curled Antony,
> He'll make demand of her, and spend that kiss
> Which is my heaven to have.
>
> (5.2.301–3)

She imagines only one kind of change in their love:

> . . . now from head to foot
> I am marble-constant; now the fleeting moon

No planet is of mine.

(5.2.239–41)

Antony becomes her "husband" (5.2.287). She imagines a realm where love is stable. As Antony's

> ... delights
> Were dolphin-like, they show'd his back above
> The elements they liv'd in,
>
> (5.2.88–90)

so she herself becomes all "fire and air; my other elements / I give to baser life" (5.2.289–90). She imagines no change in affection or sensuality; rather, she imagines these things to continue, but on the plane of the purer elements, beyond the fluctuations of earthly imperfection. Like Antony, she does not imagine a new, spiritualized existence, but rather an afterlife in which the best of this earth is raised to a higher power.[12]

She imagines a realm in which her "marble" constancy allows her to become her own monument.[13] In it desire, forever insatiable, will always lead to delight, will always be fulfilled by a perpetually devoted lover. It will never lead to fear of loss or to further desire for some greater delight. The self-perpetuating cycle of self-torture that desire fuels in this mundane world will end in a future life imagined as somehow frozen and changeless.

Yet by embracing the pure atmosphere of change and the free possibility of sexual passion suggested by "fire and air," she seems to contradict her self-imagining as "marble." This imagined stasis also seems contradicted by the fact that in this final moment she dreams of a delight in the future, of which the present pleasure of the asp is merely a prefiguration. Like Antony, she gives up this life in order to gain another. Such a state of feeling seems not to begin a new level of existence, but rather to start the old cycle of desire once again, in which the present is denied in the name of a further desire, setting a mental pattern in motion that cannot create the eternal satisfaction that she imagines, but instead eternal frustration. She is taken in by her own wish-fulfillment fantasy, just as Antony was.

Just as there was irony in the fact that Antony tried to avoid self-loss by killing himself, so there is also irony here in the fact that this suicide so much lamented by Cleopatra is actually the realization in unexpected form of her deepest wish: for Antony to prove a devotion to her that will never change.

II

Seeing this irony, we are at last in a position to appreciate the fullness with which this play presents a psychological portrait of the Buddha's Second Noble Truth, the cause of suffering. For the irony of Antony's and Cleopatra's suicides is the same as that which, in the Buddhist view, is created by desire and its pursuit of happiness as they endlessly repeat their cycle of frustration and pain. One version of this cycle makes the parallel particularly clear. It is described by Chögyam Trungpa as "the Six Realms, the different styles of samsaric occupation." Typically, each of us continually moves from one to another of these realms in a perpetually self-reinforcing dynamic of striving (Trungpa 1976a, 23). In these realms,

> we attach values to things and events which they do not necessarily have. We have definite opinions about the way things are and should be. This is projection: we project our version of things onto what is there. Thus we become completely immersed in a world of our own creation, a world of conflicting values and opinions. (1973, 131)

We impose preconceptions—what we need to believe—on our experience. Thus the particular form that our individual experience of life seems to have is actually "our own creation"—that is, at some level, our choice.

One of these six styles is called the Realm of the Gods. Its way of being suggests Antony and Cleopatra's feeling of tension between "reality" and transcendence, as well as their apparent resolution of it. This tension, as we have seen, begins with the love game in their very first lines of the play, and then seems resolved by Antony's brave pronouncement: "Let Rome in Tiber melt" (1.1.33). Such a resolution seems to put the characters on a level of being that transcends normal human striving—on the level of the gods. In this God Realm, transcendence is

> realized through tremendous struggle, is manufactured out of hope and fear. The fear of failure and the hope of gain builds up and up and up to a crescendo. One moment you think you are going to make it and the next moment you think you are going to fail. Alternation between these extremes produces enormous tension.
> ... And then pleasure begins to saturate our system, psychologically and physically. Such a breakthrough, such a tremendous achievement. We no longer have to care about hope and fear. (1976a, 25–26)

But of course Antony and Cleopatra are never able to sustain their high resolve. (A further irony is that, could it be sustained, even bliss would begin to feel like just another everyday experience, nothing special or extraordinary—or satisfying.) Instead, the lovers will repeat this pattern again and again with ever-increasing intensity. Confidence is inevitably followed by disillusionment.

And then they fall into the Realm of the Hungry Ghosts, in which one

> experiences great hunger for more pleasurable, spacious conditions and fantasizes numerous ways to satisfy his hunger.... Each time he seems about to achieve pleasure, he is rudely awakened from his idyllic dream; but his hunger is so demanding that he is not daunted and so continues to constantly churn out fantasies of future satisfaction. The pain of disappointment involves [him] in a love-hate relationship with his dreams. He is fascinated by them, but the disappointment is so painful that he is repelled by them as well.... It is the insatiable hunger itself which causes pain. (1973, 139)

Implicit in the texture of this realm is self-distrust, even self-hatred. From the Buddhist point of view, this feeling is quite intelligent, for it indicates accurate self-recognition, an intuition that the desire to make dreams real is inherently self-defeating, that it causes pain more than pleasure, that it is the desire for pleasure itself that creates pain. This feeling of self-distrust, however, is not so clearly formulated by the sufferer who is caught in the cycle. She is conscious of frustration, but not so precise about its cause or its self-defeating implications. Typically, the way out seems to be to pursue the dream still more arduously. At its most extreme, the blindness of this suffering might lead to a suicide like Antony's, a literal acting out of these self-defeating implications.

Usually, though—and this is true for both Antony and Cleopatra earlier in the play—this blindness leads into another style of samsara; not atypically, this is the Human Realm, a realm where the intelligence of self-doubt activates a kind of passion, "an intelligent kind of grasping in which the logical reasoning mind is always geared toward the creation of happiness" (1976a, 29). In this style of pursuit, there is much jealousy of others who seem to have what you want, but

> it is not simply a matter of being jealous of another person; you want to draw that person into your territory.... There is an heroic attitude, the attempt to create monuments, the biggest, greatest, historical monument. This heroic approach is based on fascination with what you lack. When you hear of someone who possesses remarkable qualities, you regard them as significant beings and yourself as insignificant. This continual

> comparing and selecting generates a never-ending procession of desires. ... There is a constant searching, a constant looking for new situations or attempts to improve given situations. It is the least enjoyable state of mind. (1976a, 30–32)

Antony's honest clarity about the internal as well as external threats to his honor leads him to try to resecure it in various ways, from marriage to warfare to the transcendence of suicide. Cleopatra's continual game-playing to draw Antony "into her territory," until at last she tries to recreate herself into a monument, to freeze a moment of imagined bliss into eternity, also seems to fit this description precisely.

Early on (for example, in act 2, scene 5), this constant search also leads her to the frustration of a fourth realm, that of the Jealous Gods. In it, she could

> deduce the possibility of heaven, the complete elimination of pain and achievement of pleasure. ... But [her] preoccupation ... makes [her] insecure and anxious. [She] must always struggle to control [her] territory.

Then, "through tremendous struggle," she may begin

> to realize that [she] has made it, that [she] is there, that [she] is in heaven. Then [she] begins to relax, to appreciate and dwell upon [her] achievements, shielding out undesirable things. It is an hypnotic-like state. (1973, 142–43)

Hypnotized in this way, Cleopatra returns at her end to the Realm of the Gods. She is intelligent enough to know that she cannot sustain perfection in this world, but too blind to give up her idea of perfection. She kills herself to preserve it. As with Antony, this self-contradiction ironically provides the psychological ground for a continuation of the endlessly repeating cycle she is trying to escape. As Trungpa writes, "One cannot help playing the game; one just finds oneself playing it, all the time" (1976a, 40). And, implicitly in the context of this play, for all time.

In these characters, then, the samsaric cycle has been played out fully. Because Antony's and Cleopatra's self-awareness is explicit, unlike that of the characters in *Julius Caesar*, these characters are uniquely positioned to enact the psychological process of the Second Noble Truth, describing how striving causes suffering. This process is further emphasized by Cleopatra's attempt to go beyond it, to find a way to the Buddhist antidote, the Third Noble Truth, the cessation of striving. But again more clearly than

Brutus, she imagines that state to be essentially the same as this one. She projects another version of the same cycle she has already projected on her earthly life. She dies still in pursuit of a way to end this "excruciating and continuous pain" described in a fifth realm, Hell. In it, one "becomes paralyzed, frozen," as Cleopatra literally tries to become in her frustration, recreating herself by "playing" herself into a monument (1973, 138).[14]

This ironic view of the lovers' self-perpetuating cycle gestures, in its turn, toward a similarity between the Buddhist perspective and Jacques Derrida's linguistic one.[15] From his perspective as from the Buddhist, for example, it might be said that Cleopatra's form of dying (in "play") dramatizes her blindness to the fact that life is always and inescapably "played," and that this always implies one's own deconstruction, one's lack of stable identity, of signification. To commit oneself to continual self-reinvention, to a process of becoming in which one role is always being substituted for another, is simply to give an appropriately "dramatic" form to the fact that we are all unanchored from a stable identity. To "play" life is to choose to commit oneself in a particularly obvious form to changing identity. *Any* character—or person or sign—undergoes such lack of identity merely by its dependence for definition on its changing contexts in any linear progression. Whether the progression is a history, a narrative of a history, or an element within a narrative like a sentence, this essential fact of dependency remains. And, in essence, it is their denial of this implication that makes it impossible for either Cleopatra or Antony to dramatize the Buddhist alternative, the Third Noble Truth.

This is not because Antony and Cleopatra equate play with reality. They are right to do so. Rather, their mistake is to *believe* in either of them. As Trungpa writes,

> if we are speaking of a way out all the time, then we are dealing in fantasy, the dream of escape, salvation, enlightenment. . . . This approach becomes an obstacle. (1973, 118)

We must face ourselves honestly, as Antony and Cleopatra sometimes do; but on the Buddhist path,

> one does not seriously play their game of hope and fear. This is why the experience of the spiritual path is so significant, why the practice of meditation is the most insignificant experience of all. It is insignificant because you place no value judgment on it. Once you are absorbed into that insignificant situation of openness without involvement in value

> judgment, then you begin to see all the games going on around you. Someone is trying to be stern and spiritually solemn, trying to be a good person. Such a person might take it seriously if someone offended him, might want to fight. If you are in accordance with the basic insignificance of what is, then you begin to see the humor in this kind of solemnity, in people making such a big deal about things. (1973, 115)

Armed with this sense of humor, one can accept the samsaric Six Realms as nothing special, therefore as not particularly threatening. And in the absence of striving to escape them, they lose their power to entrap.

Jacques Derrida explains his view of signification in language (and in all linear representations) in ways that echo this Buddhist perspective. Just as Cleopatra desires a stable self and a stable love relationship, so readers desire to invent for written work a unified structure, one of whose symptoms will be a coherent meaning.

> The concept of centered structure—although it represents coherence itself, . . . is contradictorily coherent. And as always, coherence in contradiction expresses the force of a desire. The concept of centered structure is in fact the concept of a play based on a fundamental ground, a play constituted on the basis of a fundamental immobility and a reassuring certitude, which itself is beyond the reach of play. And on the basis of this certitude anxiety can be mastered, for anxiety is invariably the result of a certain mode of being implicated in the game, of being caught by the game, of being as it were at stake in the game from the outset. (Derrida 1986b, 84)

Derrida's assumption is that language, and therefore any construction that is created in language, "excludes totalization," excludes the possibility of being unified into one coherent meaning. The reader who insists on coherence is therefore like Cleopatra: in his attempt to escape anxiety by believing in stability, he contradicts the nature of language just as she contradicts the nature of play. Indeed language, like Cleopatra's continual self-reinventions, is a "field" that

> in effect is that of play, that is to say, a field of infinite substitutions only because it is finite, that is to say, because instead of being an inexhaustible field, as in the classical hypothesis, instead of being too large, there is something missing from it: a center which arrests and grounds the play of substitutions. (Derrida 1986b, 91)

That is, language is not different from "play." Reading a text is not different from living a life. In the Buddhist view the "normal" samsaric cycle of life experience is not denied but accepted, and accepted with a sense of humor, precisely *because* it lacks a solid and stable center; samsaric experience is not other than nirvana, but is in fact its ground. Similarly, Derrida does not endow language with grand transcendent qualities, but insists instead on its finiteness, and suggests that it is in fact this very condition of being limited which is the basis of its infinite possibilities. And the cause of this centerless destabilization is the same as that for Cleopatra's role-playing and for life itself: all three take the form of an endless "play of substitution."

Derrida explains this situation in linguistic terms:

> Every concept is inscribed in a chain or in a system within which it refers to the other, to other concepts, by means of the systematic play of differences. (Derrida 1986a, 125)

Therefore, each sign depends on its contexts for its meanings. The implication of this linguistic situation is that

> the movement of signification is possible only if each so-called "present" element, each element appearing on the scene of presence, is related to something other than itself, thereby keeping within itself the mark of the past element, and already letting itself be vitiated by the mark of its relation to the future element, this trace being related no less to what is called the future than to what is called the past, and constituting what is called the present by means of this very relation to what it is not: what it absolutely is not, not even a past or a future as a modified present. (1986a, 126–27)

A sign's meaning, therefore, exists in "relation to an impossible presence, . . . as the irreparable loss of presence, . . . as the death instinct, . . . opening itself to nonmeaning" (1986a, 131). As we have seen, this perspective toward the play within language parallels the Buddhist perspective on the suicides of Antony and Cleopatra. The characters dramatize this "death instinct" as a reaction to a feared "loss of presence," a fear which implies recognition of the threat of this loss—that is, of the actuality of the "presence" of "absence." By contrast, accepting this absence with a sense of humor might place us in the state that Buddhists call *sunyata,* an emptiness in which full presence occurs *by virtue of* absence, in which one does not impose meanings on one's contexts, nor identity on oneself. Derrida's description of the "trace" within its linguistic field gestures explicitly toward a similar context:

> Always differing and deferring, the trace is never as it is in the presentation of itself. It erases itself in presenting itself. (1986a, 133)

As with the Buddhist sense of humor that allows an acceptance of emptiness (meaninglessness), so Derrida writes that our reaction to this centerless play can be

> the Nietzschean . . . joyous affirmation of the play of the world and of the innocence of becoming, the affirmation of a world of signs without fault, without truth, and without origin which is offered to an active interpretation. *This affirmation then determines the noncenter otherwise than as loss of the center.* And it plays without security. For there is a *sure* play: that which is limited to the *substitution* of *given* and *existing, present,* pieces. In absolute chance, affirmation also surrenders itself to *genetic* indetermination, to the *seminal* adventure of the trace.
>
> There are thus two interpretations of interpretation, of structure, of sign, of play. The one seeks to decipher, dreams of deciphering a truth or an origin which escapes play and the order of the sign. . . . The other . . . affirms play and tries to pass beyond . . . [this interpreter who dreams of] full presence, the reassuring foundation, the origin and the end of play. (1986b, 93)

It "tries to pass beyond" this reader who is a counterpart to the character Cleopatra, she who is blind to the way desire drives her, blind to the emptiness of her belief in meaning.

III

As we may have come to expect, *Antony and Cleopatra* not only exemplifies this "dream" in its characters, but also frustrates this "dream" in its readers. At several moments it exposes the "absence" which is without as well as within these characters, the "absence" which is within itself as a whole, and even the "absence" of an object of its own representations. As Antony prepares for his land battle, he says that through this fight he and his sword "will earn [their] chronicle" (3.13.175). This "chronicle" is the history of the event which, perpetually retold, will give him fame. In this way it is like Cleopatra's "monument." One important instance of such "chronicling" is of course directly before us: this play. The mind of the created character Antony who is contained within this play also encompasses the play, and even tries to dictate our interpretation of it. At a moment in which he contemplates recreating himself in his ideal identity, he deconstructs himself as a character by requiring us to see him as more than a character, as using this play as well as being part of it. On the level of character, this manipulation makes his heroism seem more planned than "natural," and therefore calls into question whatever honor this present narrative may seem to give him. On the level of the whole play, by asking us to believe in Antony as larger than his role, this line reminds us of what we may successfully have willed to forget: that we "believe" in him only as a convention of the theater, that in fact he is merely a fiction within a narrative that is itself a fiction. He reminds us not to believe in him, nor in his nor any other interpretation of the play.

Just before his suicide he further undermines our "normal" assumptions about both story and interpretation. Antony says,

> Wouldst thou be window'd in great Rome, and see
> Thy master thus with pleach'd arms, bending down
> His corrigible neck, his face subdu'd
> To penetrative shame, whilst the wheel'd seat
> Of fortunate Caesar, drawn before him, branded
> His baseness that ensued?
>
> (4.14.72–77)

He points out the threat of an alternative script, Caesar's, which he would avoid because he wants to be interpreted as noble. But is not his imagining of Caesar's "alternative" the very one *Antony and Cleopatra* actually represents? From the Roman point of view (and that of many scholars: see note 1 above), it would seem to be. Any narrative, it may be, contains its own "alternative," the very version of itself that it professes to be "absent." Here, however, this notion is explicit, making the conclusion nearly inescapable that interpretation is always arbitrary, even when we can be sure of the "story." However, story lines, we are also reminded here, are arbitrary as well. Even their sources, their "origins," are uncertain: Are they constructed from a factual history of "what is called the past" which can be trusted in some way to be "true"? Are they constructed (or reconstructed) by the playwright? Are they even constructed by the character, as Antony seems to believe here?

Cleopatra too shows an awareness of alternative scripts; she is determined not to play into Caesar's, where he will

> ... hoist me up,
> And show me to the shouting varlotry
> Of censuring Rome.
>
> (5.2.55–57)

Even worse, she says, there would be this treatment:

> The quick comedians
> Extemporally will stage us, and present
> Our Alexandrian revels: Antony
> Shall be brought drunken forth, and I shall see
> Some squeaking Cleopatra boy my greatness
> I' th' posture of a whore.
>
> (5.2.216–21)

She truly sees (as Dolabella confirms) how Caesar will treat her if caught. Yet if we see her as the Romans do, she (like Antony) is accurately describing what we are watching at that moment onstage, the opposite of her own interpretation. She is the "gipsy," "strumpet," "whore" whose infamy is even now, on the Jacobean stage, being exhibited in the precise form of her description: by "some squeaking Cleopatra" who "boy[s]" her. She too denies her own "reality" by reminding us that she is "played." And she too represents the alternative interpretation whose "absence" she professes.

Enobarbus echoes the greater characters:

> Yet he that can endure
> To follow with allegiance a fall'n lord
> Does conquer him that did his master conquer,
> And earns a place i' th' story.
>
> (3.13.43–46)

The falseness of this "enduring" will be clear shortly; he will have two more changes before he dies. In spite of this lack of "endurance," however, his statement is also true: he is in fact preserved in this perennially retold "story." Like the others, this moment makes us conscious of the boundaries beyond which we will not allow a representation to go. Precisely when a character insists on the triumph of his art, or a work insists on its own *reality,* it makes its *un*reality most emphatic. *Antony and Cleopatra* puts us in this position again and again, leading us at last to Cleopatra's climactic *coup de théâtre*, the internal contradictions of which erase its own signification. By this moment, any stabilizing conception we might have had of "play," and therefore of the play itself, has been erased.

Indeed, this self-erasure through "play" suggests the inherent nature of the theatrical enterprise itself. Actors can enact only those states that are truly within them; because they are in privileged space onstage, however, and because they are "not themselves," they can perform these enactments more fully than they or we normally do in "real" life.[16] One of the principal appeals of theater to an audience may in fact be this tension between the "reality" of dreams and desires that actors stage, on the one hand, and normal acts, on the other. That is, the characters Antony and Cleopatra, because they are conscious of their acting, may embody the tensions in *any* acting, and in life as well.

Jonathan Dollimore furthers this view in his discussion of actors "who strive to become one with the signifieds of their parts." He draws the conclusion that the achievement of this significance is "true identity [, which] thus thrives by repression" (Dollimore 1984, 13). Terry Eagleton also deconstructs the idea of "true identity" by recognizing it as the product of difference, then asking if there is any state that we might call "absolute" identity—or, indeed, any "absolute" at all (Eagleton 1986, 24). This question, it may be, is the one toward which all drama tends.

From this "noncentered" point of view, Enobarbus's oral reproduction (in act 2, scene 2) of Cleopatra's staged first meeting with Antony epitomizes the larger work that contains it. Like Shakespeare, Enobarbus reproduces a presumed original in a way which so insists on Cleopatra's staged magical apotheosis that we resist belief even if we are awed by the grandeur of its idea. By insisting on its significance, Enobarbus calls this significance into question. The nature of the original is therefore also called into question. The possibility of stable meaning vanishes for Enobarbus, as for Cleopatra and for Shakespeare.

What does this imply for us in the audience? Jacques Derrida indicates the possibility of a "joyous affirmation" in which such a "loss of center" is not conceived as loss, but more neutrally as a "noncenter" of "sure play," of "absolute chance" to which the reader gives himself up (as Enobarbus accuses Antony of doing by choosing to fight by sea). However, the "normal" reaction of many readers might be that of Antony and Cleopatra: retreat to some reassuring "dream," to belief in *something*—the reaction I have already postulated to *Dream* and *Richard III.*

Giulio Romano's *Sala dei Giganti* presents a very similar aesthetic situation with unusual directness.[17] It illustrates explicitly how art can mask itself and undo itself at the same time, and how this process encourages its viewers to play king's games. (This explicitness may help us to understand why Romano is the only Continental visual artist to whom Shakespeare refers in his plays. See *Winter's Tale* 5.2.97–100 and its reference to a sculptor's work which will come to life.) Indeed, perhaps because of his different artistic conventions, in Romano these implications for the viewer may seem clearer than in Shakespeare.

In this room (discussed at length in Appendix A), Romano encloses his viewer within four walls whose frescoed story seems continuous, without beginning or end. *Trompe l'oeil* effects are used to make the illusion seem real. This illusion directly threatens the viewer: it seems that the walls of the room (which are also the pillars supporting the rebellious Giants) are tumbling down—indeed, that the exit door is about to be closed off by falling bricks. The viewer, that is, is implicated in the subject; like the rebels, he is threatened with entrapment and destruction. Like them, he casts his eyes upward to see the cause of this imminent destruction, and sees the implacable enmity of the Olympian gods. The message is clear: Do not rebel.

However, there is a twist. Qualities that are normally implicit in realistic representational art become explicit in this room. "Normally," we are doubly implicated in such an art-object by the very technique that renders it "realistic," which seems to objectify it into a thing to be looked *at,* a thing separate from ourselves. Its lines of perspective lead our eye into the painting, toward the vanishing point within, even as they reach out to enmesh us by defining our vantage point, the point of view that we adopt toward it. In this room, however, our entrapment is no longer implicit, but literal. We are physically enclosed within this all-encircling painted story, and we are forced by our physical position on the same floor with the giants to take their vantage point: that of rebels being conquered.

Yet this literal rendering of the normal implications of realistic art also makes its internal contradictions explicit: the use of pastels is both "unreal" and inappropriate for the subject; the giants are caricatures rather than "real" giants; and perhaps most obviously, there are windows that open to another "reality" outside this created one. The "reality" of the threat to rebels is thus erased, allowing us emotional distance from it. We are freed to contemplate the artwork on its own terms, as art—as the

Wall fresco, *Sala dei Giganti*, Giulio Romano. Courtesy of Alinari/Art Resource, N.Y.

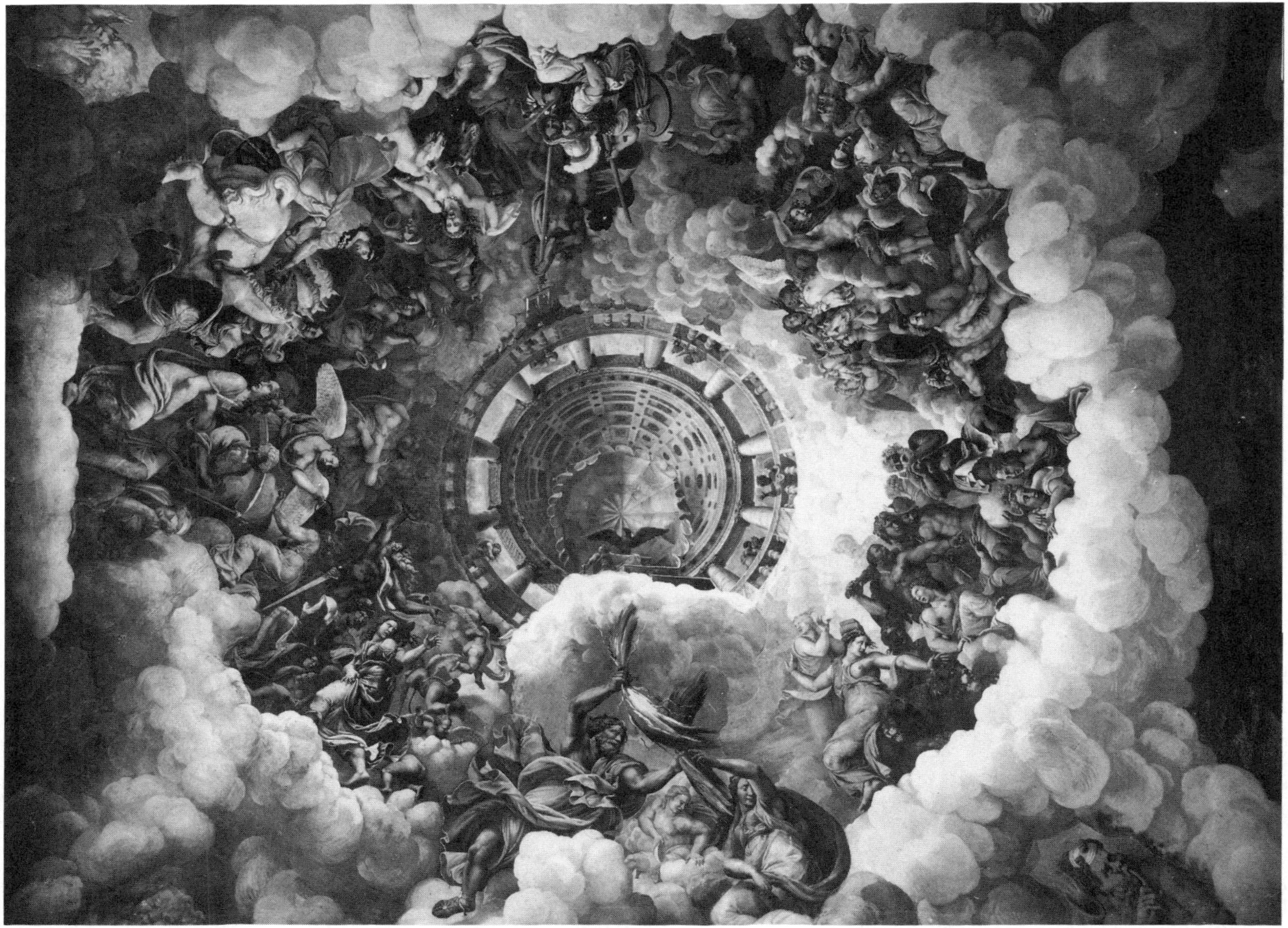

Courtesy of Alinari/Art Resource, N.Y.

artist's skillful construction of illusion. We have the leisure to contemplate the serene authority of the Gonzaga eagle reigning above the gods and goddesses. Its contrast to the fury and destruction surrounding us is comforting. So is our ability to affirm meaning. Aware of the alternative, we may choose to collude with the artist's apotheosis of his patron; we may choose to acquiesce in Gonzaga power, and in its self-definition: Mantua as the new Rome.

Romano presents the "realism" effect of his representational art in a form that is unusually explicit and threatening, yet in a form that simultaneously erases that realism and its threat. The effectiveness of his room's apotheosis of the Gonzagas depends on both aspects of this self-making/self-undoing process. In order to represent the authenticity of Gonzaga power, it undermines belief in the "reality" of its representation; in order to inculcate worship for its subject, it erases that subject; in order to speak for authority, it erases the authority with which it speaks. In each of these ways, it offers the viewer the option of accepting an "absence" of coherent structure, a "presence" of "nonmeaning." In each of these ways, it offers the viewer a choice between "deciphering a truth or an origin" and affirming "play." The room's approval by the Gonzagas and by Charles V, the Holy Roman Emperor, indicates which choice they thought the viewer would make.

In *Antony and Cleopatra,* I have argued, Shakespeare achieves very similar effects. The main characters are invested with "reality" by virtue of dramatic convention, by virtue of a complexity that seems to mirror "real" life, and by virtue of their source in history. Their linear unfolding leads up to its climax, Cleopatra's staged death. This culmination of "reality" is also the climax of her undoing, in which each of these reifying elements of the play—theatrical convention, the "realism" of self-belief, and our certainty about source or origin—have been rendered questionable, essentially empty. Threatened by disbelief on all these levels, and thus by self-disbelief as well, we might be led (as Cleopatra with her different desires is not) to accept Caesar's noble magnanimity at the end at face value. First, he confers nobility on Antony:

>   . . . let me lament
> With tears as sovereign as the blood of hearts,
> That thou, my brother, my competitor
> In top of all design, my mate in empire,
> Friend and companion in the front of war,
> The arm of my own body, and the heart
> Where mine thoughts did kindle—that our stars,

> Unreconciliable, should divide
> Our equalness to this.
>
> (5.1.40–48)

And then on Cleopatra:

> She shall be buried by her Antony;
> No grave upon the earth shall clip in it
> A pair so famous. High events as these
> Strike those that make them; and their story is
> No less in pity than his glory which
> Brought them to be lamented.
>
> (5.2.358–63)

However, consider what we have learned of Caesar earlier in the play: that he is a treacherous ally; that for his own profit he takes advantage of others' idealistic notions of honor, having no such ideals himself; and that he is a beggar for power before Fortune. In this light, these late speeches might seem self-serving. It is convenient for such a man to be able to blame the "irreconcilable" stars for his war with Antony. Similarly, it is hard not to think that, were Cleopatra still alive, she would be humiliated in just the ways she anticipated. All that Caesar can salvage from her death, however, is a reputation for noble magnanimity. And so, it may be, he too enacts a final charade.

In conscious disbelief we might, as with the Gonzagas, accept Caesar's appearance of magnanimity for the thing itself—accept the comfort of a lie. Having been shown that the dissolution of theater, history, and character implies the dissolution of the foundations of the self, we might welcome the comfort of the king as father figure, the new Caesar who rules the new Rome: James of London.

Such a conservative conclusion has been argued by Jonathan Dollimore, who believes that although Jacobean tragedies often "disclose ideology as misrepresentation" by showing its inner contradictions, *Antony and Cleopatra* seems different. He believes that this play affirms the stable power structure against individual heroism and "sexual infatuation" (Dollimore 1984, 8, 206, 217). Leonard Tennenhouse also sees this play as supporting James: in it, "the unruly woman of Elizabethan comedy was criminalized" to show how unruly the world can be without a patriarchal monarch in control (Tennenhouse 1980, 153).

However, as I have argued above, not only Cleopatra and Antony but Caesar, too, is discredited, and the inconsistencies between ideology and fact are exposed. Therefore, the cost of such a conservative affirmation is high. To reach this conclusion in the context of the present argument, we must recognize that Shakespeare deconstructs both his play and his audience in order to inscribe himself within this gift to the patron of the King's Men. If we follow him by welcoming Caesar's comfort, indeed, we might find our own version of Cleopatra's suicide (in whose significance we are similarly taught not to believe). This welcome might be our way of joining her in sympathy, even as we make a different choice, one which the play has taught us is more intelligent and less self-obsessed (certainly less self-destructive) than hers, but *not* more "true." In this view, the play raises our consciousness, but offers no alternative to playing king's games. As with the *Sala dei Giganti,* this play's "non-center" is its political strength.

As in *Merchant of Venice* and *Julius Caesar,* then, Shakespeare here leaves us without a safety net. This time, even though we may renew the struggle to string a tightrope over the abyss of disbelief and to attach it to the protective, paternal arms of King James, we will be aware of doing so within the void, aware that even if we succeed, we are in fact adrift. This play may have made the idea inescapable that meaning is erased by the very fact of its representation, that it is always our invention, and that it is essentially empty.

That is, even if we choose self-subjugation, from both the Buddhist and Derridean points of view there is a gain in this play. Our intensified awareness of the contradictions within this choice may open us to another possibility, to the threshold of another way of being. More than these earlier plays, *Antony and Cleopatra* seems to be the natural culmination of a long and methodical process. The implications for an audience of a play's self-deconstruction are worked out so fully, in such excruciating detail, that the seeds for a particular style of revulsion at the way of the world and the self—at a particular way of *understanding* the world and the self—may have been sown. If so, their growth in the viewer may be irreversible.

From the Buddhist perspective, this seeing through conventional categories of belief can lead toward the end of our desire-cycle of striving, as well as to the end of its mirror, our oppositional mode of dealing with the world; in turn, these cessations can lead to the end of suffering. Chögyam Trungpa discusses this situation in which "there's nothing to hang onto, nothing to work on, nothing to grasp onto" as a somewhat intimidating one: "Freedom from attachment to outer and inner naturally begins to bring about a sense of desolation—you can't be *here* and you can't be *there*" (Trungpa, 1976b, 132, 26). A sense of renunciation begins to develop "from having given up any clinging situations": "nothing is cultivated because you want to cultivate yourself for the good and for the great and the glory anymore" (1976b, 133). However, this is not the renunciation of asceticism, or of self- or world-rejection:

> Renunciation in this instance is not just throwing away but, having thrown everything away, we begin to feel the living quality of peace. And this particular peace is not feeble peace, feeble openness, but it has a strong character, an invincible quality, an unshakable quality, because it admits to gaps of hypocrisy. It is complete peace in all directions, so that not even a speck of a dark corner exists for doubt and hypocrisy. Complete openness is complete victory because we do not fear, we do not try to defend ourselves at all. (1973, 198–99)

Far from closing ourselves off from experience, we can be more open to it, for the very reason "that nothing extraordinary is taking place—and there is no one to project extraordinary situations taking place either" (1976b, 26). In this recognition, we can be beyond the cycle of hope and fear that desire fuels. "Desolation" may be intimidating, but it is also the basis of "freedom."

For social activists, this Buddhist perspective may seem depressing. It seems to raise audience consciousness without encouraging a change in social forms. To the contrary, it seems that if having desires and mounting oppositions to achieve them are both self-defeating, there is nothing to be done. Furthermore, if the oppressive world is merely a reflection of our own self-oppression, then even if we could do something, it would have to be to ourselves as much as to the world. Since even a Buddhist reformer is likely not to be oppositional, he or she might seem like the courtiers who play king's games in response to *Richard III* and *Dream*.[18]

However, the Buddhist assertion that a changed consciousness is possible at all is in itself revolutionary, beyond the demonstrations of Karl Marx or Michel Foucault. For one version of its social efficacy, it may be useful to remember the lesson of Bottom, and to have faith that changes in consciousness eventually lead to changes in action, that society can be worked with instead of against, pacified rather than opposed so that it *wants* change instead of fearing it.

And if *Antony and Cleopatra* gives us a Derridean glimpse of the way toward this spaciousness, several earlier plays offer glimpses of this spaciousness itself. However, before turning to them, it may be useful to remember here that once Shakespeare had thoroughly worked through the "emptiness" implications of realistic representation, he changed to the less realistic conventions of romance. We will return to the way in which he worked with these implications in the new genre in our final chapter.[19]

6
Prince Hal's Deferral as the Ground of Free Play

The Buddhist Third Noble Truth is that we can end our suffering in this world by nonstriving, by becoming desireless in the sense of being unattached to the things of this world, of not needing them to build ourselves up (Trungpa 1978b, 59). To attain this state, it is necessary to become egoless, to cease belief in oneself as a continuing, autonomous entity with a particular, ongoing identity. It is necessary to see the cinema we create, "The *Me* Show," as a discontinuous series of frames that we have spliced together to give ourselves an impression of our own continuity. If we wish to end suffering, we must no longer define ourselves as stable beings who move through life with a particular set of character traits and a particular place in the world. We must give up the idea of self-definition altogether and, indeed, give up belief in our having a particular personal identity. Then, no longer having a self-image to enhance or defend, we need no longer compartmentalize experience into desirable and undesirable categories, accepting the one and rejecting the other, then projecting these preconceptions on the world. Instead, everything that comes our way is accommodated hospitably, and with respect. We can be nonjudgmental, nonexclusive, nonsuppressive. The energy that has been blocked by repression and judgment and fear is released to flow back into our lives. It may bear repeating, however, that such a liberation is not a release from this world into another; rather, it allows us to see (and be in) this same old world in a new way.[1]

This state of being is one that we conventionally resist, just as the characters Antony and Cleopatra do. We resist it because it is fearful: we are dominated by our self-definitions, by our belief in ourselves as independent individuals—in our egos; and this liberated state kills them. *Antony and Cleopatra* exposes these conventional beliefs in its characters and in its own dramatic conventions as well; but it also gestures toward a space beyond these conventions, a space that Shakespeare had already begun to explore in *Henry IV, Part One*. This play introduces its main character, Prince Hal, as one who consciously refrains from defining his identity in terms of his present surroundings. He is conscious of being without a self-definition in the present tense, and is therefore also conscious of being in a set of circumstances on which his sense of himself is not dependent. Thus preconceived judgments need not be projected; he can do what he does for "sport," in pretense, as an actor. However, it is well to say at once that he has not come to this state through wisdom, but by being given an auspicious familial and political situation. Hal has many qualities that are not consistent with the Buddhist point of view. Nevertheless, because his present situation does not encourage him to define himself, he lives without a conventional sense of identity, and does so with equanimity. As we watch this situation unfold, we can glimpse through him several aspects of the Third Noble Truth.

I

A situation of nonidentity is possible for Hal because the uniqueness of his position makes it unthreatening. The psychological structure of his historical situation seems to be set up much as Antony's is (pleasure in the person of Falstaff seems to oppose duty and honor in the persons of King Henry and Hotspur), but the prince does not experience a conflict between these values. His rival is his father, not a competitor like Antony's Octavius, and this rival wants to give him power, not take it away. Again, like Antony, Hal is a prince rather than a ruler; he does not yet need to make choices. Most important of all, he is always conscious of his future: that he will be king and that his present situation is temporary. This awareness most particularly reinforces his ability to accommodate equably those differing perspectives that might "normally" seem to conflict.

In the very first scene he says,

> I know you all, and will a while uphold
> The unyok'd humor of your idleness,
> Yet herein will I imitate the sun, . . .

(1.1.195–97)

He will "imitate the sun" by putting himself under a cloud; his every act in this play will be a pretense, an "act" designed to enhance his public image "that when he please again to be himself, / Being wanted, he may be more wond'red at" (1.1.200–201). And yet this image he thinks of *is* in the future. For *now,* it allows deferral of self-image, and he continually takes advantage of this option. After the conclusion of their "play extempore," Hal tells Falstaff of his intention to banish him: "I do, I will" (2.4.481), yet immediately lies to the sheriff to defer Falstaff's day of judgment.[2] The play ends on essentially the same note, with Hal's "lie" to "do [him] grace" (5.4.157). His awareness of his future allows him a continual deferral of judgment in the present.

Thus he turns the present into a stage whose roles are played in the shadow of the future. In this unfolding "present," he has no "present" identity. It too is deferred, this deferral being the ground on which his ability to defer judgment is based. At the end of the play, with Hal's final lie for Falstaff, it is still being deferred. And, as Stephen Greenblatt has pointed out, even this future "self" that he will become as king is not essential and unchanging, but simply another role, this one socially defined (Greenblatt 1985, 33). It may be that there is *never* an "essential" Prince Hal. At any rate, in *Part One* this seems true, and he more than any character we have so far seen knows this about himself. He is positioned as Jacques Derrida believes signs to be in their relationship to their presumed identity (or meaning): they too *by their nature* keep their meaning in perpetual deferral. Derrida writes,

> The sign is usually said to be put in the place of the thing itself, the present thing, "thing" here standing equally for meaning or referent. The sign represents the present in its absence. It takes the place of the present. When we cannot grasp or show the thing, state the present, the being-present, when the present cannot be presented, we signify, we go through the detour of the sign. We take or give signs. We signal. The sign, in this sense, is deferred presence. (Derrida 1986a, 124)

If the prince is like a sign whose meaning is absent, this is because he is like a sign or element which,

> appearing on the scene of presence, is related to something other than itself, thereby keeping within itself the mark of the past element, and already letting itself be vitiated by the mark of its relation to the future element, this trace being related no less to what is called the future than to what is called the past, and constituting what is called the present by means of this very relation to what it is not: what it absolutely is not, not even a past or a future as a modified present. (Derrida 1986a, 126–27)

Hal, of course, gets his expectation of the future from his family, his lineage, his past. He consciously determines his style in the "present" by its relationship to that which is *not* "present." This context for existence that Hal renders explicit is one that Derrida believes to be ubiquitous, whether we consider signs in language or in life. Derrida argues further that when we see signs in this context, we must then conceive of them as players in a game, or in

> a play in which whoever loses wins, and in which one loses and wins on every turn. If the displaced presentation remains definitively and implacably postponed, it is not that a certain present remains absent or hidden. Rather, *différance* maintains our relationship with that which we necessarily misconstrue, and which exceeds the alternative of presence and absence. (Derrida 1986a, 131–32)

The prince does not differ from others in his displacement, then, but in his consciousness of it. Perhaps he most clearly acts out the implications of this consciousness at the end of the play. There he exemplifies this idea of losing and winning on the same turn by defeating Hotspur and, with virtual simultaneity, pledging to give his winner's reputation to Falstaff. In doing so, it has often been argued, he transcends either/or choices ("the alternative of presence and absence") and achieves a more inclusive way of being, a way in which the normal categories of experience, usually thought to be mutually exclusive, can rest easily together beyond compartmentalizing definition.[3] He lives within the "free play" conditions that Derrida alleges for signs in a text.

One of the implications of this state that he dramatizes is his lack of commitment to any of the worldly options he is offered.[4] Continuously in the act of deferral, knowing from the first that his anticipated and imagined identity as king is always at a distance, he is perpetually unattached. His prodigal son role frees him from being bound to either his father or his friend Falstaff. But this state of *non*attachment need not imply the lack of feeling that we associate with *de*tachment. Rather, it has to do with not identifying oneself with things, therefore not needing to cling to them or hoard them or push them away. Because it is common to see *Henry IV, Part Two* as this play's sequel, it is also common to read this first play as part of a sequence in which the blatant hypocrisy of *Part Two* is read into *Part One:* Hal's banishment of Falstaff in the second part is believed to be set up by an unfeeling, cynically self-seeking prince in the first.[5] But the reverse is equally arguable from the same facts: that *because* the prince knows all this to be coming, he can be different (deferred) here, just as, reciprocally, his deferred kingly identity *depends* on this difference, as he knows. Both sides of this second perspective reinforce his deferral of identity as being uniquely *in the present*. He is fundamentally different from what he will be later, as king; then he will have no choice but to embrace self-definition.

The freedom that Hal achieves by being unattached to his present circumstances is shown by the variety of perspectives he can take toward Falstaff. When he wishes, for example, he can see him just as his father does, with the judgmental eyes of authority. Hal foresees that Falstaff's acts will "ebb," and that they will lead to "the gallows" (1.2.27, 38); and he foresees that his value is self-limiting: "If all the year were playing holidays, / To sport would be as tedious as to work" (1.2.204–5). Yet because he sees his relationship with Falstaff as limited, he is not threatened by it as is his father (who, as present ruler, cannot defer decisions). The prince can therefore also allow himself to enter fully into Falstaff's realm. And when he does so, he finds himself quite unexpectedly beside another character who is unattached to this world, although in a radically different style.

II

This difference in style is crucial, for it gives Falstaff the ability to unfold to the prince still larger dimensions of that freedom which the nonidentity of "free play" allows. Hal's nonattachment, in turn, allows him to appreciate these dimensions, and from them to learn new possibilities for himself.

Because of this largeness of character, Falstaff can be approached from many points of view. He allies himself with the moon, as against King Henry's sun (1.2.13–29), calling theft "good government" (1.2.26–27). He stands for disorder, refusing "to understand any fixed and final allocation of authority" (Bristol 1985, 213); he is associated with the carnivalesque, and thus with Michel Foucault's "certain plebeian quality" which exists in all classes, and which represents the limit of power relations—"their underside, their counter-stroke, that which responds to every advance of power by a movement of disengagement" (Foucault 1980, 138). To the political, he is the apolitical; to the top of the hierarchy, he is the bottom; to order, he is the limit of order; to judgment, he is the flesh, appetite incarnate, time humanized (measured by physical impulses rather than minutes), the thing to be judged by authority. In himself he is judgment forever deferred. He is the play's principle of rebellious chaos reduced to a pointless old man or enlarged to an archetype. He is evil against good. In political, moral, or psychological tems, Falstaff is always out of bounds, the Other by whom the borders of convention or culture or order are defined.[6] He can be discussed in terms of any category of experience because he challenges them all equally; he challenges the very idea of categorizing experience.

Thus, in spite of his reputation, he can be said to be as unattached as Hal is to the things of this world. He is a creature of impulse, not of lust. He wants food, drink, woman, and he takes them. He has appetite. But there is nothing he must have to complete his idea of himself, nothing he lusts after, nothing actively sought or dreamed of. In this limited sense, Falstaff has no sense of purpose. As the prince says in the second scene, his clock is his belly, but it *tells* time, it does not *anticipate* it. If he epitomizes the principle of earthiness (Hal says that he "lards the lean earth as he walks along," 2.2.109), he also has the earth's physical inertia, in contrast to the vitality born of lust that leads Hotspur to his death.

However, because he is unattached to things and in this limited sense desireless, he is not bound by the earth, or by the flesh either. On the contrary, the dominant impression his language gives is of intellectual energy, not the physical slothfulness of self-indulgence. He seems, in fact, to indulge the natural fecundity of his mind and imagination far more fully than he does his body. This intellectual energy is exemplified constantly by his puns, of course, but a more expansive example occurs in act 2, scene 4, when Prince Hal has set his companion up for comic exposure as a coward and liar in the conclusion to the Gadshill incident. Falstaff seems to play into the prince's hands by lying more and more blatantly to escape the charge of cowardice, boasting about how many men he fought and killed. But as he raises the number of the killed from two to eleven, his lies become so palpable that it is impossible not to believe that he means to be found out.[7] Certainly he does not seriously try to defend himself (as a person without self-image need not). Neither cowardice nor lying is an important issue to him. He is not "exposed" because he does not hide anything, except in pretense, in playing to the conventional assumption that everyone will agree cowardice and lying to be "bad." By making his lies obvious, Falstaff shows his emptiness; by this example, he challenges Hal to perform a similar self-deconstruction.

This challenge goes further: in seeming to be unconcerned about appearing truthful, he implies that "truth" is like any other thought—something to recognize as another's belief or expectation, an idea with which to play. Michel Foucault captures something of this spirit when he writes that "'Truth' is to be understood as a system of ordered procedures for the production, regulation, distribution, circulation, and operation of statements" (Foucault 1980, 133). The "truth-value" of a statement is irrelevant to its social function. Falstaff here tests Hal's limits just as Hal tests Falstaff's, seeing how far this heir to authority will let him go not just in falsehood, but in the deconstruction of the idea of "truth" and in the deconstruction of any possibility that authority—*any* ideological stance— can be legitimated. Falstaff's challenge, then, is only partly by example. He also confronts conventional belief directly by flipping its coin over to show it its other face. He challenges Hal in this way to see what is lost by adhering to authorized belief, to extend his limits, and at last, perhaps, to abandon boundaries altogether.

Later in this episode the prince increases the pressure on Falstaff by playing his trump card, the "truth," stripping away the lies and laying bare the cowardice. In reaction, Falstaff shows still another dimension of his character, coming closer to the quality that is the basis of his mastery of situations. He at once shifts the ground of the discussion with a question: "Was it / For me to kill the heir-apparent?" (2.4.268–69). The "truth" issue is transformed into a game of intrigue, of disguise and hidden intention, Falstafff's patriotism now contrasting favorably with Hal's practical joke. Cowardice is playfully transformed into patriotism, lies into modesty; the tone shifts, our perspective turns, and suddenly we are laughing *with* Falstaff, although *not at the prince.* Falstaff survives because, being unattached to particular ideas, he is able to play with them rather than being fixed by them, and in this way he can neutralize the power of judgment. He shows the prince that he can play with ideology as well as falsehood, and feign that loyalty to authority that is the other side of the *un*truth he has just finished entertaining. In nonattachment, nothing need be rejected. In this spirit, he shows too that one can survive severe challenges without defeating the challenger, and that the oppositional mode is as unnecessary in political argument as in philosophy. Falstaff's resolution costs Hal nothing. Our laughter, indeed, repudiates the very ground on which the opposition between right and wrong, and therefore even between authority and rebellion, rests. Before Falstaff had shown what is lost by belief in conventional categories; here Falstaff shows that in the abandonment of conventional modes of operation we not only lose nothing, but in fact gain flexibility and vitality. Hal's lie shortly thereafter indicates his "present" acquiescence in these lessons.

But first, as if to lay the groundwork for the impact of this lie when it comes, Falstaff clarifies and widens the implications of his nonoppositional position—in spite of the fact that Hal's renewed challenge is even more difficult than the previous one. Falstaff is to play the father/king, and if he plays the role well, he must condemn the self that has just triumphed as the patriotic hero of Gadshill. Nor is Hal merely exposing his companion now, but sitting in judgment, first as his present self, the prince, then as his future self, the king (as Paul A. Gottschalk 1973/74, 612 has observed). As usual, however, Falstaff transforms the challenge into his own tour de force, in this case enacting the many levels of subversion.

Falstaff plays the first part of his monarchic role in parodic imitation of King Cambyses (2.4.387). Politically, by playing Henry as Cambyses, he seems to call the king a tyrant; by playing Henry as a role, Falstaff seems to call him a player king, a figure of questionable authority; and by parodying the role he plays, he seems to parody royal authority in itself. However, he also knows the disappointment Henry feels at the waywardness of his son, and gives this feeling an accurate voice too, both in its dimension as father for son, and as king for prince. He asks, "Why being son to me, art thou so pointed at?" And again, "Shall the son of England prove a thief and take purses?" (2.4.406–7, 409–10). At other times he is again subversive, but in a way that cuts against himself as well as King Henry: if, for example, Falstaff embodies the Lord of Misrule, the antiorderly spirit of carnival in which flesh and holiday are crowned, his is the voice of the commons that mocks the very authority that he himself represents.[8] Reciprocally, when he demystifies the theater by reminding us from his joint-stool throne that it is a form of royal discourse, he is also a commoner who appropriates this discourse to his own counterauthoritarian uses. He undermines himself and authority at the same time; he fulfills Hal's expectations by condemning himself and yet stands uncondemned. Still unfixed, he enacts the political implication of nonattachment that subversive ideas and ideas supportive of authority and judgment are equally valid, equally unthreatening, equally to be accommodated. In this universally hospitable frame of mind, he personifies unmeasured, uncensored fullness. He seems to have achieved that sense of humor toward life and himself in which he can see and feel "the whole ground, the open ground." In "this open situation," there is "no hint of limitation," nothing to make "a big deal" of, either through rejection or desire (Trungpa 1973, 114).

As Falstaff plays the roles of monarch and prince, then, subverting both them and himself, he is intensifying his counterchallenge to the prince, and on two levels. On one level he is daring the prince to become the authority figure he was born to be, to cease deferral. On another level, he is challenging the prince to be as good as Falstaff himself, as willing to give himself up, to continue to acquiesce in not judging. And in response,

Hal answers both levels of this challenge affirmatively. Like Falstaff, under challenge the prince enlarges.

Hal's roles here have a more literal relationship to his "reality" than do Falstaff's. He plays roles that enact his actual present (as prince) and future (as king). His playful commentary on authority is therefore closer to the bone; it is directly rather than indirectly self-targeted. Almost inescapably, given this situation, he gives his "self" up. That is, he is true to his "present" role as prince, in which in "reality" his identity (as king) is deferred, by dramatizing his "absence"—by remaining silent, except for the asking of one brief question. Judgment is deferred (as it is in the full play) until he plays his future identity as king; then he finally gives it voice. In his changing roles in the "play extempore," then, Hal epitomizes the Derridean situation of deferred identity which governs the prince throughout the play as a whole. And even when, as king in the latter portion of this little play, he does become judgmental, it is (as Falstaff says) in "practice" for this future (2.4.375), not for "real" in the present. Although he delivers the same judgment against Falstaff that his father would, he does not do so because he means to pass this judgment *now*. Instead, by showing that Hal knows the mind of his father, this judgment demonstrates his awareness of the ground that legitimizes his present deferral, as well as the ideological implications of this deferral from the king's point of view. It is in this knowledge, then, that he again chooses to defer judgment in his "real" self just before the end of this same scene, by lying to the sheriff. That is, because his answer to Falstaff's self-defense and mockery of the prince (2.4.397–432) is couched in the voice of his future "self," it legitimizes his silence as prince—even in the face of the enthronement of carnival. Falstaff's and the prince's exchanging of titles in play, then, is their way of rehearsing the rest of the play, a way of "practicing" how to "play" with the very terms by which society defines identity—not to deny the existence of these terms, but to practice how to exist *with* them rather than *within* them. Hal's lie is a commitment to continue this "practice."

The performance in act 2, scene 4 is metadramatic, then, as James Calderwood has seen (1979, 7–8). It is a rehearsal for one of its major "real" events, Hal's interview with his father in act 3, scene 2. (Indeed, from the king's vantage point, the performance epitomizes the play's situation: Falstaff seems to threaten to rule the prince, thus the future king and, perhaps, the kingdom. Even Henry's usurpation is figured by his son when Falstaff, as carnival king, accuses Hal of planning to "depose" him, 2.4.435.) It encourages us, in other words, to see Hal's specific role in act 3, scene 2, as well as more generally in his other scenes, as the play of nonattachment. This little play renders the illusional nature of the rest of the play virtually explicit. Thus it positions us in the audience to see the full play's action as the two main characters do, in a nonattached way, as transparently not to be "believed"—to see it, that is, as a Buddhist might see life: as a show (sGam.po.pa 1986, 259). We are prepared by this "play extempore" to understand how Hal the player can lie for Falstaff, and also to understand the value of this nonopposition.

Having decided at the end of the scene to continue his exploration of the possibilities of nonattachment, Hal continues to increase the difficulty of his challenges to Falstaff. He transports Falstaff from the tavern, where morality and order are relative abstractions, to the battlefield, where they take on the seriousness of life and death issues. He deliberately puts Falstaff at risk, as if the world's pressure is increasingly difficult for him to withstand. It is as if Falstaff's legitimation must now be in relation to ultimate things if he is to have value. Otherwise, if he is without value in "real" terms, Hal will have lost his alternative; he will have to cease conscious deferral and bend himself to training for the future—to come out from under the clouds. Hal's freedom, that is, depends on Falstaff. Therefore Falstaff must be pushed. And, reciprocally, this process of pushing also makes Hal's freedom from attachment clearer. Thus, immediately after his deferring lie to the sheriff, he plans to "procure this fat rogue a charge of foot," saying "I know his death will be a march of twelve score" (2.4.545–48). There is no question for Hal of an alliance with Falstaff. But still there is humor, and there is the possibility of learning. This possibility is delayed, however, because in act 4, scene 2, with Falstaff's "pitiful" soldiers, and in act 5, scene 3, with Falstaff's bottle of sack, Hal has other things on his mind.

We in the audience may see more than he during this period. We may see that under this new pressure Falstaff, though he does not change, does progressively unfold, enlarging and clarifying the implications of his stance toward life. As in act 2 he robbed money intended for the king, so in act 4, scene 2, he robs the king of the best conscripts for the army and takes bribes in the process. This time, though, he gives more explanation than before. And although the prince's attention is otherwise engaged, he too is present for Falstaff's explanation of the quality of his men: that they are good enough to be "food for powder, food for powder; they'll fill a pit as well as / better. Tush, man, mortal men, mortal men" (4.2.65–67). He describes war to the prince from the point of view of a plebeian soldier, not of a commander nor of a representative of authority. No considerations of reputation or gain enter into his assessment of war. He considers it instead as a death machine. Since its practical effect is to kill men on both sides, any live body will serve. In battle as in the tavern, he does not see king and country, or virtue and honor, but bodies. He still sees life on the level of experience, without preconceptions about its meaning (without certainty that there *is* meaning). War is not for him about winning and losing; it is not a competition for anything; it is simply a threat to life. It is fitting in every way that Falstaff does not fight well, if at all. This fact in itself embodies his critique of those who would impose their meanings on us; he speaks this critique in every way he knows how, both to the man who will be king and, of course, to us.

In act 5, scene 1, when he confronts the concept of honor, this attitude toward abstractions remains explicit. Because honor has no physical basis, it is merely a "word" (5.1.134); its composition is "air" (5.1.135). Words by themselves cannot confer "reality," any more than signs can have meaning in themselves, or selves can have identity. Falstaff's substitution of sack for a pistol in act 5, scene 3 merely confirms this view. The prince's wrenching the bottle out in expectation of a weapon is simply one more comic exposure that fails because the identity exposed was never denied. This episode reemphasizes Falstaff's lack of attachment to a particular preconception of himself.

In the final scene, as he actually faces death in battle, he takes the implications of this attitude almost as far as they can be taken. He seems to die: "He [Falstaff] falls down as if he were dead" (stage direction, act 5, scene 4, after line 76). Of course, he is *not* dead, but he lies there on the stage next to Hotspur, *seeming* so both to Hal and to us. We too are surprised, then, when he returns to life. However, our reaction is as it was with the bottle of sack in act 5, scene 3: we do a double take, and suddenly realize that once again he is being consistent with himself. Without a sense of honor, why should he not pretend to die? Once more he shows his ability to play with ideas, first in act and then in word, by turning the conventional meaning of the word "counterfeit" around. He shows its "emptiness"—its *many* uses and its dependence for meaning on an individual's sense of context:

> . . . I am no counterfeit. To die is to be a counterfeit, for he is but the counterfeit of a man who hath not the life of a man; but to counterfeit dying, when a man thereby liveth, is to be no counterfeit, but the true and perfect image of life indeed. (5.4.115–19)

Denying once more the value of abstractions, he poses them as "counterfeit" values, as alternatives to "life," energy, vital signs.

More: as James Calderwood has observed (1979, 7), here he is metadramatic. By seeming to us to be dead, then rising, he enacts the theatrical idea that a counterfeit can seem real. As in act 2, scene 4, he reminds us here that the play is a fiction; he gets us to see *him,* as well as the play as a whole, in the same way that *he* sees the events within the play: they are a "show" to play in, or to watch being played. [9] So reminded not to take him seriously, we may come to acquiesce in the Buddhist vantage point, from which it is this very seeing through the counterfeit's claim to "truth," seeing through to the ideological emptiness of experience, of act and idea and word and theater equally, that allows us the mental and emotional equanimity called freedom. In this nonbelief, we can indulge these counterfeits, enjoy them, and let them enter our lives. One of Falsaff's main themes throughout this play is the paradox that life becomes more full as its lack of certain meaning becomes more transparently plain. As we learn to concentrate on particularity in itself, without assigning it value, withou falsifying it by the assignment of an ideology, it actually takes on an importance of its own, in itself. The metadramatic form of his presentation in this particular context leads us toward seeing in this way.

To Falstaff, this counterfeit, *un*certain aspect of things is all that is certainly "true." It is not at all surprising, then, that he says of the apparently dead Hotspur, "How if he should counterfeit too and rise? ... Therefore I'll make him sure, yea, and I'll swear I kill'd him. Why may not he rise as well as I?" (5.4.122–26). And so he stabs him in the thigh, adding his sense of touch to his eyes' testimony. Falstaff must know more than anyone how the appearance of one thing may turn into another, for the flux of things is the quality in which he lives.

Therefore, when he picks up *truly* dead ("counterfeit") Hotspur and puts him on his back and lugs him about, this is not only a comic version (perhaps a parody) of the morality play's vice or devil taking the damned soul offstage—another parodic play within the play; it is also a physical demonstration of who is truly alive and who is truly dead. [10] In metadramatic form he presents a visual contrast between the value of honor and identity, on the one hand, and the value of life unfettered by ideology, on the other. The honorable Hotspur is, even in the words of the prince, merely "luggage" (5.4.156). The morally ordered view of the world is still deferred in the prince's mind—present only in its "absence."

Indeed, from this point of view this scene is a recapitulation of the whole play. As we have seen, Hal's "presence" is a function of his knowledge of his deferred future, and of the consequently deferred idea of order. It is this very presence in absence, this "trace" of order and identity, which renders Falstaff unthreatening to conventional minds like ours, that once more legitimizes him and allows us (like Hal) to see his value. Falstaff depends on Hal for his appeal to us, and his metadramatic parody prepares the way for us to appreciate Hal's reaction.

III

The characters who insist on trying to define themselves in the present, who want to defer nothing, are different. From the point of view of authority, for example, Falstaff's triumphant devil-figure would seem an outrageous sacrilege. And indeed the play emphasizes this difference by counterpointing the two perspectives: as Falstaff triumphs on the battlefield, so do the king's forces. Fully to understand Falstaff's impact on the prince, then, as well as his impact on us, it seems necessary to contrast him with the king and the rebel Hotspur, i.e., those who seem to stand most powerfully in contrast to Falstaff's attitudes.

The play portrays the king and his kingdom very clearly at once. They are both in crisis. Henry makes the point explicit: "So shaken as we are, so wan with care." He has daubed his country's "lips with her own children's blood" (1.1.6). His aggression against Richard II seemed justified by Richard's own sins, epitomized by his violation of Henry's rights of inheritance. But righting those wrongs involved Henry himself in the commission of further wrongs: rebellion, murder, usurpation. Now full of guilt, his preferred method of making things better is further aggression, this time in a Crusade to the Holy Land against people of another religion and nationality. He makes the self-defeating nature of his oppositional stance toward the world quite clear. It inflicts misery on others and on himself as well. Indeed, this misery is infecting the entire nation: he cannot leave for a foreign war of atonement because his earlier aggression has taught others at home how to act in his own style. Civil war threatens. "Right" and power are separate. To solidify power (and therefore the self-image of the powerful) is an endless struggle, the opposite of nonstriving desirelessness. Henry craves righteousness so much that he will kill for it.[11]

Nor do the identity and power of kingship bring content. Henry is caught in a mental vise. He believes that only the exercise of power can right wrongs, yet violence begets violence. He is caught in a viciously painful samsaric cycle of violence, guilt, insecurity, violence. Unlike Falstaff's, Henry's vision of safety is of a world hardened into an immobilized status quo with himself cemented atop it. It is an image of self-entrapment, a denial of life that corresponds closely to the Elizabethan portrait style discussed in chapter 2.

In this embattled frame of mind the king is very "practical," very quick to sense threat, yet frequently caught in irony. In act 1, scene 3, for example, he clearly sees the insurrectionist spirit behind Hotspur's noble language, yet two scenes earlier he would have preferred to have this young man as his son (1.1.79–90). Hotspur and Henry speak the same language, apparently unlike the prince; they both deal primarily in power, and use words to cloak it or to exercise it. Hotspur indeed is a would-be usurper, a youthful image of the aging king. As the rebel whose presence is required for the guilty king to legitimize himself, yet who frustrates the desire for atonment by keeping him from his Crusade, Hotspur embodies the ironically self-defeating aspect of the king's desire, forcing on Henry the pain of frustration in which desire always ends. In this sense, in fighting Hotspur, the king fights himself. By the end of the play, Henry's death is not distant.

Hotspur fits this image well: he is even more full of desire for honor and reputation than is the king. We might even say that he makes this play world's conventional value system, the one upheld by the sovereign and all his lords, clear by exaggerating it, by putting its qualities closer to the surface. He shows that the desire for honor is not unlike other forms of lust:[12] "By Heaven, methinks it were an easy leap, / To pluck bright honor from the pale-fac'd moon" (1.3.202–3). No image is too grandiose for his craving. His righteous anger (1.3.129ff.) and greed, as is exemplified by the rebels' splitting up English territory in act 3, scene 1 without regard for the good of the kingdom, are simply other forms of the same irrationality. His lust for reputation, indeed, crowds out more domesticated desires. Lady Percy asks,

> For what offense have I this fortnight been
> A banish'd woman from my Harry's bed?
> Tell me, sweet lord, what is't that takes from thee
> Thy stomach, pleasure, and thy golden sleep?
>
> (2.3.38–41)

In seeming contrast to Falstaff and Hal, Hotspur's energy is based entirely on desire, on the need to satisfy a craving that will puff him up in the present. For Henry, already king, the craving is also for righteousness, but in his case it is more defensive than aggressive. They are different faces of the same adversarial attitude toward the world. Hotspur dies, and Henry will follow shortly. Thus they expose the limiting nature of the "reality" that Prince Hall will inherit; by contrast, they make Falstaff look more sane, and certainly less lustful. Their examples not only encourage Hal's difference, but also enable it. Representing what he will be, they are the difference from which he in turn must differ, the difference he defers. He depends on them for his freedom to find an alternative, a "different" way of dealing with both life and power in his unfolding present.

It is not immediately apparent, however, that the prince uses this freedom, for as Falstaff's tests progressively intensify, Hal seems to turn in the king's direction. He becomes a valorous and skillful warrior-prince, praising Hotspur (5.1.86–92), gracefully conceding that he has "a truant been to chivalry" (5.1.94), courageously offering to fight his rival in single combat "to save the blood on either side" (5.1.99), fighting on in battle despite a wound (5.4.1–14), and at last completing his transformation by killing his rival. Up to this point, he spends the second half of the play gratifying his father. Only after he has succeeded does he give us a glimpse of a "different" attitude toward this new and honored posture.

When Hal kills his rival, Hotspur falls beside Falstaff. Standing over their corpses, the prince expresses his attitude toward the alternatives his world has seemed to offer. He speaks first to his most recent choice, saying of Hotspur,

> When that this body did contain a spirit
> A kingdom for it was too small a bound,
> But now two paces of the vilest earth
> Is room enough.
>
> (5.4.89–92)

Its danger past, Percy's ambition is seen to reflect a noble spirit. Nonetheless, Hal's view of it is ironic. Hotspur's "spirit" overreached itself. He graciously bestows respect: "Thy ignominy sleep with thee in the grave, / But not rememb'red in thy epitaph!" (5.4.100–101). But he is aware of Hotspur's "ignominy." He stands apart from the man whose reputation he has won for himself. He does not identify himself with his fallen rival, and his irony distances him from Hotspur's ambition—from Hal's own deferred identity.

His attitude toward Falstaff is similar: affectionate but distanced, aware that Falstaff too represents the ironic "vanity" (5.4.106) of human life: "Could not all this flesh / Keep in a little life?" (5.4.102–3).

Then Falstaff returns to life and, with his "luggage" on his back, claims to have killed Hotspur. The prince, at the height of his honor and glory, the champion of order who has broken the back of civil war, chooses to continue to defer judgment, just as he must defer his role of king. Further, this deferral of judgment is on Falstaff's own terms: "For my part, if a lie may do thee grace, / I'll gild it with the happiest terms I have" (5.4.157–58). Having won the honor that he and all the audience had hoped he would from the first act, he gives it away to the man who seems least to deserve it, and does so with a lie. With this lie, Hal enacts the same ironic skepticism about honor which his elegy over Hotspur's corpse has just enunciated. This attitude may not be the same as Falstaff's earlier explicit denial of honor, but it shows his difference from Hotspur: he is not obsessed by honor, not entrapped and limited by it (see Dessen 1986, 66–68, 87).

One can argue that his skeptical irony is symptomatic of a more general cynicism about all ideal values, and on a less philosophical level than Falstaff's. One can argue that in lying, he is simply doing what comes naturally to the honorable and powerful, as Hotspur lied about his prisoners in act 1, as Henry may have done to Richard II, as Hal, in playing behind a cloud, has been implicitly doing throughout the first half of the play. It may be that his callous playing with Francis the drawer in act 2, scene 4 is simply the most obvious example of his willingness to exploit people for his own amusement, as well as for less trivial political ends. It may be that he indulged Falstaff in order to learn the language and thoughts of subversion so that authority might better contain them. Or perhaps he did so to appropriate Falstaff's plebeian voice for a general, society-wide affirmation of the present power structure. It may even be that by giving the subversiveness of Falstaff its voice, Hal demonstrates the need for authority in this society, thus again legitimizing his and his father's hierarchical positions.[13]

In the same vein, the irony of his acquiescence in the final lie may seem to suggest that the prince is playing with Falstaff, rather than being gracious to a friend: "If a lie may do thee grace, / I'll gild it with the happiest terms I have." To one of the governing class, "grace" requires truth, honor, noble birth. A "lie" cannot confer it. The comment may seem to demean Falstaff, to be an ironic reminder of his subordinate status.

However, in this lie that gives away the honor and reputation earned in defeating Hotspur, the prince gains nothing. Whatever advantage he can gain by being with the fat man in the tavern has already been achieved.[14] To the contrary, it is Falstaff who gains: in *Part Two,* some believe him to have been Hotspur's conqueror. And from Falstaff's nonideological perspective, a lie *can* in fact give "grace"—that is, approval. The lie, then, seems not to function merely as self-serving cynicism on the prince's part. We need to inquire further.

In act 2, scene 4, Hal had parodied Hotspur (101ff.); in act 5, scene 1, seen his nobility; in act 5, scene 4, destroyed him, then viewed his ambition ironically. In this variety the prince shows his awareness that we are mortal and limited, that no value is ultimate, and that several attitudes toward the same value are possible. Although he has earned honor, he is not seduced by it as Hotspur is. Still prince, still aware of the order and kingship that will be his, the present in this way "vitiated" by the trace of the future, he continues to defer judgment. Because he knows that this "lie" will not be his last word on Falstaff, it *can* be his last word *here*, in this play. He chooses once more not to judge, to remain unattached to the ideology that a self-image in the present would require. He becomes a warrior great enough to beat the play's rebel champion, then seems to confer the honor of this victory on the character who had denied its value. Honor becomes the plaything of both characters, and equally, despite their different ways of playing with it.

IV

At this point, then, Hal exemplifies the possibility of the coexistence of apparent opposites, the lack of need to make either/or choices. He refuses to set himself off from Falstaff in appearance or stature. He holds the royal imperatives of self-image and ideology in balance with an appreciation of the more primal, earthy level of experience, seeing both limits and value in each, uncommitted to either. Winning, then giving away the reputation gained by this victory, he acts as if the process of enactment itself, not the result, is what matters. It is as if, uncommitted to self-image or ideology, he need not be bound by goals. Identity deferred, he is able to play with ideas without believing in them and thus, like Falstaff in his more limited setting, to be their master. For Hal, it may be, warfare is not essentially different from playing extempore, for it is the quality of being extempore that is crucial, whatever the role.[15] In this spirit, each act or thought becomes local, limited to its specific context, rather than meaningful in a more general way. Yet because this local event and its specific context are all there is in a particular place and moment, it is also an "ultimate," in spite of its lack of "meaning." Viewed psychologically, we could say that because it does not carry the pressurized weight of ideology or ulterior motive, it does not produce tension and distraction. In an act extempore, the prince can bring his full concentration to bear on the thing he does now because nothing else is. Alert yet relaxed, he can act efficiently, marshaling his full resources for the present occasion. Thus Hal, the man whose "lie" confirms the idea that all of his princely scenes from act 3, scene 2 on have been "acts," is able to overcome in honorable combat the warrior Hotspur for whom honor is an ultimate value. The prince is in a kind of free play that seems similar to that described by Derrida both for signs and their counterparts in a play: characters. In his victory and "grace" afterwards, Hal shows the fruitful aspects of this mental situation. He shows that free play facilitates both sanity and efficient action in the world. It is what a Buddhist might call "skillful means."

Trungpa's writing illustrates this Buddhist idea. In such a non-meaningful situation, he asserts,

> the thought process and the emotions are transparent and they are taking place in the midst of nowhere, in space. That spacious quality, when everything operates and occurs in space, is the positive space of skillful means, of working with everyday life-situations. In fact, the creativity and the positive aspect of the emotions and life-situations can only be seen through experiencing the space. . . . [T]hen there is no hesitation at all. (1976a, 66)

Trungpa explains more fully that "the fundamental nature of the emotions, is just energy." They have no particular object. In our samsaric illusion we attach emotions (like desire) to our mental projections, believing these projections to be true outward things, and thus also believing that we need whatever things we have attached our feelings to. But when you are

> able to relate with energy, then the energies have no conflict with you. They become a natural process. So trying to suppress or getting carried away by the emotions becomes irrelevant once a person is completely able to see their basic characteristic, the emotions as they are, which is shunyata. The barrier, the wall between you and your projections, the hysterical and paranoid aspect of your relationship to your projections, has been . . . seen through. When there is no panic involved in dealing with the emotions, then you can deal with them completely, properly. Then you are like someone who is completely skilled in his profession, who does not panic, but just does his work completely, thoroughly. (1976a, 67)

When well developed, this quality of being comfortable with one's emotions and situations (projections), of working with them extempore—

without attaching preconceptions about oneself or the world to them—leads to

> total confidence without a reference point. Just fully being skillful involves total lack of inhibition. We are not afraid to be. We are not afraid to live. We must accept ourselves as being warriors. If we ackowledge ourselves as warriors, then there is a way in, because a warrior dares to *be*, like a tiger in the jungle. (1976a, 121)

Without the reference point of our self-image, our idea of our solidified selves, it is possible to achieve power,

> a further expression of the confidence of skillful means. Skillful means is the confidence to step up to the edge of a cliff and power is the confidence to leap. It seems to be a very daring decision, but since there is no reference point, it is an extraordinarily ordinary situation; you simply do it. (1976a, 122)

Prince Hal is leaping off such a cliff by embracing widely disparate, apparently contradictory postures: warriorship, drunkenness, trickery—even lying. He approaches accommodation with most of the range of experience offered by the play, yet seems unbound by it. He seems a free person because none of the roles he is offered is used to fix a particular identity. In this state of nonattachment, however, it is not that there are no strong feelings, such as hatred or friendship or love, but that one is not dominated by them. Like ideologies, feelings come and go. We have them whether we have goals or not, whether we believe in particular solidified selves or not. We are human; inescapably, we think and feel. But because nothing needs to be achieved, nothing needs to be sought, avoided, or clung to. In this nonattachment, one lives in the flux of things, knowing that nothing endures; one experiences this knowledge as a source of power rather than weakness—in Hal's case, the power to continue to lie for Falstaff even as he conquers Hotspur. Yet because one has no alliance with ideas or people or things, one is, in this state as in jumping off the cliff, essentially alone.

V

The deferring, aloof, ironic, yet playful Prince Hal well illustrates both the power and the challenge of this situation. If *Merchant* left us in a frightening psychological free fall, Hal seems in the next year to offer an example not of how to escape this fall, but of how to live fruitfully while falling. His example may have offered Shakespeare the strength for his further exploration of the fearful samsaric realms in *Julius Caesar* and *Antony and Cleopatra*.[16]

We in the audience have been prepared to appreciate this example of the prince in various ways. Because Hal's deferral of judgment is based on his awareness of his future role, he has taken the political threat out of Falstaff's dis-order. Knowing Falstaff will someday be judged, we can enjoy Hal's participation in his companion's zest for life here, and even in his destruction of ideology. (The king's final speech reinforces this condition. Its optimism about the continuing civil war, while giving the prince a leadership role against Mortimer, is a concluding reminder of the inevitable restoration of that order.) In addition, Falstaff's metadramatic actions (his kingly "play" in act 2, scene 4, and his resurrection in act 5, scene 4), combined with Hal's own, remind us that Shakespeare's play itself is an illusion. Just as the prince's deferral pacifies us into appreciating disorder within the play, Shakespeare, by effacing the play's "reality" value, pacifies us into colluding with its unconventional political/ philosophical implications for life outside itself. Hal's "difference," his nonoppositional exemplum for both life generally and politics in particular, becomes viable for us because it seems to efface not only its own validity, but also the validity of the dramatic form that is its expression.

In previous plays, we have seen that the cost of challenging authority is to discredit the expression of that challenge by the use of metadramatic techniques. This play might seem to repeat the formula that subversion is acceptable if it somehow negates itself. However, there is a "difference" here too: in setting up a nonoppositional model, this play denies the need to discredit subversion *or* to credit authority. Despite the conflicts within it, this play, through the example of Hal, at last refuses to set the two in opposition. Rather, they are shown inevitably to be each other's *différance,* each the necessary condition of the other. To see this transparent, tentative nature of apparently solid things and ideas is not in *Henry IV, Part One* to discredit them, but to give them value. Thus legitimized, subversion need not be violent and destructive, like Hotspur's; it can be pacific and constructive, allowing freedom because there is the "trace" of order and authority in it, as Hal's deferral shows. Only those characters who deny the validity of the "different," who hold an adversarial perspective toward life, are discredited. Their assumption that political and moral problems must be solved by strife is therefore also discredited.

This play is not so much an exposure of specific means, however, as of the mental suffering that such an adversarial attitude inflicts. Prince

Hal's great warriorship shows that battle is not in itself "bad"; if used in a proper frame of mind, it may prove fruitful. But neither the king nor Hotspur can solve problems with violence; rather, they create and enlarge them. Henry's ambition has led him to guilt and defensiveness and discontent. Hotspur, who emulates the king's belief in honor, as well as in civil war as a legitimate means of redressing wrongs, is also like the king in perpetuating violence, not ending it, for he too is driven by his perpetual dissatisfaction. If he were to become king, this pattern would surely continue. The play displaces this conventional model of action in the world, and replaces it with Hal's nonadversarial alternative by positioning it squarely in the foreground. In the realm of policy at the end of the play, his last word is consistent with this view. He moves toward rapprochement with erstwhile enemies by freeing the Douglas.

Hal, then, exemplifies a new political possibility for Shakespeare: that one can stand for peace and justice without subverting either authority or oneself. For the first time, we see a character who, like us, plays the king's game, but without the consciously willed self-subjugation that a contest between rebellion and obedience seems to require. Rebellion, therefore, becomes unnecessary. Being unattached to self-image, Hal can "play" this game, yet play it truly, with love for his father. He can play it so well that the king sees it (accurately) not as a power game, but as true loyalty. Pacified, he no longer requires it, and gives the prince command. By the end, Hal is in a position to teach authority how to "play" the power game without being attached to it; unthreatened, she might play it without repression.

With such a prince, the interdependence of subversion and loyalty is shown in a way that pacifies other conventional political issues as well. Questions of whether subversion is active or contained, or whether it serves authority or rebel, become moot. One need not win at the other's cost, as Prince Hal shows by winning and then giving Falstaff his victory. In this play, the transparency of the art of resemblance effaces meaning, such that it comes close to embodying the play's political/philosophical implications. Unlike the other plays we have studied, here self-effacement is fruitful, freeing a full range of being.

However, this is not a position that Shakespeare maintained. Eventually Hal will be entrapped by his long-deferred identity, just as the king is now. And whatever we may applaud in Falstaff, he takes his pleasures very seriously. His fear of death shows that he too is attached to the solidity of his own life, even if it is unlabeled. Rather than coming from the kind of inner wisdom that an accomplished meditator might achieve, Hal's posture seems instead to depend on the play's exposure of its Derridean situation of deferral. This privileged moment of similarity to a Buddhist vantage point, that is, seems to stem from its special political cicumstances in this particular history. Nonetheless, it is a space in which some of the fruitful aspects of a way very like the Buddhist one have been explored.

7
Further Glimpses of Free Play in *Hamlet* and *King Lear*

I

Hamlet is different. Although it is true that the play and its title character have several striking similarities to *Henry IV, Part One* and its Prince Hal, Hamlet is unlike Hal in *choosing* deferral rather than being forced into it by the situation of having a living father.

Nonetheless, the similarities are important. They define the conditions in which free play is achieved in Shakespeare. Each main character is a prince; by the end of the first act, each has received his mission in life from his father/king and each has formulated a plan to role-play (Hamlet will "put an antic disposition on," 1.5.172). In each case, too, this "playing" points toward the mission to be completed in the future, even as it is the form of present deferral or delay. In addition to being in this situation of Derridean "absence," each character deals with an unhealthy present rulership in which the king clings to belief in a "real" self-image. In each case, that is, the main character is set up as a potential reformer whose deferral, in combination with his lonely separation from the values of the world he inhabits, allows him a privileged mental position. The aloneness of this deferral, emphasized by role-playing, enables him to explore perspectives toward life that are alternatives to those prevailing in his (and our) societies.

In a larger view, these plays prepare their audiences to accept an alternative vision by emphasizing their own metadramatic qualities. In the case of *Hamlet,* however, these qualities are more explicit and, like the character himself, more puzzling. Thus just as Hamlet defers (delays) his ultimate identity as reformer-avenger, so, James R. Siemon argues, does the play conclude with "an ultimate deferral of significance" in which everything "both is *and* is not" (Siemon 1985, 195, 242).[1] From the very first scene onward we are beset with questions and mystery, and at its end the play continues to pose questions. For example, has it been the story Horatio promises at the end to tell (5.2.339–40, 379–86)?[2] If so, can we assume his telling to be unbiased? And in this metadramatic conclusion, what are the political implications of Fortinbras's statement that Hamlet, "had he been put on," would "have prov'd most royal" (5.2.397–98)? Is the character "put on" the throne to be thought of as an actor "put on" the kingly stage? Does the tendency within and without the play to psychoanalyze Hamlet turn up any more "essential identity" than with Prince Hal? Is there not an exposure here of the theatrical nature of England's crown as well as Denmark's?

Hamlet is full of theater within theater, full of pretense extempore as well as formally scripted and enacted, all of it raising questions about the nature of both appearance and reality. The opening military ritual of the changing of the guard fails to reassure even its practitioners of the stability it is meant to provide. The guards' questions about a ghost shatter the prescribed order of things, and continue to haunt the gorgeousness of the court in scene 2, where Hamlet himself takes on the undermining role and reemphasizes the court's hollowness. The play begins by emphasizing the difference between "seems" and "is," yet even when the ghost *seems* to give his son a glimpse into the secret truth of things behind their outward appearance, new questions arise. "And shall I couple hell?" Hamlet asks (1.5.93).

Nearly all the characters are involved in playing at pretense, often on several levels. Polonius is typical. He advises Laertes "to thine own self be true" (1.3.78) in terms that require deliberate self-falsification: "Give thy thoughts no tongue, / Nor any unproportion'd thought his act" (1.3.59–60), then in act 2, scene 1 instructs Reynaldo in the pretenses required to spy on this son. He tells Ophelia not to see Hamlet any more, then in act 3, scene 1, as part of his own spy program for the king, he looses her on this same Hamlet. Spying on Hamlet is particularly concentrated in act 2, scene 2, where not only Polonius but also Rosencrantz and Guildenstern take part, while Hamlet himself hides behind his antic disposition. Roles and counterroles form the very texture of court life.

Hamlet, however, forces us to see his pretense not only as part of a court intrigue, but as a philosophical issue as well. He puts the metadramatic aspect of this issue in the foreground by discussing institutionalized pretense in the theater. When he tells Rosencrantz and Guildenstern that he is disillusioned with both himself and "this most excellent / Canopy, the air, look you, this brave o'erhanging / Firmament" (2.2.299–301), he refers to the "real" world as it is represented in this theater. He reminds us that this life onstage *is* represented rather than real. There then follows a discussion of the status of adult, as opposed to boys', acting companies, a discussion which includes a reference to the Globe (2.2.327–62). If, before, the representational quality of the theater was emphasized, here the real-life theatrical situation in London is brought into the play. A little later, we are reminded of the character Hamlet's acting ability: he tries acting Aeneas's lines, complete with a false start (2.2.449–64), and Polonius (predictably) compliments him for his skill. The character and the actor who plays are fused; we are reminded by this rehearsal that the present performance of *Hamlet* is enacted by real people like ourselves, that it too was rehearsed, that it is as much deliberate pretense as the play within the play that he is developing during this scene, and at the same time equally charged with "reality."[3]

In the movement of the first half of the play, this emphasis on pretense and its significance gradually intensifies. The pretense of the spies is solidified into Hamlet's acting, directing, even collaborating on the writing of the formal play within (2.2.540–43). His soliloquy after the players leave makes these ideas almost explicit. Referring to the first player and his role, Hamlet asks, "What's Hecuba to him, or he to Hecuba, / That he should weep for her" (2.2.559–60)? He compares himself—a person who, in the context of the play, has a "real" reason to shed tears—with the player king who does not, but who actually does weep. Life in the play is represented rather than real, yet theatrical illusion is more expressive, and in this sense more "real," than life. Illusion and reality collapse into one another. In and out of the theater, the play seems to imply, they are of one ambiguous substance.

Thus in this play *Hamlet* especially, "the play's the thing / Wherein [to] catch the conscience of the King" (2.2.604–5). It will "catch" Claudius not because he will think it "real," but because it *represents* a particular version of reality (in this case, a *ghost*'s), making it public. Even if (as in this case, in act 3, scene 2), nobody else in the (stage) audience understands that it is an accusation, the accused will know because he knows the truth to which it refers. He will know that what he had believed to be secret is not, that the playwright also knows it. Thus the "real" power in the pretense derives not from its verisimilitude, but from its emptiness, its transparence as a representation of another's thought. This thought is the deeper secret behind the secret truth behind appearance that becomes visible in *Gonzago*.

Just before this enactment begins in act 3, scene 2, Hamlet illustrates the importance of transparence by giving an acting lesson to the players. Here he is concerned with the *style* of representation through acting. His preference is for a moderation that echoes Polonius's advice to Laertes: Do not overact, but "be not too tame neither" (3.2.16), for

> the purpose of playing . . . is, to hold as 'twere the mirror up to nature: to show virtue her feature, scorn her own image, and the very age and body of the time his form and pressure. (3.2.19–24)

This mimetic theater can *show* truth, but it does not pretend to *be* that truth. It is not even a copy, but a reflection; it reveals what is normally unseen. Its illusion is closer to the heart of reality than is "reality" itself *because* it is not reality, but a mirror.[4] It offers a privileged perspective. Thus Hamlet judges unskillful actors to be unnatural persons ("some of nature's journeymen had made" them, "and not made them well," 3.2.33–35).

The dumb show is another instance of the truth-value of transparent illusion. It tells the story of the past whose end we know: the marriage of Gertrude and the coronation of Claudius. It is the beginning of their story, the part before *Hamlet* began and on which the ghost has filled us in. It is therefore prefatory to *Hamlet* as well as to *Gonzago*. The pantomime shows the secret essence of the real (in *Hamlet*), as Hamlet says it should. And because we see the ghost's full story here, including the murder and the murderer's reciprocated love for the queen, the speaking play can be (as it is) interrupted without loss of clarity. Indeed, because we know the full story line, the king's interruption intensifies the moment in the court theater when suddenly he leaves the audience to become the principal player.

The style of this dumb show is as important to us as we know it is to Hamlet. It must be quite different from the full mousetrap in acting style, in pacing, in costume. Its convention is that it is a mimed preview. In style and in function it reminds us (and the stage audience) that it, and therefore the play it previews, is scripted, rehearsed, a representation. Thus although the mousetrap itself will seem more naturalistic by contrast, as its script comes closer to Hamlet's "real" intention (it embellishes the dumb show's version of the past by inserting the nephew as murderer), we are constantly aware of its emptiness, and therefore of the truths behind it. Its full effectiveness in the present depends on our seeing that while it tells the prehistory of *Hamlet,* it also threatens the king with a future catastrophe.[5] This present performance, that is, contains those qualities that Derrida insists the stage of "presence" always will contain: traces of the past and the future, "constituting what is called the present by means of this very relation to what it is not" (Derrida 1986a, 127). Through the dumb show,

Gonzago and thus *Hamlet* collapse together into transparence. Claudius replaces (becomes) the player king; the mousetrap becomes the full play's epitome in both form and story.[6]

Hamlet's conclusion is also in the form of a play within the play, another court entertainment, this time a game of dueling into which reality intrudes even more dramatically than in the mousetrap: both the participants/actors and the stage spectators actually die, some according to script and some extempore. If the mousetrap was *Hamlet*'s epitome, then the duel, which is its twin and sequel, collapses reality into theater, and vice versa, with even greater explicitness.[7] It is a climactic affirmation of the power of theatrical illusion on its own terms: it has power because it forces itself to be seen as illusion.

I will return to this idea later, to analyze how it works itself out in this ending. First, though, it will be useful to see how the title character functions within this metadramatically "emptied" play.

II

Hamlet can be unruly and disturbed, but he can also be moral and rational; at times insensitive and even casually cruel, he can be sensitive to others, as well as to the finest philosophical nuances of his universe. For most of the play he is full of such inconsistency, a fact that leads to as many interpretations of his character as there are of the whole play. He opens the play in a malaise: he would like to dissolve "into a dew" (1.2.130). When the ghost gives him a mission to live for, he is both frightened ("And shall I couple hell?" 1.5.93) and ecstatic:

> Haste me to know 't, that I with wings as swift
> As meditation, or the thoughts of love,
> May sweep to my revenge.
>
> (1.5.29–31)

He thinks of those "more things in heaven and earth" that exceed philosophy, plans his "antic disposition," yet feels that "the time is out of joint" and says, "O cursed spite, that ever I was born to set it right!" (1.5.166, 172, 188–89). This careening from mood to mood, even from rationality to apparent insanity, will continue through much of the play. It is almost as if Shakespeare had decided to present an example of the Buddhist view of the "self": its discontinuity, its status as a sequence of individual pictures rather than the smoothly consistent movie narrative that we invent from these pictures in order to construct a self-image, in order to build the security of an idea of a continuous and consistent *self*. In this inconsistency, Hamlet continually commits himself to his mission, then (it is usually argued) delays, defers action, and asks questions both of himself and the universe. Unlike Prince Hal's, Hamlet's deferral is not an accident of timing, but his choice, a product of his temperament. This fact is important in our understanding of his character at the end. Unlike Hal, Hamlet must change. Only when he becomes comfortable with both his deferral *and* the mission he defers, when neither serves as an identity to cling to, does he fulfill his mission. Only when he has given himself up to the possibility of death—given up the idea of self-identity—can he achieve it. As Derrida would have it, presence can occur only in its absence.

The form of his deferral also reveals an important aspect of Hamlet's character. It is clear that he believes that he delays his revenge. In soliloquy after soliloquy he berates himself for it: "O what a rogue and peasant slave am I" (2.2.256ff.); "To be or not to be" (3.1.64ff.); "How all occasions do inform against me" (4.4.34ff.). Even the ambiguous ghost of act 3, scene 4 (is it in fact a hallucination?) feels it necessary to remind him about his "almost blunted purpose" (3.4.111). However, it is arguable that these soliloquies reflect, and therefore emphasize, Hamlet's own self-doubts more than the reality of his situation. The ghost's reminder, for example, occurs fewer than eighty lines after Hamlet has skewered Polonius, asking expectantly, "Is it the King?" (3.4.26), then reacting in disappointment to the corpse, "I took thee for thy better" (3.4.32). We might wonder how often Hamlet must kill someone to satisfy this voice, to whomever it belongs. Nor is it necessary for us to agree with his belief in his delay elsewhere. Having heard the ghost in the first act, Hamlet sets up a test of its truthfulness, the mousetrap. We might think this stratagem a bit long-winded, but it is effective. Whether or not *we* believe that Hamlet delays, then, *his* belief that he does seems exaggerated; it therefore emphasizes his tendency to self-doubt, and helps to place this self-questioning in the play's foreground.

From the Buddhist point of view, this self-questioning quality is crucial. Of the six styles of samsara (the Six Realms discussed in chapter 5), one, the Human Realm, is characterized by this quality. It is the most fortunate realm to inhabit. Chögyam Trungpa writes that it is

> in the Human Realm that the possibility of breaking the karmic chain or the circle of samsara, arises. The intellect of the Human Realm and the possibility of discriminating action allows room to question the whole process of struggle. There is a possibility for the . . . [individual] to

> question the obsession of relating to something, of getting something, to question the solidity of the worlds that he experiences. (Trungpa 1973, 146)

It is not that pain and inconsistency are avoided in this realm, but that they can be recognized. Indeed, because one can see one's own inconsistency and occasional lunacy in this realm, its pain is likely to be more intense, and therefore the reaction, the struggle, the writhing, the inconsistency, may also be more intense than usual. Hamlet is aloof, biting, even cruel to almost everyone in the play except Horatio, and especially to those for whom he most deeply cares, Ophelia and his mother. In the Buddhist view, this increased awareness of the pain of samsara is a necessary stage in the process of transforming it.[8]

When seen in the spirit of this self-questioning that Hamlet's soliloquies emphasize, the mousetrap is extraordinarily well-conceived. As P. J. Aldus has seen, it does even more than verify the ghost's allegations and threaten the king: it creates a no-exit situation for Hamlet himself (Aldus 1977, 163). If Claudius is guilty, he will not miss the threat; hearing the threat, he will not fail to protect himself by acting first. Hamlet knows his man, and builds into the mousetrap his own self-entrapment, proof against his belief in his own tendency to delay. He builds into the mousetrap a situation that will force him to act on the ghost's instructions if they prove legitimate.

The "To be or not to be" soliloquy, occurring in the midst of his preparations for this play within, shows the quality of mind in which he builds this self-entrapment. It is a statement of his recognition that to continue "To be" is "to suffer / The slings and arrows of outrageous fortune," to be stoically fatalistic, while "not to be" is to be actively heroic, "to take arms against a sea of troubles, / And by opposing, end them (3.1.55–59).[9] The "nobler" course is the second, and Hamlet is already in the middle of it. He has just finished choosing a play and rehearsing it in the previous scene, and in the next will oversee its performance. The "troubles" of this speech would seem to refer to his current obsession, the king's guilt, and to his self-doubts and hesitancy in dealing with it. "Not to be" suggests Hamlet's recognition that to set things right against the king, as he is currently trying to do, will cost him his life. This idea, of course, reinforces his self-doubt about his "resolution" (it was not so long ago, at 2.2.577, that he accused himself of being "pigeon-liver'd"). Now he applies to himself the musing that "conscience does make cowards of us all" (3.1.83, 82). His self-doubt allows him to recognize his weakness; this recognition, in turn, allows him to try to come to terms with it. To prevent the effects of cowardice, he springs his trap on himself as well as his adversary.

From the Buddhist point of view, Hamlet's self-reproaches are a problem as well as an opportunity. The assumption behind them is that there is a solid self to reproach. Although apparently negative, they satisfy one's sense of self-importance. We cannot succeed in destroying self-belief by self-reproach, for even the willed exercise of self-destruction is an act of this same self, enhancing its sense of its own virtue. And yet by simply watching oneself, by seeing oneself clearly without apology or defense, one can use self-consciousness against itself. Gradually, the ways of the self and its thinking can be seen through—seen as repetitive habitual patterns. At last, although they do not go away, they become familiar, no longer disturbing. We can relax with our old selves, and this relaxing can make us new: the watcher, necessary at first, is deprived of his function and dissolves. "Conscience," which Hamlet says creates cowardice, no longer exists. We become what we do in the world: pure action, skillful means.[10]

Hamlet goes through a change somewhat like this in the middle of the play. He has engineered his situation so that after the *Murder of Gonzago* he has no more choices to make. He and Claudius are now mutually aware antagonists. With no exit possible, Hamlet feels increasingly free from the need for self-reproach. He is sometimes actually joyful in this danger, as he is immediately after the play within: "O good Horatio, I'll take the ghost's word / for a thousand pound. Didst perceive?" (3.2.286–87). And almost at once he calls for music.

Of course, he cannot sustain this mood. He is almost feverish with the ghost and Gertrude in act 3, scene 4; and in act 4, scene 4, as he goes to the ship for England, he reproaches himself a last time (4.4.32–65).[11] After this, though, there are no more self-doubts, and no more self-accusations about delay. He gradually wears his fears away until his preoccupation with himself dissolves in worldly action. Hamlet transcends the normal boundaries of this world not by trying to escape them, nor by trying to be heroic or transcendent, but by committing himself wholly to the facts of his world—to the ghost and his own conscience, to the past and the future in their absent "presence"—regardless of cost or profit, as a matter of necessity.

During this time when Hamlet's self-questioning gradually dissolves, a new clarity of vision emerges. We see it first in the precision with which he traps himself in the mousetrap. He perfectly anticipates Claudius's response to his little play: the king opens act 3, scene 3 by registering the mousetrap's threat: "I like him not, nor stands it safe with us / To let his madness range." And, in response to the threat, Claudius at once begins his counterattack: "He to England shall . . . " (3.3.1–4). It is therefore quite natural that Hamlet, having set up the provocation for a countermovement, should anticipate the nature of that countermovement as well. His remarks about the "letters seal'd" (3.4.202) show that he does; it is therefore also unsurprising that he knows enough to exchange these letters at sea. Once the mousetrap confirms to him his ability to see through the apparent honesty of the king, Hamlet's vision cuts through everything.

Even when he mistakes the identity of the spy in Gertrude's bedroom, this mistake is more interesting for the glimpse it offers of the way Hamlet's mind has begun to work than it is for the identity of the victim. This once guilt-ridden, self-reproachful young man kills his beloved's father, thinking him to be the king, and feels absolutely no remorse. He is disappointed ("I took thee for thy better"), but he feels no guilt: "Take thy fortune; / Thou find'st to be too busy is some danger" (3.4.32, 33). In Hamlet's view, Polonius himself is to blame. He is the king's spy.[12] Hamlet knows this in the instant, and his emotions are now synchronized with his knowledge.[13] His lack of guilt shows that he is no longer imprisoned or obsessed by the past. Accepting it as part of his "present," he no longer clouds his mind by second-guessing himself; it is in fact this acceptance that allows him to be alert, clear-minded, quick to strike when the moment presents itself at the end. And this acceptance is set in relief by its contrast with his antagonist. In act 4 it is Claudius whose "hectic in [the] blood" rages (4.3.66). Threatened by the killing of Polonius, Claudius's composed self-confidence begins to falter just as Hamlet is finding self-confidence himself.

In act 4, scene 7, Hamlet continues the pattern of closing off self-questioning at the same time that he acts against Claudius. His warning letter to the king is at least as unnerving as was *Gonzago*, and even more obviously self-entrapping. Hamlet can be patient in act 5, scene 2, because he himself has constructed the atmosphere in which something *will* happen, as well as because he has achieved new clarity and equanimity.

He shows one mental side of this new equanimity when he is with the grave diggers in act 5, scene 1. They stage a mirthfully ironic scene of *memento mori*, a kind of dance of death in which they dig up old bones in order to open a grave for new ones. Ophelia and Alexander and Yorick, the beautiful and the great and the common, the new and the old, all are seen to be equal in their mortality, as the bones of their corpses intermingle. Hamlet responds to this situation by recognizing that death and disintegration involve them all, including himself: "To what base uses we may return, Horatio!" Yet he is unthreatened by this recognition. Instead, he joins in the grave diggers' ironic humor:

> Alexander died, Alexander was buried, Alexander returneth to dust, the dust is earth, of earth we make loam, and why of that loam whereto he was converted might they not stop a beer-barrel? (5.1.202, 207–12)

In thus accepting the inevitability of his own death, Hamlet completes the questioning process of the "To be or not to be" speech in act 3, scene 1. He sees that he, like Alexander and Yorick, is worm bait, whatever he chooses, even if he chooses "to be." His antic dialogue with the king in act 4, scene 3 about the corpse of Polonius (he is "not where he eats, but where 'a is eaten," 4.3.19) has now become his vision of his own reality as well. Ironically, in finally accepting his mother's view that anybody's death is "common" (1.2.72), he is not disposed to give up revenge. To the contrary, content now "not to be," he is ready "to take arms" and perform his mission.[14]

The personal relevance of this enabling *memento mori* theme intensifies when Hamlet discovers (at line 242) that his beloved Ophelia is dead, and follows Laertes' leap into her grave. Surely he is asserting his love and sorrow in common with Laertes. But in this self-dramatizing act, as with the dumb show and the letter, he is also intensifying his war of nerves with the king. He warns Laertes in the king's hearing, "Though I am not splenitive [and] rash, / Yet have I in me something dangerous, / Which let thy wisdom fear" (5.1.261–63). Like the dumb show, too, this situation in the grave suggests a rehearsal for the action to follow: hand-to-hand combat with Laertes while the king and court look on. In a strange way, it suggests as well Hamlet's acceptance of the duel's aftermath; he says that Laertes may be buried quick with Ophelia, and so will he (5.1.279). It is as if he is trying on the death he knows awaits him. Intimations of the future are palpable within the present.

In this new acceptance of full presence, including its traces of both past and future, Hamlet sees that from this "indiscretion," this leap, he has learned something: "There's a divinity that shapes our ends, / Rough-hew them how we will" (5.2.8, 10–11). This sounds at first like religious fatalism, an unBuddhist-like acquiescence in the laws of some higher power. However, three times now, counting the leap into the grave, Hamlet has deliberately intensified the atmosphere of threat that surrounds the king. Although Hamlet does not plan the form of the final confrontation, he has made sure that such a confrontation will occur. This speech, therefore, indicates neither passivity nor fatalism, but another aspect of his mental clarity. Because he now accepts his destiny and its consequences, his mind is no longer clouded by anxiety about the future.[15] With this clarity, he himself takes the initiative in the fifth act.

And yet he is also compassionate. Having accepted himself, his situation, and his limits, he has nothing to defend, no need to be defensive. He can feel grief in common with Laertes for a dead father and for the dead Ophelia (5.2.75–78). He sees himself in another person, even in the one who will be his executioner, and he asks Laertes' forgiveness as they prepare to duel (5.2.226). Under still greater provocation at the end of the play, Hamlet will "exchange forgiveness" (5.2.329) with him. Hamlet has had a hand in the deaths of all Laertes' family and, in return, Laertes kills him, but in the end they attach no blame to each other. Each has acted as he has felt he must. Hamlet, then, is purged not only of guilt and anxiety and self-questioning, but of their roots which, according to Buddhism, lie in the neuroses of passion (desire in the sense of needing, grasping, clinging), aggression (defensiveness, self-protection), and ignorance (belief in the solidity of the self and the world).[16]

He believes, instead,

> There is special providence in the fall of a sparrow. If it be [now], 'tis not to come; if it be not to come, it will be now; if it be not now, yet it [will] come—the readiness is all. (5.2.219–22)

Again, this would seem like passive acquiescence to fate, if not to a god, were it not for the final clause, "the readiness is all." Its emphasis falls on his psychophysical state. All that matters is that he be ready to act when the time for action comes. He seems strangely passive in that he does not plan the particular occasion, but it is only strange because we are unfamiliar with the Buddhist form of desirelessness; he knows that the occasion will occur sometime, and that at that time he will perform the deed. He is desireless, then, not in the sense of being uncommitted to anything, but rather in the sense of being absent, of not needing this revenge to define himself by, or to make a self from. Revenge is not a building block for Hamlet, but simply an act he will perform. He is at peace with his destiny, including his own extinction. As Joseph Summers argues (1984, 63), he is poised, not passive; he is both relaxed and alert; he is in a psychophysical state prized by Buddhist meditators.[17]

Although both Claudius and Hamlet have shown that the pretense of play can be an instrument of political strategy, Hamlet now exemplifies another spirit of play. Like the players in the mousetrap, in this duel he is a performer in a game not of his own making. Like his situation in the world, the game of dueling in which he finds himself is governed by arbitrary rules; his "identity" is an arbitrary role assigned by these rules, not a definition of the essential self; and in this staged play Hamlet acts as he never has before. Although he is aware that there is danger in the court, he accepts the game as a game, as if without suspicions. He does not take his rapier and go straight for the king, ignoring Laertes. He plays the game according to its surface rules, apparently innocent of its subterranean agenda. Only when he is unfairly struck, and then learns about the poison, does Hamlet turn to his mission. Instantly he knows that this is the moment, and his role changes.[18] He duels with the royal spectator who is in fact the center of the real spectacle, as he was in the mousetrap. Against all odds, and on both levels of the game, he wins. And in killing Claudius while defeating Laertes, Hamlet collapses *Hamlet* into the staged duel. Play is reality. In play, he enacts revenge. Hamlet epitomizes *Hamlet.*

Earlier, we anticipated this climactic and explicit affirmation of the power of transparent theatrical illusion. We can now see that Hamlet's emptiness of "self" makes this statement of dramatic power possible. Further, we can also see that this emptiness exemplifies a kind of equanimity described in Buddhist literature, a state of mind-body synchronization that enables efficient action in the world precisely because it is nonaggressive. Exposed to Hamlet, worldly expectations are turned upside down. In this ultimate theatrical moment, the corruption of court theatricality is contrasted with the spontaneous effectiveness of Hamlet's. The emperor is fully exposed. He is as weak as he was threatened and unhappy.

Chögyam Trungpa's summary description of such effectiveness, and of the attitude which is its mental/emotional ground, leads so directly to Hamlet that it bears repeating:

> Fully being skillful involves total lack of inhibition. We are not afraid to be. We are not afraid to live. We must accept ourselves as being warriors. (Trungpa 1976a, 121)

This state is an ultimate denial of authority: of oneself as subject, and therefore of whatever authority claims power over that supposed subject. Authority's rug is removed from its headquarters. Hamlet is simply "ready," poised in present potentiality, without allegiances. Trungpa speaks of such a person:

> You have no need for territory so your space becomes a public park, a common ground, no-man's-land. No-man's-land is free ground, not

subject to any laws of any government. You are free to do anything there, no one can make any demands upon you, so you can afford to wait, to be patient. (Trungpa 1976a, 114)

Hamlet not only exposes royalty in the play, then, but also exemplifies a practical alternative.

III

Still, a character may threaten established authority within a play, yet not threaten it in the world outside the play. In *Hamlet,* however, as in *Henry IV, Part One,* we have an unusual theatrical situation. For one thing, the play exposes the emptiness of Claudius's court ceremonies so remorselessly that they might well suggest the elaborate fictions of England's Gloriana as well.[19] For another, it presents an exemplary alternative to conventional attitudes toward authority, and in the person of a prince. Perhaps most crucially, the play's conclusion involves the audience directly in this alternative perspective.

Dying, Hamlet says,

> You that look pale, and tremble at this chance,
> That are but mutes or audience to this act,
> Had I but time—as this fell sergeant, Death,
> Is strict in his arrest—O, I could tell you—
> But let it be. Horatio, I am dead,
> Thou livest. Report me and my cause aright
> To the unsatisfied.
>
> (5.2.334–39)

He seems to speak to the still living stage audience that does not yet know Claudius's secret. But of course we know that the tale that Hamlet bequeaths at his death will end the invisibility of secret rule by force, will unmask the pretenses of power games. Not content with Claudius's death, Hamlet will have the king's secret, and his subterranean way of playing, exposed. He will cause the story *Hamlet* to be made as transparent to its own surviving participants, the characters, as it already is to us. For we know the core of the story Horatio will tell. It may be, we have just watched its rehearsal in the theater. The surviving characters are put at our level of understanding, at least in potential.[20]

In another way, however, we are far beyond them. Hamlet's dying words remind us once again that we have been watching a representation of the story of a story. The ghost, the dumb show, *Gonzago, Hamlet:* in different styles, details, even tenses, each has told a version or part of the same core narrative. We know that Horatio's retelling will in some way be a repetition of what we already know, but also that in some unpredictable ways it will be altered by his individual perception of things. In Hamlet's final command, then, we get a sense of story as an endlessly repeated cycle. We had thought it was over, but now we know it will begin again, circling back on itself (as Terence Hawkes suggests), perhaps in another form, telling perhaps another truth. Frederic Jameson argues that all

> texts come before us as the always-already-read; we apprehend them through the sedimented layers of previous interpretations, or—if the text is brand-new—through the sedimented reading habits and categories developed by those inherited interpretive traditions. . . . [Thus] interpretation is here construed as an essentially allegorical act, which consists in rewriting a given text in terms of a particular interpretive master code. (1981, 10)

As Hamlet's dying wish directs our attention to yet another telling of his story, it reminds us that a teller tells what he wants heard, and that the shape of the story he tells is a product of what he himself was ready to hear, or know, when it was told to him. And this is not the end of the story's variability for, like the teller, we too hear the (probably very different) story that *we* are ready to hear. In Hamlet's final command, that is, the truth-value of the story just seen, as well as of the one to be heard, is problematized. The variety of *Hamlet* interpretations bears notorious testimony to this problematizing that Hamlet begins—at the play's end. We are reminded that the play we have just seen is *our Hamlet*, and only incidentally Shakespeare's. Like Horatio, and perhaps like Shakespeare himself, we are trapped in the endless cycle of retelling the same story again and again, because we will always tell the story of our own perceptions and understanding and personal history. Hamlet's command, that is, begins us, the play's readers or audience, on a mental journey that renders us as transparent as the play and its title character; it empties us, like the play, of "truth."[21]

Involving us in this process of turning back, this endlessly self-emptying/self-retelling/self-reenergizing process, it captures us in a spectator's version of the experience of goal-lessness. As in a circle there is no ultimate destination because there is no beginning or end, so on the Buddhist path there is no goal. To strive for nirvana is by definition to fail, for nirvana is the state of being without strife, without goal, free in space and time. Life is one moment, then another, that we must experience fully one at a time, without looking backward or forward for those "traces" that are inevitably present anyway, without our efforts, *because* they are "not."

By putting us in a state of dislodgement like that, *Hamlet* positions us to appreciate Hamlet's similar dislodgement, to appreciate that we need not be aggressive or oppositional in relation to the unmasked royal theater of Elizabeth (or any ruler) in order to effect reform. The poise of alert patience can mature into social change, perhaps even into revolutionary change. In making his art transparent, then, Shakespeare is like Hamlet, inscribing himself within his threat to established authority, inviting our collusion with him in rejecting the late Elizabethan model of monarchy, suggesting that a different, perhaps younger, player is needed. But at the same time he does not suggest active resistance; in spite of the form of Hamlet's own action, the character's example exalts the virtue and transformative power of a patience very like that espoused by Buddhists. Risky though this strategy may be for the playwright, it seems to have been subtle enough, or pacific enough, to pass into performance. Because it did so, we have in Hamlet as well as in Hal an example of the fruitfulness of life in free fall over the personal abyss that opens when the Elizabethan tightrope snaps.[22]

IV

King Lear too has an astonishing moment in act 4, scene 6 of *King Lear* when his orientation toward himself and the world seems very like a Buddhist's. That he does not sustain this moment may suggest Shakespeare's own ambiguous relationship to it, *Hamlet* notwithstanding.

If Hamlet is different from Lear in his ability to sustain his stance until his death, it may be partly because he *chooses* his deferral, then consciously explores its implications as he grows into them, and partly because he dies never having had to take the crown. King Lear, of course, not only wears the crown at the beginning of the play, but mimics Shakespeare's new ruler, James, in his insistence on absolute sovereignty both as father and as king.[23] He so believes in the trappings and flattery that attend his office that he exemplifies anybody's description of blindness; his belief in his self-image as king/father is solidified by his belief in a world of complete obedience.

When the trappings and obedience fall away, then, his self-image also crumbles. Whether or not this process is meant as a cautionary example for Shakespeare's king, it is clear that Lear's pain forces him to interrogate his own assumptions about both the world and himself, and that lifting the veil of his illusions drives him mad. The climax of this process is act 3, scene 6, the hallucinatory trial of Goneril and Regan. It represents Lear's final crazed attempt to impose justice on a world in which, as this scene shows, justice is absent, and the desire for it therefore insane.[24]

However, as Lear's madness is an index of the degree of his original blindness, the unfolding of acts 3 and 4 shows that the apparent alternative, rationality, is also intolerable. Cornwall and Regan, like Edmund and Goneril, are clear-minded about their objectives in the world and efficient in achieving them. Their difference from Lear and his sympathetic/pathetic followers is emphasized by the fact that their scenes are counterpointed with his throughout the third act. As Lear's anguished madness climaxes in act 3, scene 6, so their rationality climaxes in act 3, scene 7, with the physical blinding of Gloucester. In act 4 their desire for power and possession, the motive behind their rationality, is then concentrated into a new image. It is feminized in the characters of Goneril and Regan, and given the form of a possessive sexual lust that, in the final act, culminates in their murder of one another.[25] Albany's prophetic assessment, "Humanity must perforce prey on itself, / Like monsters of the deep" (4.2.49–50), seems accurate. Both the new world characterized by Edmund's "Now, gods, stand up for bastards!" (1.2.22), with its attack on bloodlines, and the old world with its proclivity toward blind tyranny, are discredited in the play. In the ambitious new rulers of the play's midsection, as in the Lear of acts 1 and 2, a character's sense of psychological security requires the hardening of heart and mind against others. Both worlds are in a kind of panic.

Blind Gloucester's moral response to this world without apparent values—his attempt to avoid contesting the gods' "opposeless wills" (4.6.38) by futilely insisting on justice—is suicide. To him, this world without options is grotesque; to us in the audience, as Ian Kott has argued, Gloucester himself may seem grotesque as well. He is its helpless victim, a buffoon pantomiming his belief that a simple tumble on a flat stage is a fall from a great cliff. And if we laugh at Gloucester even as we pity him, we will feel ourselves to be at the same dead end he feels himself. There is, as he learns, no exit—for him or for us. We also do not know what to believe.[26]

At this point Lear enters and briefly dramatizes an alternative. This new Lear, although still mad, is quite unlike his old self; he is of course unlike Edmund and Goneril and Regan as well, and also unlike the now "resigned" Gloucester. As his madness has passed its climax of rage and reached catharsis, it has swept his self-belief away. He is no longer in anguish, therefore; his mood has quieted, even sweetened. He accepts the grotesque situation of the play and dissolves it into unimportance. Unhinged from all conventions, he seems to accept his lack of status and justice. Indeed, Lear not only sees such personal expectations to be absurd, but joins this absurdity, personifies it, even provokes it into a game. Playfully, at times joyfully, he turns our puzzled disillusionment into fun.

Lear's own fun may be most clear at his exit. The Gentleman and attendants come in to take Lear to his daughter Cordelia, but the father does not expect kind treatment:

> No rescue? What, a prisoner? I am even
> The natural fool of fortune. Use me well,
> You shall have ransom. Let me have surgeons,
> I am cut to th' brains.
>
> (4.6.190–93)

He imagines being captured by an enemy who might release him for ransom. Given his "sovereign shame" (Kent, 4.3.42) about the injustice he has done Cordelia, and his knowledge of the world's inhumanity, this may seem a reasonable assessment. He accurately assesses his brain's malfunctioning as well. It seems reasonable for him to wonder if he will be killed rather than ransomed:

> *Lear.* I will die bravely, like a smug bridegroom. What? I will be jovial. Come, come, I am a king. Masters, know you that?
> *Gent.* You are a royal one, and we obey you.
> *Lear.* Then there's life in't. Come, and you get it, you shall get it by running. Sa, sa, sa, sa.
>
> (4.6.198–203)

Lear has not lost touch with the world outside him. If his attitude toward possible threat is new, it is because his attitude has changed, not his ability to assess his situation. Indeed, if anything, his perceptions are *more* accurate than before, not less.

In this new attitude, his opening line's pun makes light of the idea of death. Even life itself is a thing to play with now, rather than cling to. In this "mad" new playfulness, then, he tries on an old role, that of king. Surprisingly, the Gentleman accepts it, and Lear understands that he does: "Then there's life in't." Although he is not out of touch with "reality" (his recognition of Gloucester at line 177 suggests this same awareness), however, he does not fall back into self-belief after the Gentleman acknowledges him as king. Instead, since against expectation the world once more takes him seriously, he will enjoy this regained status for the moment before it is again swept away. Seeing that his commands will be obeyed, he does not assume a regal demeanor, but the reverse: he converts the "life in't" into a game of chase and find, and runs off the stage in this child's play. He has discovered what title and command are useful for; he uses for fun the title that once defined him. Unattached to the world, yet inescapably within it, he plays the "self-existing show" of life, seeming to relish its quality of "performance," of "living theater" (Trungpa 1975, 160). It is not that he thinks things better than they are, but the opposite: he has fun because, mad, he can face how awful they are. He can enjoy the absurdity of kingship. For this brief moment, he converts samsara to nirvana.

He enters this scene in the same spirit, mockingly feigning kingship: "No, they cannot touch me for coining, I am / the King himself" (4.6.83–84). His following speech continues this pose in the related language of a military commander, concluding with a mock sentry challenge:

> Give the word.
> *Edg.* Sweet marjoram!
> *Lear.* Pass.
>
> (4.6.92–94)

Lear creates his own mental frame of reference, and imposes it on those around him. Edgar and Gloucester cooperate, as will the Gentleman, so that he can follow his own whims freely. In the process, Lear will show us the wisdom in his madness, his own sense that his changing moods *are* in fact whims, insubstantial in themselves.

Even when he falls into self-pity or rage, his perceptions seem just:

> they are not men o'their words; they told me I
> was every thing. 'Tis a lie, I am not ague-proof.
>
> (4.6.104–5)

> And when I have stol'n upon these son-in-laws,
> Then kill, kill, kill, kill, kill, kill!
>
> (4.6.186–87)

He knows where he is and where he has been in this world. When he is gay, it is not because *he* is out of touch, but because the *world* is. The old roles he once believed in are now perceived as jokes. Unattached to his self and his world, a kind of sweet renunciation allows him to go through the motions of the world's conventions without taking them seriously. He is in the mental state of just "an ordinary citizen," for whose world

> there is no country; it is stateless. And this stateless country extends to the rest of the universe. Because it is stateless, there is the possibility that . . . [people] could begin to feel a sense of signing themselves over to outer space. (Trungpa 1976b, 34)

To be a ruler with such a perspective on the world requires a profound sense of irony:

> Ay, every inch a king!
> When I do stare, see how the subject quakes.
> (4.6.107–8)

This ironically detached amusement is the fundamental lesson he has learned from his experiences. When Gloucester says, "O, Let me kiss that hand!" the king responds, "Let me wipe it first, it smells of mortality" (4.6.132–33). His nonattachment extends even to ultimate things, and beyond the individual to the species, yet without disabling his enjoyment of them. He is a free man. [27]

One important basis of this freedom is shown when he speaks to Gloucester. Lear is the only character in the play who can talk to Gloucester about his blindness directly and on his own level, as if blindness were just another form of experience, no more dreadful than many others that he himself has known. He does not shy away from the most difficult facts, but instead confronts them:

> Get thee glass eyes,
> And like a scurvy politician, seem
> To see the things thou dost not.
> (4.6.170–72)

There is the virtue of honesty in physical blindness, a virtue ironically missing in the conventional, seeing world. In the pain of lost sight there is the strength of knowing one's limits, of knowing that one does not see, and of pretending nothing.

In the next scene he is sane, but he nonetheless retains this direct, illusionless approach to difficulty for a little while. Very simply, he surrenders himself to his wronged daughter: "If you have poison for me, I will drink it" (4.7.71), and he sees without embellishment that he is "old and foolish" (4.7.83). Serious rather than game-playing here, he still takes no refuge in self-image. He remains "stateless." Trungpa's remarks once more seem particularly descriptive:

> When a person is completely exposed, fully unclothed, fully unmasked, completely naked, completely opened—at that very moment he sees the power of the word [sunyata, emptiness]. When the basic, absolute, ultimate hypocrisy has been unmasked, then one really begins to see the jewel shining in its brightness: the energetic, living quality of openness, the living quality of surrender, the living quality of renunciation.
>
> Renunciation in this instance is not just throwing away but, having thrown everything away, we begin to feel the living quality of peace.... Complete openness is complete victory because we do not fear, we do not try to defend ourselves at all. (1973, 198–99)

Having given himself up, Lear transcends Terry Eagleton's formulation that "actors are, so to speak, signifiers who strive to become one with the signifieds of their parts; yet however successfully they achieve this we know that such representation is a lie" (1986, 13). Lear, as well as his audience, seems to know that his "parts" are but roles, at first in act 4, scene 6, when he is freed by madness from conventional self-belief, then when he carries this wisdom back into his world of sanity in act 4, scene 7.

However, he cannot maintain this renunciation. Having found that Cordelia forgives and loves him, he falls into dependence on that love. He retains his knowledge of the hollowness of politics and power:

> ... so we'll live,
> And pray, and sing, and tell old tales, and laugh
> At gilded butterflies, and hear poor rogues
> Talk of court news; and we'll talk with them too—
> Who loses and who wins; who's in, who's out—
> And take upon's the mystery of things
> As if we were God's spies; and we'll wear out,
> In a wall'd prison, packs and sects of great ones,
> That ebb and flow by th' moon.
>
> (5.3.11–19)

But he cannot live without Cordelia's love, a love which he imagines as a continual undoing of his error-prone past:

> We two alone will sing like birds i' the cage;
> When thou dost ask me blessing, I'll kneel down
> And ask of thee forgiveness. So we'll live . . .
>
> (5.3.9–11)

From the Buddhist point of view, the problem with this posture is not his love for Cordelia, but the *nature* of that love.[28] The problem is that Lear needs it; he depends on her love for his own equilibrium. He thinks the lesson in Cordelia's love is that if one loves, one will get love back. But Cordelia, who loved her own unloving father in act 1, has already disproved this by exemplifying a love that is unconditional. Love is a gift freely given because it is felt, not a commodity offered in expectation of a profitable return. It is ironic, then, that this unconditional love is what Lear hopes to capture in a prison, reenacting again and again the disproof of his belief. The reason Cordelia's death kills him is not that he loves and makes himself vulnerable, but that he does not love and make himself vulnerable enough. As with his kingship in act 4, scene 6, so here with love: if he is to preserve his equanimity in this cruel world he must give himself up utterly; he must love Cordelia enough not to ask anything in return. But of course his need is too great for this; his love becomes part of a business deal and, as it so often does, the world conspires with the lover to effect a foreclosure. As Trungpa writes,

> Love and compassion are vague terms; we can interpret them in different ways. Generally in our lives we take a grasping approach, trying to attach ourselves to different situations in order to achieve security. Perhaps we regard someone as our baby, or, on the other hand, we might like to regard ourselves as helpless infants and leap into someone's lap. This lap might belong to an individual, an organization, a community, a teacher, any parental figure. So-called "love" relationships usually take one of these two patterns. Either we are being fed by someone or we are feeding others. These are false, distorted kinds of love or compassion.
> . . .
> However, there is another kind of love and compassion, a third way. Just be what you are. You do not reduce yourselves to the level of an infant nor do you demand that another person leap into your lap. You simply be what you are in the world, in life. (1973, 211–12)

As his "sanity" matures, Lear requires the security of a loving frame of reference, of an environment which, though spatially limited to a prison, nonetheless performs the vital function of echoing his thought, thus confirming his idea of himself and his place. In this state of mind, of course he dies when Cordelia does. And we in the audience, not at all unlike him, of course pity him; and of course we think this play gratuitously cruel, snatching the supports out from under Lear just when he had seemed to learn something, just when he had begun to teach us to hope again for some justice in this world of the play. Edgar's concluding speech directs our attention to his suffering; in doing so, however, it turns away from Lear's wisdom in act 4, scene 6.

Shakespeare may have begun in this play to represent another subversion of conventional and official thought, but it is not sustained until the end. Although, as Jonathan Dollimore points out, the play does "make visible" the "social process and its forms of ideological misrecognition" (1984, 191), its concluding effect is different. The concluding effect is instead, as Jan Kott suggests, of a grotesque world that forms "a criticism of the absolute in the name of frail human experience" (1964, 92), a representation of cosmic injustice (see Susan Snyder 1979, 168). Though bleak, this ending allows us the luxury of complaint, a complaint in which we can imagine our solidarity with our species: "Misfortune isn't our fault; the world (and/or the gods) is unfair."

Nor do the metadramatic moments in the play undermine this conclusion. Although several of the characters play roles, these roles usually seem anchored to the interior "reality" of the narrative, rather than emphasizing its artificial and "made" quality, as if they saw the play from the outside. To be sure, the cruelty of the ending is, from the point of view of narrative inevitability, gratuitous; it might even seem Shakespeare's deliberate erasure of the positive direction the narrative seemed to have taken. But even if this recognition leads our attention back to the author, and to an attempt to read his intention through the now transparent artwork of the play, the ending does not turn us toward Lear's inadequacy in the "birds i' th' cage" speech, and thus does not lead us to a critique of conventional social roles, including power roles. Rather, again, Edgar's conclusion emphasizes the ordeal of suffering humanity in a difficult universe.

Indeed, it may even be that Edgar, who is the legitimate heir of an earl and is directly bequeathed the crown by the current ruler Albany, represents a chastened and youthful version of Lear. He has shadowed many of Lear's experiences as mad outcast during the play, seems to believe in the virtues of the old hierarchical system, and has enough youthful energy to reinstate it. Seen in this light, the ending threatens no one, subverts nothing. Although the play as a whole may act as a warning about the abuses and blinding qualities of absolute power, such a warning leaves the hierarchical system itself unquestioned.

In this play, then, Shakespeare glimpses another way, but closes it off. The insights of Buddhism are open to anyone. Their maintenance, however, requires sustained, directed effort; this is extremely difficult without the guidance of a tradition and a teacher.

Epilogue:
The Tempest

In writing of the metadramatic quality of this play's epilogue, John Greenwood voices a common perception:

> As Prospero dissolves the illusion of the island and frees Ariel, we must dissolve the illusion of the drama and free Prospero.... As Prospero is called upon to forgive the characters in the play, we are called upon to release Prospero, and thus we become aware of the play's power to stir in us a sense of grace.... Here then is art as life, beyond rational control, and yet, strangely enough, here is art under the very considerable and mature control of an acknowledged master. (1988, 184)

In his epilogue this master, Shakespeare, has the character Prospero ask us, the audience, to confirm our collusion with both the master and his creature.[1] Indeed, the two relationships are reciprocal. We are asked to release Prospero from our "spell" by "prayer." Becoming white magicians, offering a supplication to God, we reenact the righteousness of Prospero's power, and thus confirm it. This confirmation, in turn, acknowledges the power of Shakespeare's play to transform us into Prospero's image. We are not only to be consciously complicit in Prospero's character and action, but also to be fully aware of their author.

Prospero makes the play's artificiality explicit as early as his marriage masque. He announces, "Our revels now are ended," then becomes startlingly ambiguous:

> These our actors
> (As I foretold you) were all spirits, and
> Are melted into air, into thin air,
> And like the baseless fabric of this vision,

> The cloud-capp'd tow'rs, the gorgeous palaces,
> The solemn temples, the great globe itself,
> Yea, all which it inherit, shall dissolve,
> And like this insubstantial pageant faded
> Leave not a rack behind.
>
> (4.1.148–56)

Are these palaces, temples, the globe and "all which it inherit" part of the revels' "vision," of the Globe Theater "itself," or indeed of the greater world outside it? As we balance the possibility of all three, in our minds they coexist.[2] They are all the subject here, and their equation with ourselves in the audience is at once made plain:

> We are such stuff
> As dreams are made on; and our little life
> Is rounded with a sleep.
>
> (4.1.156–58)

The epilogue, then, simply extends this equation, and opens it out so that we are included within the texture of the play. Becoming like Prospero, we complete its action. As we do so, the play enters "reality." Reciprocally, we become its players. The play's self-deconstruction is its form of self-assertion, as both Derrida and Buddhists might expect. By accepting the convention of the theater, by choosing to use "hands" and "breath" respectively to clap and to voice approval of this play, we also choose to accept our inclusion within it. It will not seem surprising, then, if we wish to explore the implications of Prospero's self-deconstruction, as well as the nature of Shakespeare's power in this metadramatic moment, since we are implicated in them both.

For Prospero the roles of actor at the end, and of author/producer of act 4's masque, are only two of many. He also plays ruler, magus, and father during the play, putting on and taking off costumes at need; in addition, he stages an earlier play within, the storm in the first scene, immediately after which he lets us in on its secret as if from backstage, as if we were his as-yet-unacknowledged accomplices from the very beginning.[3] For him and therefore for us, dramatic roles and knowledge of their production coalesce as early as act 1, scene 2. From this perspective, we might even think this play to be Shakespeare's anticipation of *Las Meninas,* since one of its main subjects is its own manner of representation. However, far from "eliding" its subject, as Michel Foucault alleges of Velázquez's painting (1973, 16), *The Tempest*'s story content becomes *more* emphatic for us because, colluding in its creation, we are as enmeshed in it as Prospero.[4]

And as Shakespeare is, for not only is he too implicitly inscribed in this work by its explicit unmasking of its own construction, but also by the fact that within this construction there is a maker, a magician who repeatedly refers to his power as "art."[5] Shakespeare is implicitly seen not only *behind* the play by virtue of its transparence, but also *within* the play in the person of its main character. Thus when Prospero faces us in the epilogue, his identity gone—he has not only given up his magical power, but he has also lost his role in the now concluded story—it is as if character and actor and author have been collapsed into one figure who speaks to us directly as if we were all on the same level.[6] To clap is to be directly implicated not only *in* Prospero's art and Shakespeare's, but *with* the artist himself.

Like *Las Meninas, The Tempest* is still more complicated by the additional inscription within it of the reigning monarch. For Shakespeare, this is the figural god/father who rules still another island than Caliban's and who, like a good father to his kingdom, teaches us in the audience, as Prospero does the other characters, the Christian/Stuart virtues of love, humility, forgiveness, and marriage.[7] Can it be, then, that Prospero's request for applause is actually a veiled command? It is surely not strange that such a play would be chosen for the celebration of James's daughter's wedding; in such circumstances, how could the epilogue *not* be heard to end in a command? Like the transparent artistry of a perspective drawing, the transparence of this play does not lead us merely to see further and further into it, so that its plays within plays create a kind of infinite regress.[8] Rather, as in Romano's *Sala dei Giganti,* it encloses us within it until, at last, it is ourselves we see—ourselves not only within the social context constructed inside the play, but also within the social context that surrounds and produces the play, a social context that the play implies by reinforcing.[9] Under the watchfully expectant eye of Prospero, then, we are profoundly conscious of many reasons why our hands are clapping: to applaud the play's excellence as an entertainment; to applaud the author's excellence as a maker of entertainments; to applaud King James, whose virtue the play represents; to applaud the author for his applause for the good king; to show that we are like the character and author and king in virtue; and lastly, perhaps, to show that we consciously choose to join the author in his willed self-subjugation to the monarch.

We are made conscious of the political power of a work of art that forces its audience to adopt a deconstructive stance toward it. This is where "representation, freed finally from the relation that was impeding it"

(Foucault 1973, 16) leads—to a reinforcement of its powerful relations with its subject and that subject's social implications, a reinforcement that functions by drawing its audience within it.

One of the values within the play in which we seem to collude is the Trinculo-Stephano-Caliban grouping's parodic condemnation of Sebastian's and Antonio's usurpation theme. Another is the colonization of the play's only female character, Miranda, into the naïve obedience of a fairytale daughter (presumably as a model for Princess Elizabeth, as well as for all women).[10] A third is the enslavement of Caliban, apparently justified by his attempted rape of Miranda and his continuing desire to take power from Prospero. That is, we approve a prescription for social order under the aegis of a benevolent father/king. This powerful man seems to exemplify virtue: he teaches humility, the giving up of belief in one's personal ability to control one's destiny, and the trusting in a higher power instead. Thus the mariners in the storm fall "to prayers" (1.1.51), like Alonzo and Ferdinand. Thus Alonzo renounces power in favor of love for his son when the illusory banquet is snatched away. And thus Ferdinand carries logs for Miranda, and she for him. Willed service is freedom, a virtue which Prospero seems to mean to teach to Sebastian and Antonio as well. When he plans to drown his book, he also seems to adopt this lesson for himself; and when he appears powerless before us in the epilogue, he seems to ratify this adoption. He seems at last to enact what he teaches: self-surrender, a Buddhist as well as a Christian virtue.[11]

However, this is not all our clapping implies. As many scholars have shown, this virtue is not unambiguous. For example, Caliban's pain and sense of injustice are given a clear voice. Indeed, because the island was his, inherited from his mother, Prospero may as justly be called a usurper as Antonio.[12] Thus for the dispossessed, the value of language—of having a voice—is denied. Caliban's only "profit on't" is that he knows "how to curse" (1.2.363–64).[13] In addition, Caliban's claim that Prospero had been kind to him at first and that in return Caliban had shared his island and its good things with Prospero (1.2.332–39)—a process repeated with Stephano and Trinculo in act 2, scene 2 (see especially 2.2.160–77)—is a tale just like that which Michel de Montaigne attributes to the Spaniards as he condemns their arrival in the New World (in "Of Coaches," in the Florio translation). Caliban's place in the play, then, does not fit neatly into a pattern that glorifies the king. It encourages us to read between the lines.

Doing so, we might wonder if Prospero's extended historical disquisition in act 1, scene 2, is not his own revisionist history of the island.[14] For us as for Miranda, he certainly claims to be a benevolent "schoolmaster" whose care has

> made thee more profit
> Than other princess' can, that have more time
> For vainer hours, and tutors not so careful.
> (1.2.172–74)

He not only tells us what to believe, but expects gratitude for doing so. In recognition of this self-serving expectation, too, we clap at the end.

There are other problems. For example, when he remembers Caliban and his group and ends the marriage masque, Prospero's lost composure suggests his less than total control over himself and others (4.1.139–45). And it may be that he deliberately entraps Sebastian and Antonio by setting them up in a situation specifically designed to bring out their worst traits—that Prospero *wants* them to sin in order to justify humbling them.[15] However, perhaps the most crucial problem is his own surrender of power, his show of practicing the humility he has taught others. For one thing, it occurs only after the island has been made safe for this surrender, when Prospero can believe that "at this hour / lies at my mercy all mine enemies" (4.1.262–63). Ariel's report summarizes this situation in detail (5.1.7–19). *Then,* securely in control, confident that they are all "spell-stopp'd" (5.1.61), he announces that he will give up his magic (5.1.50–57), and forgives them (5.1.28–30, 78).[16]

In addition to the fact that he is a pragmatist even in virtue, surrendering only when he is confident that it is safe to do so, there is also a question about whether or not in fact he *does* give up power at all. The arranged marriage between Miranda and Ferdinand may seem ideal, but it is certainly political: it will place a male who is untainted by sin on the thrones of both Milan and Naples; the territory to be governed by Prospero's own blood descendants (through Miranda) is actually enlarged. At the same time, he gets personal vengeance on his "forgiven" brother Antonio by effectively disinheriting him.[17] From this perspective, we clap for the *show* of virtue that hides the Machiavellian beneath.

Prospero's final "acknowledgment" of Caliban, "this thing of darkness" (5.1.275) and "a bastard" (5.1.273), is similarly double-edged.[18] From a royal perspective this may seem a gracious gesture of condescension to a creature who is unworthy of it because of color, descent, and ill will. He is a "native" to whom this island will be left only by default. Indeed, the transfer of title is far from complete. Perhaps the "bastard"

Caliban is "acknowledged" so that this primitive island will remain in some sense within Prospero's family's control? This view is certainly consistent with the father's use of his daughter's idealized marriage. However, it may also indicate Prospero's self-awareness; it may be his acknowledgment of some darkness that he sees within himself ("this thing of darkness I / Acknowledge mine"), perhaps some figural kinship with Caliban? It may show the insecurity that fuels the royal nightmare of instability which he then causes to occur in "reality" on the isle, justifying his creation of his Machiavellian self.[19]

If King James's image is thus exposed by Prospero, however, the play offers no alternative example we can turn to. We must applaud, even though in doing so we are acting out not only our audience part in the conventions of theater, but also our enmeshment with a problematic Prospero, with the author who engineers his exposure, and even with the now problematized king who is its object, standing behind as well as within the play. To consciously choose to play our part in this theatrical situation is to acknowledge our own exposure as much as the king's. The self-deconstructive elements in *The Tempest* at last dissolve all the play's complex layering into the single act of our applause, concentrating our awareness on the fact that we choose to play this king's game. We clap for social stability, knowing its price to be the lost integrity of feigned virtue and service. Stephen Greenblatt's suggestion about *Henry IV,* that a voice is given to the dispossessed in order better to contain them, seems to extend in this play beyond the characters to include both the author and his audience. As if to confirm Jacques Derrida's ideas, Shakespeare's self-deconstructive play seems to affirm royalty by the very act of exposing its negative qualities.

Our alternative to clapping is silence, since other responses might be hazardous. Possibly we could force Prospero to remain before us, unfreed from the stage, vulnerable and exposed. Possibly we could force the king in the audience to face himself and his courtier Shakespeare through the person of Prospero.[20] Possibly we could encourage the king's self-awareness by our creation of a silent public space in the theater. However, this seems unlikely in the audience, and anyway is not encouraged in the play itself, which seems not to move toward such a perspective on self-transformation. It problematizes self-surrender, as we have seen, in the character of Prospero.

I have argued that there are glimpses of a different perspective in other plays. However, each of these cases seems to require special circumstances. In the case of Prince Hal, a situation of deferral is tolerable because it is self-limited. In *Hamlet,* the antagonist is so identified with corruption that he seems dissociated from current social or political ideology outside the theater; the king can be killed by a hero who is both princely and dissociated from all self-definition. With Lear, the character is dissociated from the "normal" because he is mad. In such cases, not only does Shakespeare's deconstructive stance toward his art display its emptiness of unproblematized significance; it also allows us, through our collusion with a character who mirrors this quality of the play, to see this emptiness as a possibility in life, to learn a stance toward life outside the theater that a Buddhist might think wise.

It may be, indeed, that a play's self-deconstruction, and its characters', is the necessary method of expression for this kind of wisdom, for emptiness implies a fullness of being which, by virtue of its contrast to the limited nature of language, cannot be explicitly stated. Shunryu Suzuki writes of Zen Buddhism,

> The more you understand our thinking, the more you find it difficult to talk about it. . . . There is apt to be some misunderstanding, because the true way always has at least two sides, the negative and the positive. When we talk about the negative side, the positive side is missing, and when we talk about the positive side, the negative side is missing. We cannot speak in a positive and a negative way at the same time. So we do not know what to say. It is almost impossible to talk about Buddhism. (1970, 90)

Jacques Derrida makes a very similar observation about language when he writes, "The sign represents the present in its absence" (1986a, 124). "The present" exists only in relation to the other tenses, and thus "is called the present by means of this very relation to what it is not: what it absolutely is not" (1986a, 127). Direct verbal expressions of full being, of the "present," are therefore impossible—or possible only "under erasure"—for the "emptiness" of this state consists precisely in "being" beyond words and concepts. Its fullness *depends* on such emptiness. But if it cannot be directly stated, it *can* be exemplified, and our eyes *can* be prepared to recognize it. This is the reciprocal function of the unusual character, and of the parallel attitude engendered in an audience by a play's self-deconstruction. Shakespeare's emphasis on metadramatic moments is one of his great strengths.

However, in most plays Shakespeare seems not to allow emptiness to become a positive example. His plays deconstruct themselves again and again, but Shakespeare has no tradition to draw on that could clarify and reinforce the importance of this act, then guide him to its deepening.

Again and again, his self-deconstruction subsides into an exposed acceptance of his theater's conventions. He even seems to use it as an instrument of state, a way of subverting *all* options, not as an example but as a way of forcing us to reinscribe ourselves within his art's submission to established authority. Thus the conventions of royal discourse contain him and us in *The Tempest*'s epilogue as much as they do Prospero. And although it may be, as Jonathan Goldberg argues, and as the many dimensions of Prospero suggest, that the king is also contained by his own discourse (1983, 20), this is cold comfort for us; although *he* is exposed, it is *we* who bend the knee.

Yet even in these plays of subjugation, as Shakespeare makes us conscious of accepting this stance with him, he also shows us the Buddhist alternative by seeming to erase it. To Derrida, "Being" is absence: "Always differing and deferring, the trace is never as it is in the presentation of itself. It erases itself in presenting itself" (1983a, 132, 133). To Trungpa also, the fullest "being" requires a situation in which

> you and your projections, you and the world outside, becomes [*sic*] transparent. This involves removing the dualistic barriers set up by concepts, which is the experience of shunyata, the absence of relative concepts, emptiness. (1976a, 65)

Similarly, with Shakespeare, as well as with the implications of his work, our relationship is dialogic. The essence of his self-deconstructive plays is their oscillation between what is said and what is not, each of them both present and absent at once. The "significance" of these plays lies in this relationship—this dialogue between the spoken and the unspoken of which their self-deconstruction makes us conscious. His plays are continually unmaking the fullness of emptiness, thus making this fullness visible. If Shakespeare, at last, does not exhort us to social or personal change, then, he may be unique in keeping that option alive, continually reminding us that if we will have significance, we must pretend it. He bequeaths to us, that is, a tension, an inner friction that can, in each of us who chooses to attend it, mature to "readiness." He does not seem to feel the need for instant answers and quick reforms. He does not encourage an adversarial attitude toward his worlds. We can be citizens and expatriates at the same time. Trungpa writes,

> At the point of having seen the complete picture of samsara, of having completely understood its mechanism, nirvana becomes redundant. In

what is called the enlightened state, both samsara and nirvana are freed.
(Guenther and Trungpa 1988, 23)

In such a state of awareness, the illusions of life become like a delightful "magic show" (sGam.po.pa 1986, 295). It is the possibility of this show that Shakespeare's self-deconstruction, even in its acceptance of the status quo, leaves us, the possibility of a revolutionary state of mind in which everything, including revolutionary social change, becomes unpredictably possible.[21]

The self-referentiality that lies behind Shakespeare's self-erasures seems to have been immanent in Western art from its beginnings. It may be that he brings this tendency out more fully than others, but this is a difference of degree rather than kind. The wisdom of emptiness has always existed in our experience, as Christianity's tradition of negative theology, as well as the Western tradition in art, testify. Although it has not yet been formalized into a main Western tradition, it remains close to our surfaces, available in its absence. Shakespeare, even in his most socially acquiescent plays, makes this absence palpable.

Appendix A:
The Sword of Prajna in the Visual Arts of the Continent

Although the art of resemblance seems to showcase the significance of its subject, the thing its art "resembles," this kind of art also tends to emphasize the fact of its presentation of this subject. By making its own constructed nature transparent, it typically undermines its apparent intention of "resemblance." Thus the mimetic visual arts, regardless of style, have inherent within them a tendency to self-problematization. Indeed, the effect of this art on its viewer seems most powerful precisely when this tendency is dominant. And this tendency, I have argued at some length in chapter 2, leads the viewer to a Buddhist-like awareness of both the subject *and the viewer oneself* as pretense, as entities to take seriously only in full awareness that their (our) identities are in fact also problematized. I have argued that this tendency has kept such a Buddhist-like view available below the surface of the Western tradition in the visual arts—available, as it were, in its necessary absence of direct statement—from earliest times until (at least) Shakespeare's. This appendix will sketch some examples of this tendency for the purposes of indicating its extent in time, its variety, and the range of possibilities that it had come to offer by the end of the sixteenth century.

The self-referentiality that tends to problematize this art of resemblance in the West becomes visible as early as the Minoan civilization of Crete (i.e., before 1500 B.C.). The Archeological Museum in Iraklion displays many examples of representational sculpture, as well as "realistic" scenes and figures painted on various forms of pottery and on walls; such depictions, brilliantly colored, come mainly from Knossos. Also within this early period, there are several examples of illusionism in ceramics. Pottery is fashioned to fool the eye into believing the pottery is made of some other material than it is: thin metal, or wood, or woven basketry (see Hans Georg Wunderlich 1983, 258–59). And, on the opposite end of the spectrum of mimetic styles, there is already an explicitly self-reflexive piece. A sarcophagus from the palace of Agia Triada in the south of Crete seems to picture on its side the rites of the dead; in the extreme right of this picture is a sarcophagus very like the one on which the picture has been painted, in use within the ceremony it depicts. This piece presents itself and its context explicitly to us. In its transparence as art, in its very act of announcing its status as a made object, it also establishes its ritual significance. The paradox that the power of the imitative arts derives from their artistic transparence, especially when what is imitated is of this world (medieval and Byzantine artists often having other ends), begins at once, and in several forms. It is as if each style implies the others, or gives impetus to the others.

The variety of styles that express this internal mechanism expands remarkably under the pressure of the circumstances of different historical moments. In order to get a sense of the range of this variety within a brief compass, I will here confront the art of resemblance at selected limit points where we can see it in the act of changing its relationship toward the thing it represents. In order to get a sense of its ubiquitousness in the Western tradition, I will arrange these limit points chronologically. However, I wish to emphasize that these examples are far too selective for their order to be conceived as a diachronic history.

One such limit point occurs in Ravenna in the late fifth and sixth centuries. It is clear that here, in this time, artists and their patrons had a choice. Roman skills with perspective (in wall painting) and illusionism (in stucco pillars sculpted in relief, and in stone statuary, both designed to look like real wall- or ceiling-supports) are evident in Pompeii—for example, in the House of the Vetti and in the Oriental House. So is an interest in "realistic" animal and human figures. In the mosaics of Piazza Armerina in Sicily, there are even clearer examples of background scenes that are in themselves landscapes, rather than grounds of flat color or of multicolored abstract design. Not surprisingly, these interests were carried to Ravenna. In the mosaics of the baptistery of the cathedral and even more fully in the mausoleum of Galla Placidia, both dating from the middle of the fifth century, realistic figures are often depicted; in addition, in the Galla Placidia the pictures are mainly either full realistic scenes or, if one figure is dominant, the backgrounds are typically full-color landscapes.

When, in the next century, the artists of the emperor Justinian take a different direction in Ravenna, it is clear that this new way is a choice. Particularly in the Church of S. Vitale, where a supreme political statement is being made to help consolidate Byzantium's appropriation of the Western empire, this change from "realism" to a Byzantine iconographic style seems obvious. It is a style that harmonizes with its politico-theological subject to sanctify the new government. Leading to the altar space are scenes from the Old Testament. As we approach the altar, we follow a progression of human figures who lacked Christian revelation, but whose power and righteousness prefigure it nonetheless. Arriving at the altar itself, we encounter the Christian emperor and empress, arranged at the head of this series of heroic humans as if they are the double climax to the human development we have been tracing. They face each other on opposite sides of, and raised just above, the altar. They are depicted as icons, not individuals, against a flat gold background. Only their feet rest on a green ground, as if to express their earthly sphere. They seem by both placement and stylized posture to represent the summation of earthly majesty. Christ is between them, directly behind and above the altar; he is raised slightly higher than they, against the same gold ground except where his lower half rests on a blue sphere. As Justinian and the empress Theodora are the culmination of righteous earthly power, Christ is the source and justification of that power. It seems no accident that these rulers flank the Lord around his altar; they represent their reign as an earthly extension of Christ's. They are the earthly pillars on which Christ and the Church rest in this world. Power and religion unite in this carefully composed presentation of Justinian and Theodora.

The rich and multicolored stones that form the floor and wall designs of the basilica, as well as its Greek plan, further accentuate the sense of Eastern magnificence with which the monarchs invest themselves through this church. Otto von Simson (1948) writes that this style "epitomizes the spirit of Byzantine culture." This art

> is at once sacred symbol and precious toy. Byzantine man was a *Homo ludens*. To him the world was a theater, created and directed by the Divine Poet. . . . With the detachment which is at once the detachment of contemplation and of playing,

he could "see the abstract in the concrete." Within the church, its supreme ceremony, the mass, was a "liturgical drama" which

> transcended the sphere of worship. It embraced the political world and mirrored man's existence on earth and in the life to come.

Because art was patterned on "the reality beyond realities" (Von Simson 1948, viii), Agnellus writes that he and his contemporaries

> did not experience aesthetic enjoyment but were overcome by awe and fear as if in the presence of sacred reality.

Their idea of "imitation" was "magical" (Von Simson 1948, 79). It was a perfect style in which to make a Byzantine political statement to the West.

In Ravenna, then, and perhaps in medieval art generally, the turning away from realistic imitation must be seen in this context. Implicitly self-reflexive and self-problematizing, this kind of resemblance seems less useful in the circumstances and to the purposes of the new rulers. The hieratic style that they adopted instead was already associated with Byzantium, and thus with themselves. It was also better suited to its object of imitation—these rulers in their relationship to the *other* world—and better suited as well to its message: the divine sanction behind their earthly power. What Murray Roston observes about one aspect of the art of realism may be true for the whole: Byzantine and medieval artists "had only 'lost' the art of physical perspective in the sense that modern artists have lost it, as no longer serving their needs" (1987, 47).

Yet despite this lack of "realism," S. Vitale's representation of the emperor and empress is still an art of resemblance. Michel Foucault's criterion for an art *not* so characterized is that it must "separate the representation from its relation to its object." Clearly, this art does not make such a separation. It is still an art of "resemblance," but it is a style of resemblance that, related to another world, avoids self-problematization in this one.[1] The choice of this style in this situation for these purposes, indeed, strongly suggests that the patrons of this art so fully understood the tendency of worldly mimesis toward transparence that they could develop a way of exploiting this art. The effects they achieved, as we shall see in our discussion of Masaccio, nonetheless depend upon an attitude toward resemblance that is similar to that held by illusionist artists at the extreme other end of the mimetic spectrum.

Another limit point occurs six centuries after the high moment of Ravenna. The Siennese master Duccio di Buoninsegna (1255?–1318), working just half a generation before Giotto, stands poised at the transition between the Middle Ages and the Renaissance. His transitional situation is complicated by the fact that both his backward- and forward-looking qualities are strongly suggestive of contemporary Byzantine (Eastern) style, although specific sources have not been identified. After Ravenna, the iconic aspects of this style spread all over Europe, so the indebtedness of his medieval side is not surprising.[2] However, there is a further Byzantine mediation: part of Duccio's presumed anticipation of Renaissance art, the facial expressions which seem more natural than iconic, is perfectly consistent with the contemporary practices of Byzantine painters during the Paleologian Renaissance, which also began in the thirteenth century (see White 1979, 55–58; also Stubblevine 1979, 7, 28). A splendid example is in the church of the Panaghia Kera in Kritsa, near the northeast coast of Crete. However, Duccio is also indebted to contemporary developments in the West: he worked with Cimabue at Santa Maria Novella in Florence, and it is probably from this work that he learned his new sense of volume, space, and monumentality (Stubblevine 1979, ix). Even his iconic figures have a sense of depth that is foreign to the Byzantine style (White 1979, 57).

This combination of traditional and new qualities (the latter probably Eastern as well as Western) puzzled Vasari, who came to Duccio from the other side of the Renaissance, after the new Western style had been fully realized and codified. Vasari preferred Giotto, whose "concentrated study of the individual object" focuses his paintings, and implies the kind of close observation of "real" detail that could lead him to represent accurately what he saw—for example the receding walls of buildings—without using the rules of perspective (White 1979, 167). To Vasari it is Giotto who "completely restored that art of design, of which his contemporaries knew little or nothing" (Vasari, 1965, 57), who made a decisive break with the crude traditional Byzantine style and brought to life the great art of painting as we know it today, introducing the technique of drawing accurately from life. (1965, 58)

"Duccio, in contrast, deals not with the focused, concentrated view but with the multiplicity of things," with diffusion rather than concentration. His depictions of constructed things like buildings are therefore often "oblique"; when he can avoid them, he does (White 1979, 167). But, possibly for the same reason, he may in a particular way be "more complex" than Giotto (Stubblevine 1979, ix). Although, as with Giotto, Duccio in his *Maestà* places the Virgin and Child at the center of his composition, her glory is not only in herself, but in the influence she spreads over the many saints arrayed on either side of her (not *around* her, so that the viewer's attention, having completed its circle of the figures surrounding her, will inevitably turn back on her at their center, but stretching *away* from her). There is no question that she is the most important figure, but emphasis flows out into all corners of the painting. Indeed, our eye can rest with these outlying figures. Because many of their faces look away, or at us, they do not draw us immediately back to the Virgin at the center. Certainly Giotto painted some immensely complex scenes (not to mention the Scrovegni Chapel itself), but usually there is a narrative scheme that organizes and directs our attention. This is part of the "design" that Vasari admired. With Duccio, however, the organization is usually more symbolic than narrative. It is therefore often less explicit, less concentrated, more diffuse. The this-worldliness that in Giotto is given its full force so that it can show the immanence of the divine in earthly reality is in Duccio always qualified. His "realism" is mediated by Byzantine practice, both traditional and contemporary. His sense of volume and depth is expressed in traditional compositions and through figures whose posture suggests the iconic as much as the "real."

Paradoxically, this Byzantine mediation between the past and present moment allows Duccio a kind of artistic freedom that is not present in Giotto. This is clear, for example, in Duccio's many paintings of the Madonna and Child. The Child is often dressed in a red or rose or skin-colored gown, the half-length Madonna in a black hooded one, and the background is a gold (like contemporary and Ravennese mosaics) sometimes shading toward rose (as in the *Maestà*, where it sets up a contrast with the golden halos of the saints). Under the Virgin's hood may be a thin line of red or rose, so that in her headpiece she echoes the gown of the Christ Child (as in the *Madonna in Trono con il Bambino e Sei Angeli*). Frequently, as in Byzantine art, the design on the black gown is composed of thin lines of gold, almost matching the background color; their directions alone must tell us how the gown is folded, for when Duccio uses this simple plan the black in the gown has very little variation. His interplay of light and shadow in gowns can be extremely realistic when it is not ornamented by these thin gold lines, as for example in his most famous painting, the *Maestà*. However, when the gowns are ornamented with gold lines, as in the *Madonna di*

Maestà, Duccio di Buoninsegna. Courtesy of Fotografia Lensini Fabio, Siena.

Madonna di Crevole, **Duccio di Buoninsegna. Courtesy of Fotografia Lensini Fabio, Siena.**

Crevole or the *Madonna con il Bambino e Sei Angeli,* this interplay is muted. Clearly, in this kind of stylized painting, he chooses to use a flat background in both gown and field. The iconic quality of the figures is emphasized.

This symbolic presence is of course the dominating motif of these paintings. At first our attention is drawn to the mother. Her monumentality is commanding, as is the contrast of her black gown with the background gold. Enfolding the child, she draws us further into the picture's center. However, because this center is relatively static, our eye is drawn to the color, to the stark red against the black gown, and then to the other side of the contrast, to the black gown itself (this is particularly striking in the *Madonna di Crevole*). Here we trace the intricacy of those golden lines that tell us how to "read" her gown and hence her posture. It is as much in those golden curves and verticals as anywhere that Duccio's artistry shows; they are understated in their thinness, but they are set off against black, and they are drawn, one pure and simple line and then another, in seemingly endless variation and harmony, almost as if pursued for their own sake. To try to "read" that gown is to become lost in the maze of their grace, just as in the *Maestà* we can lose ourselves in the saints stretching away from the Virgin. Yet these lines are not broad enough to obstruct our consciousness of the mother and child. Even in tracing those lines we see the black beside it, are conscious of the monumental gown and the mother who wears it. If we are lost in these lines, we are lost in lines that define the Virgin, lost in the grace with which they endow the painting's main subject.

The freedom of these lines, then, is not indulged for its own sake. For one thing, they are disciplined into abstract harmonies. For another, this separation from the object they adorn is precisely what empowers their unencumbered grace, what allows them to endow that object, the Virgin, with their harmony. Not only do we not need to concentrate on the worldly realism of the object for it to achieve this grace, but we do not need to concentrate on the object itself, any more than we do on the other elements in the painting. Indeed, just the opposite: to insist on concentrating on the Virgin's or the Child's face in, for example, the *Madonna di Crevole*—to concentrate on the more realistic aspects of the painting, or (from another point of view) on those aspects of the painting which, if it were mainly realistic, would be the intended focal points—is to deny both of them the grace they achieve when we look away from them to other parts of the composition. This is at least one basis for White's diffused "multiplicity of things."

In Duccio, then, at the moment when realistic imitation begins once more to enter Western art (whether from the East or from Florence), the full effect of a painting often depends on looking both at the focal point, the Virgin and Child, and away from it (toward other figures in the *Maestà*, toward the pure harmony of lines in the *Madonna di Crevole*). This is different from Holbein in convention, but similar in the experience of viewing. In Duccio and in *The Ambassadors,* to look away from the title object is to enrich that object, to return to it in consciousness of an enlarged context. The differences in their conventions have something to do with the fact that Duccio was still working with the Byzantine tradition, while Holbein was working with the realistic one developed during the fifteenth century. But it is remarkable that Duccio uses abstraction and diffusion to achieve an effect closely related to that which Holbein achieves by requiring the viewer to take two successive vantage points. The art of this-worldly resemblance seems to imply that in some way we must turn our eyes away. Nothing is as it seems at a glance. When "it" *is* as it seems, it has been mystified, as the rulers of Ravenna demonstrated.

The demystification of "reality" in this art of resemblance does not diminish in the fifteenth century, when artists were so routinely constructing paintings with "seeming" reality that their techniques had developed into conventions (for example, Kubovy suggests, the use of linear perspective to arrange compositional space, to create an illusion of depth, to focus viewer attention, and to imply a vantage point from which to view the work).[3] Indeed, as the status of "realism" solidifies, its contradictions also become more explicit. A quality of exaggeration or playfulness, the result of deliberately overdoing these conventions, makes their skill at "seeming" become itself one of art's main subjects.

Paolo Uccello (1397–1475), for example, sometimes used his knowledge of geometry, a part of his knowledge of the realistic techniques of perspective, to simplify the world's appearances from the way they are normally perceived to the way they should be. In his *Battle of San Romano* (1456?) he created a world dominated by horses, by the knights astride them, and by their spears. The horses, however, are not "real" beasts, but idealized; they are composed of arcs of the most perfect of forms, the circle. The counterpoint of these circular shapes is a forest of lines, the long spears—some pointing to the sky, some lying broken on the ground, a few lowered to the attack in a horizontal position. Mediating between horses and spears, arcs and lines, and far less dominant than they, are the knights, in the main a faceless armored mass portrayed in subdued neutral colors; their harmony with the horses partly depends on the fact that they too are drawn more with a series of arcs than with the irregular contours of realism.

Possibly it was not only the subject, a symbol of civic pride (a Florentine victory over Siena), which prompted Lorenzo the Magnificent to have this series hung on the walls of his bedroom, nor was it the only cause of his grandfather Cosimo's patronage. For this painting is technically a tour de force: it makes some of the *tools* of perspective (lines and arcs) stand out more strongly than its object, the knights and the "reality" of their victory. It is as if rendering visible the wonders of the technique of "seeming" is so important to both patron and artist that they are placed in the forefront of our attention. Surely their prominence in the painting indicates at the least that they were perceived as adding to, rather than subtracting from, the glory of the Florentine triumph that the series "seems" to claim to represent.

Of course, another standard of taste is possible. We have seen this to be true, for example, in Vasari's remarks on Giotto, where a propagandistic attitude

Section, *Battle of San Romano*, Paolo Uccello. Courtesy of Alinari/Art Resource, N.Y.

Sir John Hawkwood, Paolo Uccello. Courtesy of Alinari/Art Resource, N.Y.

toward realism justifies a glorification of the Renaissance, his own age, at the expense of the so-called Middle Ages. Given what we have observed about the *Battle*, this attitude makes his lamentation over Uccello almost predictable:

> ... if only he had spent as much time on human figures and animals as he spent, and wasted, on the finer points of perspective. Such details may be attractive and ingenious, but anyone who studies them excessively is squandering time and energy. (1965, 95)

He has nothing to say of Lorenzo's bedroom paintings in his life of Uccello, but his criticism of one of Uccello's frescoes, an equestrian portrait of Sir John Hawkwood (1436) in Santa Maria del Fiore, Florence, suggests the limitation of his taste:

> Unfortunately, Paolo's horse has been painted moving its legs on one side only, and this is something which horses cannot do without falling. Perhaps he made the mistake because he was not in the habit of riding and not as familiar with horses as with other animals. Anyhow, but for that the painting would be absolutely perfect: the horse, which is very large, is done in beautiful perspective. (Vasari 1965, 101)

Two things in this passage are relevant to the present discussion. One is that Uccello was perfectly capable of handling the conventions of realism, both in perspective and in the anatomy of horses, in a way that would please even Vasari. *The Battle of San Romano* emerges therefore as an act of choice that pleased the major patrons of his time. Vasari's was not the only standard of taste.

The other is that Vasari, the great exponent of "sane" perspective, misses the interesting fact that in this painting Uccello used *two* systems of perspective, not one (see Kubovy 1986, 119–26). This framed fresco depicts a monument which takes up half the pictorial space, rising from the bottom of the painting to an imposing height. Atop it are the horse and rider. The lower perspective system places the viewer beneath this monument, looking up, so that we see the bottoms of its two successive tops where they extend beyond their base. In this system, the monumental quality of the city's remembrance of its warrior is emphasized, as we would normally think appropriate. In addition, this perspective system places the viewer in a vantage point which is roughly the same as our actual viewing position on the floor of the cathedral, as we look up at the monument painted on the wall. This first system of perspective not only helps the painted monument to seem "real," but solidifies our experience of this "reality" by confirming our known physical relationship to it.

A different system of perspective is used for the horse and rider. If we were to see them from below as we do the monument, the belly of the horse would be extremely prominent in the picture, and we would see Hawkwood himself at a fairly oblique angle. His dignity would be compromised. Therefore, although the horse and rider are far above the viewer's head, so that we stand on the cathedral floor looking up at them, the second system of perspective presents them as if they are nearly on our level. This second system, that is, contradicts our knowledge of our own physical position relative to the painting, in order to achieve the effect of endowing its object with dignity. Uccello manipulates his contradictory systems of perspective with such skill that even Vasari does not notice. This invisible manipulation is the inverse side of that same art of resemblance that is displayed in the *Battle;* in this later painting, the very tools of the art, we might even say its manipulative implications, are made visible.

Vasari, blind to the self-contradictions of the style he admired, is the exception who proves the rule. This tendency lying behind the art of resemblance—the urge to expose its own quality of pretense—was neither short-lived nor confined to Florence. The Venetian Vittore Carpaccio (1465?–1526) illustrates this fact in another style.

His way was more whimsical than Uccello's. He did not give it the center of attention. As Patricia Fortini Brown has recently demonstrated, his work always creates the pretense of realism. Possibly influenced by Leonardo's Venetian visit in 1500, Carpaccio mastered all of his age's devices of imitation, even when his subject was a vision of an alternative world (197–218, esp. 216–18). Yet he too plays with the conventions of his art. *The Miracle of St. Tryphon* (1507?), in the School of St. George, for example, has a low border of unidentifiable flowers along its bottom edge, from the right corner to the center. They are all roughly the same shape, size, and dull brownish-green color. Then, slightly above the bottom border and to the left of center, three off-white stairs rise toward the right, toward the raised place where the main action is occurring. The line of flowers is slightly raised at this point and becomes (or merges with; it is ambiguous) a decorative pattern on the lowest of the three steps of the stair. Suddenly, that is, the flowers have entered the picture; no longer bounding its outer limit, they now decorate something *within* the picture. They climb to the second and third steps as well, decorating the entire stairway. This decorative motif, that is, intrudes into the left-central foreground of the main scene, leading to the central platform where the main subject, the miracle, occurs. The flowers' color contrast makes them stand out far more obviously against the white stair than they do against the darker ground of the bottom, and thus their presence as an element in the picture is far more emphasized than is their presence at the painting's border. In addition, one of the flowers on the first step rises beyond its decorative size and touches the second step. It seems not decorative but "real" (alive); it has grown out of its decorative pattern. This fact, in turn, problematizes the rest of the flower motif: Is it a motif, or are we to think of the whole line of flowers as "real" flowers? And if we do, how can they grow out of the second and reach the third stair? Both their place (within or bounding the picture?) and their mimetic status (decoration or "reality"?) are ambiguous.

Carpaccio's patrons for this work were the owners of the School of St. George, the Knights of Jerusalem, and they wished to honor Dalmatian sailors who had served Venice. Hence the painting's subject, St. Tryphon; he was the patron saint of the Dalmatian city of Cattaro. In pleasing the Knights, the painter was also pleasing Venice, for these knights had been "an integral part of Venice's plans for a Crusade in 1464" (Brown 1988, 69). In giving the texture of reality to an imaginary scene, then, Carpaccio's representation has political implications for each of two masters. That he problematizes his flowers seems to show that part of the pleasure of the painting, and thus its power to do its work, depends on subtly reminding its patrons that it *is* a representation, a compliment or gift specially constructed for them. By making visible his skill at manipulation, at transforming an object before our very eyes from convention to "seeming" reality, Carpaccio implies the same artificial status for the seemingly "real" narrative of St. Tryphon's miracle. This implication turns seeming reality into art-object, picture into gift. By undercutting its own status as "reality," the painting enhances its value to its patrons.

Artists of the Renaissance often achieved a similar self-problematizing effect without such explicit visual statements as those made by Carpaccio or Uccello (or Holbein or Velázquez). Instead of *exposing* their art, some artists seemed to *disguise* it, to try to fool the viewer's eye into believing in its reality. These illusionist works do not visibly compromise the status of their conventions, but instead stay conscientiously within them; they avoid inconsistency and self-contradiction. They are of interest in this discussion because if their surface "reality" is to be believed, they seem to be the conclusion to which the art of resemblance would naturally lead. They create a kind of ultimate limit case because they seem to be unambiguous, to encourage belief in their own realistic status.

It is therefore interesting that their actual effect is the opposite. What such paintings show in fact is that the self-contradictions of resemblance are inherent in its very conventions, rather than invented in particular paintings by particular artists. Illusionist paintings demonstrate the paradox that the more a work of art seems "real," the more the viewer's attention is thrown on its "seeming," then to the skill with which the conventions of the art are concealed, and at last to the artist whose skill we find ourselves admiring. The more an artist seems to deny the presence of his conventions, the more the viewer is aware of his doing so. Michel de Montaigne represents all Renaissance artists of resemblance when he writes directly to us, "Thus, reader, I am myself the matter of my book" (1948, 3). He makes explicit what Michael Kubovy argues the viewer is always conscious of in illusionist painting: of being "in collusion with the artist" himself (1986, 83). This effect is the opposite side of the coin presented in the art of Justinian and Theodora, in which self-problematizing is avoided precisely by *not* pretending to be "real."

From the Minoan example in ceramics, we might not be surprised that illusionism in painting begins in the Renaissance as soon as the necessary skills, particularly in the use of perspective, have been mastered. One instance is Masaccio (1401–28). In 1427 or 1428, after he had finished his famous realistic work in the Brancacci Chapel in Florence's Church of the Carmine, he executed *The Trinity,* a perfectly realized *trompe l'oeil* fresco, in Santa Maria Novella. He painted a tomb, such that at first glance the viewer thinks it really is a tomb, not a painting of one. Directly over it he executed a realistic painting of a chapel that certainly gives an illusion of reality, but which is (unlike the tomb) clearly a painting. The whole, then, is a fresco seeming to recreate a common actual situation: a real tomb with a sacred painting above it. The fresco employs two forms of illusionism, one to make an object (the chapel) seem realistic and another to make a different object (the tomb) seem actually present in three-dimensional space. This early, then—at the time of the maturity of Donatello and Brunelleschi, but before Alberti had codified these ideas of perspective—the most extreme form of the art of resemblance in painting was already being exploited. Indeed, Joan Gadol argues that the work of these three "had a tremendous impact upon Alberti and gave a decisive turn to his development"; he was studying their achievements as he wrote *Della pittura* in Florence in the years 1434–36 (1969, 6). Even *trompe l'oeil* cannot be seen, then, as a later and more sophisticated version of realism. It exists side by side with realistic painting from the very beginning. It must be seen, rather, as an inherent implication of this style and its conventions, available when a painter thinks it useful.

As we have seen above, a further implication to which such illusionism leads is the viewer's awareness of the artist's presence in the work. Andrea Mantegna (1431–1506), working fifty years later than Masaccio (from 1471 to 1474) on the *Camera degli Sposi* in the Ducal Palace in Mantua, pushes this implication to its limits. He lined the walls of a relatively modest-sized room with realistic frescoes glorifying the Gonzaga family. Then he went further, adding illusionism to his realism. By painting columns and connecting arches up the walls and across the ceiling, he created a *trompe l'oeil* effect, deceiving our eye into seeing an almost flat ceiling as if it were a dome; the prime structural components of the room, unifying all its elements, are in fact an optical illusion.

This much is perfectly straightforward, although it exploits the total architectural space more fully than did Masaccio. The artist lives up to his contract to glorify his patron and his family, and also places that glorification in a room that seems harmonious. In addition, he supplies his patron with an artistic "wonder," a work whose skill calls attention to itself by momentarily fooling the eye of the beholder into believing in its reality (see Kubovy 1986, 77). The room really does seem to be domed, the patron's artist skillful, and the glorification justified by its setting and good taste.

However, Mantagna has a few more artistic tricks left before dismissing us from his room. On this "dome" he paints a ceiling fresco whose object is a circular opening through which we see the sky. The use of perspective and architectural illusion give us the momentary impression that we are looking *through* the ceiling—the painted surface—into a larger "reality" (the sky) that we know in fact to exist above the ceiling. Although fleeting, this impression is different from what is achieved by a more conventional realistic landscape, one

The Trinity, Masaccio. Courtesy of Alinari/Art Resource, N.Y.

Ceiling fresco, *La Camera degli Sposi,* Andrea Mantegna. Courtesy of Alinari/Art Resource, N.Y.

frankly situated within a painting. As Kubovy observes, Mantegna was exploring "the relation between the virtual space represented in the picture and the real space in which the spectator stood" (1986, 7).

Of course, we quickly adjust. It is in fact a *painted* sky. But Mantegna's games in this fresco are not yet exhausted. On this ceiling, he paints a circular railing that seems to surround the opening to the sky, perhaps to protect people on top of the roof—on a roof garden—from falling through it into the room where we stand looking up. In fact, several people are painted on this ceiling, standing beside this railing. Indeed, we suddenly notice, three of them stare directly down, making eye contact with us.

At once, our relationship to the fresco is changed. *They* are looking at *us*. No longer a fiction imitating "reality," this fresco suddenly presents itself as if it has an existence independent of its viewers. We normally think of a painting as executed in order to please potential viewers. We think of ourselves, the viewers, as conferring legitimacy on the artwork. But here, it is as if we are interlopers, as if we have disturbed a party. The painted figures staring down at us are disorienting.

Now perhaps we are a bit cautious about standing under the naked penises of two putti and the bare buttocks of another—particularly since all three are on our side of the railing above the ceiling, rather than securely behind it, like the other figures.

This caution might be reinforced by another part of this ceiling scene: a large planter of citrus trees is uncertainly balanced on the edge of the wall by a long stick. If the stick were to waver (or be moved only slightly), that heavy planter, it seems, would fall—on us. We notice this fact in part because our attention is drawn to it: the three figures who are meeting our eyes, observing us observing them, and doing so with a certain humorousness that is hard to interpret, are placed just beside this large and threatening planter. On its other side are two ladies *not* looking at us. However, one of these is a black serving woman who is staring very fixedly at that stick whose position seems crucial to the planter's equilibrium. Indeed, carrying the "fun" a bit further, we can now see (thanks to the room's recent restoration) that the hand that rests ambiguously on this crucial stick is the hand of this black servant .[4]

Once again we do a double take, and once again of course the double take is decisive: this *is* after all merely a painting. In seeming to take itself seriously as reality—that is, in seeming to believe in itself—illusionism has overreached its possibilities. It has demystified itself into a transparency. The skill of the artist manipulating his conventions becomes another focus of our attention.

As with the example by Carpaccio, then, this room asserts its status as an art-object complimentary to its patron. It makes us aware that it is itself an article of exchange. This awareness, in turn, allows to be inscribed within it both sides in the transaction of which it is a part. Because it has problematized its "reality," it has a double object: the Gonzaga world that it represents, and the artist who created that world and who stands quite assertively behind it. This double presence is appropriate, for their relationship is symbiotic. The patron pays the artist, and the artist creates the patron in glory. Is the apparently tenuous but nonetheless perpetual containment of the black serving woman, then, the creation of skillful Gonzaga rule, or of the skillful artist's illusion? Is the artist himself a version of the master or servant? Reciprocally, might Lodovico Gonzaga be a type of the glorified artist, maintaining this tenuous balance in society among apparently competing interests? In problematizing his conventions and even his object of imitation, Mantegna (like Carpaccio) expands his elaborate compliment to his patron.

Two generations later, working in the same city for the same family, Giulio Romano (1499–1546) achieved a similar effect in a still more extreme style of illusionism.[5] His greatest single building is the Palazzo del Te (1527–34); its most famous room, the *Sala dei Giganti,* was probably the main basis for his fame in the sixteenth century. This room was a major tourist attraction; judging from the account of Gregorio Comanini in 1591, it would seem that it "was the reason so many foreigners came to Mantua" (Verheyen 1977, 54). The parade of visitors included the emperor Charles V, who toured the Palazzo twice, in 1530 and 1532 (while the work on the *Sala dei Giganti* was still in progress), and Vasari in 1541. It concentrates within itself those aspects of the building's overall style that are crucial to this discussion.

Egon Verheyen has shown that in this room (as in the Palazzo generally) Romano was competing with his predecessor, Mantegna, by importing the new Roman taste in art; he was honoring the Gonzagas by creating in Mantua a new Rome.[6] As in the *Camera degli Sposi* in the old Ducal Palace across the city, Romano's *Sala dei Giganti*'s walls and ceiling were covered by illusionist frescoes glorifying the family of his patron. However, Mantegna's pictures are static posed scenes. Their object of imitation is this family and its household. Each is discrete, individually framed at eye level by a painted decoration that also covers the walls from the viewer's waist down. By contrast, Romano's pictures are dynamic and full of movement. Their subject is the rebellion of the giants against the Olympian gods, and the viewer in this room is fully enclosed within one continuous painting. "Ceiling and walls join in one overwhelming illusion, which originally was mirrored by another since the pattern of the floor continued into the painting" (Verheyen 1977, 128). There is no "decoration" at all, no framing device.

At the center of the ceiling is the underside of a domed cupola crowning the home of the gods; in a three-tiered ring encircling the ceiling and, from the pictorial point of view, just below this dome, are the gods themselves, some in animated conversation, some appalled at the power of Jove in action as he hurls thunderbolts down from on high. Below, at ground level, with columns and rocks tumbling upon them, are the giants themselves. They are falling, or already prone; they look up at their conquerors with defiance, awe, fear, pain. Even the greatest of rebels, pretenders to the glistening, golden throne of Olympus standing resplendent above us on the ceiling, are powerless against the righteous force of the universal ruler. Indeed, their rebellion causes not just them, but their very world, to crash to the ground.

Although this scene is not explicitly about the Gonzagas, it is unmistakable in its immediate political reference. And its message is far more direct and threatening, more overtly imperious, than Mantegna's. It represents hierarchical power as absolute, as irresistible.

To see this picture, obviously, we must be inside the room. We stand at ground level, completely surrounded by the giants, enclosed by this scene from which there seems no escape. The walls, including the one with the door through which we entered, are painted in *trompe l'oeil* to seem as if they are tumbling down. Not only the giants', but also *our* columns and brickwork seem to be collapsing; the door itself is about to be sealed shut. Unlike the situation Mantegna creates in which viewer and artwork are clearly separate from one another, each staring back at the other in a standoff so that the viewer must recalculate his relationship with the art-object, here the viewer seems trapped inside this work of Romano's. As he makes his actual political referent less explicit, he makes the viewer's involvement with it far more immediate and dramatic.[7]

John Greenwood partially explains this effect by relating the frescoes' quality of continuously unfolding, rather than presenting a discontinuous series of discrete pictures, to one aspect of perspective:

> Romano's inventive pictorial narratives forsake the clarity of Renaissance one-point perspective for an endless stream of compositional motion in which individual figures are thoroughly submerged. . . . The eye must follow the narrative from event to event in order to gather the entire story. (1988, 115)

That is, Romano forsakes the aspect of perspective which, in a framed picture, implicitly draws the viewer into it. By making his painting continuous instead, he *literally* encloses the viewer into it. What is *implied* by one-point perspective is in this work experienced directly. At the same time, it avoids the built-in contradiction between realism and the convention of framing. Romano takes the idea of realistic imitation to its limit in this direction. No wonder that Shakespeare refers to him as

> that rare Italian master, Julio Romano, who, had he himself eternity and could put breath into his work, would beguile Nature of her custom, so perfectly he is her ape. (*The Winter's Tale* 5.2.97–100)

Yet, like the examples of other styles of resemblance that we have examined, this work too subverts itself. In spite of our being surrounded by these giants, we are also distanced from them; we do not share their danger and fear (Verheyen [1977, 53] emphasizes our role as spectators). This distancing effect is the result of several factors. For one thing, as Frederick Hartt observes, "although the room collapses around us, the tempietto remains intact" (1958, 154). And since the walls are not falling on us in the center, but on the giants on the periphery, we are not immediately threatened. For another, the giants are not realistic giants.[8] They are much larger than human size, and dwarf the human spectator, as giants should; yet, despite the carefully accurate anatomy, there is something on the verge of caricature about their faces and gestures. Each is perhaps too simply an extreme representation of a simple attitude. For a third, the colors do not reinforce the feelings of the scene. They are generally pastels of middle and high value, too light to evoke the heavy violence and strong emotion of the action. The dominant colors among the giants themselves are warm greens, suggestive more of rest and reassurance than of anguished defeat. And for a fourth, there is the fact of windows: the illusionist scene presents glimpses of deep landscape spaces beyond the falling walls, but these walls are themselves penetrated by windows through which we can see real landscapes outside the building. In literally seeing through the illusionist painting by looking out these windows, we cannot fail to be aware of the illusionist art within as a work of human construction. John Greenwood asserts this quality to be typical of Romano: he (like Shakespeare) creates "an art that comments on art, ... thereby calling attention to its own artificial quality" (1988, 28).

Nevertheless, despite our recognition that it is illusional, despite our knowledge that there is an outside to this inside, we are totally enclosed in its seamless fiction. Its compositional thrust is upward more than outward. Sharing the same ground with the painted giants, we follow their eyes upwards to the gods. We too see from the giants' earthbound vantage point; we too see the perspective and its vanishing point receding into the dome of the gods over Olympus. We are with the rebels, like it or not (Hartt 1958, 156).

Yet we know more than they. We entered this scene after the rebellion began. We see the power of the gods' reaction, and the rebellion's failure. Given this superior knowledge, the very fact that we share the giants' space, that we are trapped here with them, is a powerful impetus for us to distance ourselves from their situation. We can be grateful that we are not directly threatened; the stability of the tempietto is reassuring. The enclosing use of space that gives Romano's work its feeling of direct reality is also its aspect that most powerfully pushes us away from it. The more its composition draws us into it, the more we resist. We rejoice in the hierarchy that keeps us safe. Romano, in creating a new and extreme style of self-subverting illusionism, makes us aware of our willing acquiescence in Gonzaga power. We gladly enter into collusion with him.

During Shakespeare's time, at the end of the sixteenth century, Annibale Carracci (1560–1609) takes illusionist art to a still further limit point in his work in the gallery of the Farnese Palace in Rome (begun in 1597). He uses the now familiar combination of "realistic" painting and *trompe l'oeil* effects to make painting seem to transcend itself, but not to portray three-dimensional actuality. Instead, it pretends to be three-dimensional *art*. The transparence inherent in the art of resemblance is expanded so that this art's subject seems to be a conversation about its own artistic nature. The dialogue that a viewer must have with any work of art is here incorporated into the artwork itself.

Carracci's frescoes on the upper walls and ceiling of this gallery are "realistic," but with frames painted around them in a manner reminiscent of Mantegna's. However, these frescoes are also intermingled with painted imitations of statuary. Some of these "statues" are so placed on the walls as to seem to be architectural supports for the ceiling at the same time that they serve as decorations. Others are of lounging onlookers. Still others are within circular frames, forming panels which depict scenes from heroic legend. Some of these statues have the color of white marble, and some are given skin color, but all are triumphs of *trompe l'oeil*. They all seem really to be statues.[9]

However, the "realism" is of several different conventions. A realistic statue needs three dimensions and good anatomy, but not the color or perspective required for a painting. Yet some are skin-colored and some not. The different kinds, decorative ceiling supports and lounging onlookers, skin-colored and not skin-colored, stare at each other, and at the paintings that surround them. Sometimes, the stare is returned, as if one art form were in conversation with another. Equally, it is as if the form of artwork were unimportant, as if indeed the very conventions of art were unimportant. The conventions of realism for one form contradict the conventions for the other. Each calls the other into question. Yet the more fully each seems to follow its own conventions, the more powerfully each seems realistic on its own terms; and, hence, the more powerfully each makes a statement *against* the "reality" of the other. Unlike Romano and the other artists we have analyzed, Carracci calls his illusion of the real into question not by making parts of it *un*real, nor by carrying one aspect of it so far that it is potentially threatening, but by making too much of it *equally* real.[10] As a result, the questions his work poses go beyond an exposure of its "realism"; they penetrate into the nature of illusion itself.

Regardless of differences in epoch and style, the visual art of resemblance seems always, from Uccello to Carracci, to contain within it, as part of its inherent nature, reminders that this resemblance is only a mirror. Velázquez's visually explicit statement of this fact half a century after the completion of the Farnese Gallery simply suggests that such art had by then reached its ultimate limit. It always casts its reflection back on itself; it always implies its own construction. Therefore, always presenting itself as an art object, a gift, it always and inescapably inscribes its artist within it. It represents its creator as a servant. Its purpose therefore seems always to have less to do with imitation than with service to a patron.[11] As the art of realistic resemblance became increasingly fashionable, this statement of service became more and more emphatic. What was once taken for granted and thus submerged, as for example in Duccio, was by the time of Shakespeare forced into the foreground of the viewer's consciousness. Although the conventions of the art of resemblance necessarily leave it unstated, the instability of its "reality" is powerfully present.

A Buddhist, of course, would see the presence of this phenomenon not only in art, but also in life. Indeed, from the Buddhist view, the true "reality" of the art of resemblance resides precisely in this exposure of its own instability. And it is this quality of "play" in life *and* art which, to a Buddhist, makes each of them delightful.

Appendix B:
Shakespeare's Access to Renaissance Practices in the Visual Arts

We have seen that a self-referential, self-deconstructive attitude toward one's art is quite natural in the Western tradition. It is therefore possible to imagine a Shakespeare who works out the implications of this approach on his own as he explores the possibilities and limits of his chosen theatrical profession and workplace. However, it is also possible that he learned something of this approach from visual artists, then adapted it (with many of his playwright colleagues) to theatrical uses.

In considering the availability of Renaissance Continental artistic developments in Shakespeare's England, it is important to take note of an observation by Roland Mushat Frye: Elizabethan portraits do not generally show a knowledge of Italian developments in perspective (1980, 323–37). However, this portrait style did offer Shakespeare an opportunity to know an art form with important similarities to the medieval iconographic heritage. Further, this style in portraiture (typically a likeness of the subject against a shallow, flat or nearly flat, usually dark background that is sometimes populated, like the subject's dress, with symbolic images) was in fact an international sixteenth-century style.[1] It was typical at the court of Francis I, for example (thirty-two excellent examples of the type hang in the long gallery at Blois), as well as at the court of Henry VIII. The use of this style might therefore as well suggest the artists' and patrons' awareness of contemporary Continental practices as the reverse. Certainly both Francis and Henry themselves, as well as their courts more generally, were well aware of recent developments in Italy. So was Elizabeth in Shakespeare's time.

In the same spirit, but from a different point of view, Elizabeth Truax argues that not to use perspective may simply mean that the artist is conducting a mannerist experiment, not that he is ignorant of it (1980, 15). Indeed, under the Tudors the works of Hans Holbein the Younger and Robert Peake show little use of perspective; when it is used, it is played down. Yet in his altar panels of the Passion in Basel, Holbein shows his thorough mastery of this technique. Even in his portrait of William Warham, archbishop of Canterbury (now at Lambeth

Palace), there is clear use of the perspectival technique of foreshortening in the representation of the Bible by his side. Under Mary, William Scrots is less shy about its use than he had been previously; a similar change toward the use of perspective occurs in Robert Peake's work after the death of Elizabeth.[2] Although there is an iconographic spirit in the portraiture of Elizabeth and her court which has some affinity with medieval practice, it seems that this work is created by artists who are fully aware of contemporary European trends in the arts, and who are working within a court and under a monarch also aware of them.

It is not unlikely that Shakespeare would have shared in this knowledge. Elizabeth Truax believes that "Shakespeare shows [in *The Rape of Lucrece* and *The Winter's Tale*] acquaintance with Renaissance art in a style analogous to that of Giulio Romano, the one painter he calls by name, and of the school of Fontainebleau he was instrumental in founding. The influence may have come directly—he could have seen Mignon's etchings in England, or Giulio Romano's frescoes in Mantua . . . " (1980, 28; see also Waage 1980, 67–71, and, for a more indirect source, Ziegler 1985). However, whatever the source, Elizabeth Truax asserts that "Shakespeare is working in the mode of Renaissance artists" (1980, 28). If he knew the work at Fontainebleau, then Rossi and Primataccio and possibly Leonardo, all of whom worked for Francis I, could have been familiar to him as well. In this general vein, Leonard Ashley speculates that because Shakespeare was in the Southampton circle, which was steeped in things Italian, "it might be assumed that Shakespeare's information from printed sources about Italy was supplemented by acquaintance with Italians or Englishmen of Italian descent resident in London" (1980, 49).

Behind this speculation about Shakespeare himself lies our more certain knowledge that literate England in the 1580s and after was devouring information about Italian Renaissance culture. John Florio made a good living as an Italian teacher; Ben Jonson satirized his countrymen's vogue for the Italianate in both *Every Man in his Humour* and *Volpone.* More generally, Frederick O. Waage asserts that "the decades following 1590 witnessed a revolution in English aesthetics and experience of the visual arts" (1980, 57).[3]

In architecture, this change began with John Shute's *Firste & Chief Groundes of Architecture* (1563), based on firsthand knowledge of Vignola, Palladio, and Michelangelo; its influence was "widespread" (Nellist 1967, 176). As Elizabeth's new nobility constructed "many great houses of a size and scale not seen before," they increasingly showed Italian influence "either direct from native craftsmen or through the interest created by visits to Italy itself" (Nellist 1976, 177). The architect Robert Smythson illustrates the time's adaptation of Italian Renaissance principles to English houses in places as diverse as Longleat in Wiltshire (1567–80), Wollaton Hall in Nottinghamshire (1580–88), and Hardwick Hall in Derbyshire (1590–97). Ben Jonson shows how general this tendency became by lamenting it in "To Penshurst."

However, English interest in and indebtedness to Italian art and culture generally began much earlier, at the court of Henry VIII.[4] Hans Holbein the Younger exported this influence after Dürer had introduced it to northern Europe. Indeed, England almost seems after 1526 to emerge "as a haven for artists dissatisfied with the deteriorating conditions on the Continent" (Stechow 1966, 130–31). Elizabeth Truax refers to a "main body of artists who stayed in England to decorate Henry's great palaces" (1980, 15). One famous example of Henry's patronage illustrates this interest in the most up-to-date Italian fashions in art: his order for a Brussels tapestry based on the Raphael cartoons now housed in the Victoria and Albert Museum, London. These cartoons are themselves painted in full color, and are generally acknowledged to represent a high point of Raphael's art, having been done in the last four or five years of his life (in 1515 and 1516). It is interesting that the young Giulio Romano was one of Raphael's assistants on this project, working with the master in Rome at age sixteen (Reynolds 1974, 3, 7).

Although it is not unusual to think that after Henry, Protestant England's art was separated from the main currents on the Continent, such a view distorts the situation in the middle decades of the sixteenth century, and is demonstrably false for the last two decades under Elizabeth. Aside from the brief visit of the Flemish mannerist Antonio Mor in 1554 and of the Italian mannerist Federigo Zuccaro in 1575, there was the extended residence of William Scrots (from 1545 until 1553/4). As "official successor to Holbein," he and his circle sustained that knowledge of the Continental Renaissance which Henry's court had developed (Strong 1969, 19). Elizabeth Truax is therefore able to assert that most of the artists who built "the manor houses and [painted] the stately portraits of the newly enriched nobility in the days of Elizabeth were artists from Flanders who had developed Italianate skills" (1980, 15).

However, it is Nicholas Hilliard (1547–1619), "the most important artistic personality of the Elizabethan age" (Strong 1969, 48), who made the English artistic connection with the Continent most explicit. He spent 1576–78 in Paris; between 1597 and 1603 he wrote the mannerist *A Treatise on the Arte of Limninge* which includes knowledgeable references to the technique of Dürer, Rosso, and Raphael (Stechow 1966, 171). In addition, he refers familiarly to *A Tracte Containing the Artes of Curious Painting*, a work of mannerist theory by Paolo Giovanni Lomazzo published in Italian c. 1585, and in an English translation in 1598. Lomazzo, in turn, states his familiarity with Leonardo, Correggio, Titian, and Mantegna, as well as with Vasari, Michelangelo, Raphael, and Rosso.[5] And although Hilliard himself is primarily known as a miniaturist, "his impact on large-scale painting . . . was immense" as well, even after his own work lost favor (Strong 1969, 48).

In the nineties, this artistic circle widens, and its connections to the Continent solidify. Hilliard's pupil Isaac Oliver (1556?-1617) succeeded his master as favorite court painter. A mannerist, he copied and drew directly from the work of Parmigianino, and studied many other Italian masters; he also "was familiar with the work of the Clouets and the French court painters of his epoch,"[6] as well as the Flemish. His ambition was in fact "to be an historical painter working in the Venetian manner, but on a small scale . . . " (Auerbach 1961, 17, 15). He visited Venice in 1596 (Strong 1969, 68).

Two other significant painters of the nineties and after were Marcus Gheeraerts the Younger, a Flemish exile who was "the most important painter working in England between *circa* 1590 and *circa* 1620," and John de Critz, also from the Low Countries. The latter was so successful that he was named Sergeant Painter (jointly with Robert Peake) in 1605. The degree to which this constituted a close artistic circle may be suggested by the fact that the sisters of de Critz "married the Gheeraerts, father and son," while Marcus Gheeraerts's sister married Isaac Oliver (Strong 1969, 70, 75). There can be little question that in the later Elizabethan age, painting on every scale was dominated by a group of artists who were thoroughly conversant with recent Continental artistic practices.

Moreover, these artists working in England were not at all the only models available to an interested student. Professor Frye observes that "by 1600 or even before, English art collections included representative examples of Continental painting, and there is evidence not only that Shakespeare knew some of them," but also that he "was aware of the visual principles of linear perspective" (1980, 41). The long galleries of the great Elizabethan houses, indeed, were said by Haycocke in 1598 already to be "carefully furnished, with the excellent monuments of sundry famous Masters, both Italian and Germane" (Lomazzo [1598] 1966, vi). Leicester's collection was so large that he had to "spread it over three houses" (Strong 1969, 50). Therefore, an Elizabethan interested in the arts could know a great deal. Edmund Spenser wrote, with reference to the woodcuts published with his *Shepherd's Calendar*, that "Michelangelo could neither amende the best, nor reprehende the worst!" (Woudhuysen 1982, 678).

James, of course, was a far more zealous patron and collector than Elizabeth. Under his and Prince Henry's lead, Continental tastes were more directly reflected in English art. In fact, Roy Strong sees Henry as "a new baroque prince" who blends a taste for medieval chivalry with his zest for the new (1969, 38, 81–83). However, this was merely the official culmination of that enthusiasm and knowledge and experimentation whose momentum had been increasing for at least two decades, since Hilliard in the 1580s. With growing intensity, nearly two centuries of Italian and then Northern European artistic development touched England all at once in these final decades of the sixteenth century. The high tide of the Renaissance and the experiments of mannerism came together in Elizabeth's England at the time of Shakespeare. Even the beginnings of baroque style in the work of Annibale Carracci might have been known, but this is very uncertain. Still, at the very time when Shakespeare was writing *Henry IV, Part One*—namely, 1597—Carracci was working on his frescoes in the Farnese Gallery, creating a series on Bacchus with a very Falstaffian blend of sensual energy and physical lethargy. As Rudolf Wittkower writes, these frescoes were, "next to Raphael's Stanze and Michelangelo's Sistine ceiling . . . acknowledged for no less than two centuries as the most important landmark in the history of modern painting." This greatness was sensed at once. "Drawings by the Carracci were eagerly studied and copied while they were still alive . . ." These copies, spread all over, were "the equivalent of our photographs"; it was "not always easy to distinguish between original and copy" (Wittkower 1952, 14, 19, 20).[7]

Although details about the influence of the visual arts on Shakespeare remain uncertain, it is likely that Shakespeare faced—and mastered—the challenge of assimilating two centuries of Continental aesthetic development into his young, still flexible theater.

Notes

Introduction

1. For a fuller account of Trungpa's life, see his own *Born in Tibet,* and Rick Fields 1986, esp. 308–38.

2. Indeed, I find no persuasive evidence that any clear tradition of Buddhist practice or thought was available in Europe during the Renaissance. The thoroughly Christianized biography of the Buddha (given the names St. Josaphat and St. Joasaph) was well known in England and on the Continent throughout the Middle Ages and Renaissance, but offers no hint of distinctly Buddhist ideas. There seem instead to be only shadowy resemblances in the time of Shakespeare. For instance, the Gnostic roots of Christianity combine ideas derived from the East, from Stoics and Platonists as well as Hindus and Buddhists. Renaissance humanists found emphases on the inward life and on detachment from a world of flux and impermanence in their studies of Stoic, Neoplatonic, and Epicurean philosophers. Although Byzantine Greeks flooded Europe in the fifteenth century, the Hesychasts' use of Buddhist-like meditation techniques (mantra and breath control, particularly) seems not to have had much influence, despite its having become in 1351 part of the official dogma of the Eastern Church, and despite one of its foremost exponents' having been a principal speaker at the Council of Florence in 1438–39. Although Mircea Eliade and Carl Jung have argued that various Buddhist- and Taoist-related purification practices were preserved in the Renaissance West by the continuing practice of the ancient art of alchemy, this too seems a tenuous connection. Nor does the gradual development of trade with the East seem to have resulted in widespread religious or philosophical cross-fertilization, however transformative it was in other ways for European society.

For readings in these subjects, see particularly Eliade 1958, 202, 281–91; Eliade 1978a, 226–27; Eliade 1978b, 56, 62; Fields 1986, 13–30; Geanakoplos 1976, 26–27; Geanakoplos 1961, 113, 179–86; Gill 1961, 114, 186–88; Jonas 1963, 158, 173, 200, 207, 286; Carl Jung 1967, 122–48; Nichol 1979, 40–56, 76; and Radhakrishnan 1940, 230.

3. See, for example, on authorship, Michel Foucault's "What is an Author?"; and on this issue's relationship to the stability of Shakespearean texts and the role of the critic, Jonathan Goldberg's "Textual Properties." The best-known recent account of "reinventions" of Shakespeare is probably Gary Taylor's. G. Douglas Atkins's survey of and commentary on deconstructionist views of the critic's role is also useful (especially 60–61, 87–88).

4. For the conception and legitimation of this view that a literary work can be

dynamically dialogic, containing a variety of competing voices, see Mikhail Bakhtin's *Dialogic Imagination,* for example 270–87. However, I dispute his idea that it is only the novel that displays this characteristic "heteroglossia," and that poetry (implicitly including Shakespeare's) is by contrast monologic.

5. Stephen Greenblatt's phrase is "the circulation of social energy," the subtitle of his *Shakespearean Negotiations.*

This is probably also the place to differentiate my work from R. H. Blyth's pioneering *Zen in English Literature and Oriental Classics,* published in Tokyo in 1942 by the Hokuseido Press. Mr. Blyth's method is to quote passages that seem to him to express Zen, a quality that, "though far from indefinite, is by definition indefinable, because it is the active principle of life itself" (1960, 2). These passages are cited without regard for their speaker or their dramatic context. While Mr. Blyth's clarity about Zen, and about Buddhism generally, is inspiring, his view of the Shakespearean text is unproblematized, uncontextualized, ahistorical. Because my view of the texts is different, so too is my application of Buddhist principles to them.

6. In *Renaissance Self-Fashioning,* Stephen Greenblatt argues similarly in developing his idea of a "*poetics of culture*" that literary criticism "must be conscious of its own status as interpretation," and that we cannot "decisively separat[e] works of art from the minds and lives of their creators and their audiences." He says, "the questions I ask of my material and indeed the very nature of this material are shaped by the questions I ask of myself" (1980, 4–5). For variations on these views, see Jonathan Goldberg's discussion (1988, 216) and G. Douglas Atkins's survey of ideas (1983) on the reciprocal relations between reader and text (especially 51–52, 84–85).

7. For a discussion of the similarities between Buddhist and Derridean deconstruction from the point of view of philosophy/comparative religion, see Coward 1990 (especially 125–46); Loy 1987 and its elaboration, Loy 1988; and Magliola 1984 (especially 87–129). Although these writers differ among themselves, they each center on the seminal Mahayanic figure Nagarjuna in his relation to Derrida.

Derrida's difficulty in addressing the enhancing or fruitful side of "absence" is well illustrated by his "How to Avoid Speaking: Denials," an essay which addresses the problem of affirmation. Because direct affirmation is impossible (presence exists only as absence), Derrida moves at once to negative theology and asks of it a series of questions:

> Is there some discourse that measures up to it? Is one not compelled to speak of negative theology according to the modes of negative theology, in a way that is at once important, exhausting, and inexhaustible? Is there ever anything other than a "negative theology" of "negative theology"? (1989, 13)

Near his conclusion, Derrida finds affirmation only by negation:

> Being *is not* (a being, that is) and . . . it *would have always had to* be written *under erasure,* . . . an erasure that would above all have nothing negative about it! (1989, 60–61)

And thus even prayer is impossible, for

> If there were a purely pure experience of prayer, would one need religion and affirmative or negative theologies? Would one need a supplement of prayer? But if there were no supplement,

if quotations did not bend prayer, if prayer did not bend, if it did not submit to writing, would a theology [sic] be possible?

Interestingly, Buddhism is a religion without a theology—without belief in an external deity. It may be that this fact illuminates its ability to describe the experience of fruitfulness in "absence" which eludes Derrida. For unlike him, Buddhism is not caught in a logocentric tradition. Again, see David Loy for a discussion of this fact.

8. Several recent studies from different vantage points have expressed strong reservations about the "totalizing" view of the power of social authority, and also about the related view that authority can always "contain" all the subversive elements which might otherwise prove threatening. For example, see Peter Stallybrass and Allon White on the "transgressive" aspects of Mikhail Bakhtin's ideas about carnival; James C. Scott's 1985 study of the strategies of resistance to authority among the powerless in a Malaysian village, esp. pp. 314–35; Annabel Patterson's 1989 argument against the ability of Elizabethan authority to maintain its containment of "the popular voice" in its theater, or even to maintain a consistent policy toward the theater, esp. pp. 23–25; and Walter Cohen's 1985 argument that popular and aristocratic interests under Elizabeth and James were actually similar in significant ways, and that in any event "absolutism" was in this period never more than "partial" (esp. pp. 26–30, 136–51).

9. Trungpa discusses the interrelationships among language, the world, and emptiness (sunyata) in Trungpa 1975, 150–52, 165–68; and 1988, 71–72.

10. Along with Trungpa 1973 and Trungpa 1976a, perhaps the best general introduction to Buddhism is Suzuki 1970.

Chapter One. Pacifying Action in *A Midsummer Night's Dream*

1. This and all subsequent citations from Shakespeare's plays are taken from *The Riverside Shakespeare*.

2. For a discussion of the complexity of Bottom's wise foolishness from the perspective of the comic convention of the fool, see Willeford 1969, 137–39; for a more abstract view of the fool's relationship to Christian and to Zen Buddhist wisdom, see Willeford 1969, 230–35. Mikhail Bakhtin (1984, 260) connects the fool to the "wisdom" of the festive.

3. Most readers see change, often associated with metamorphosis, as ubiquitous in the forest. C. L. Barber writes, "The woods are established as a region of metamorphoses" (1959, 133). Noel Purdon believes that the play adopts the "central emblem of the moon," and that it is this "lunatic" moon's influence that creates a "kingdom of metamorphosis" (1974, 179–80). See also James A. McPeek (1972, 69), Stephen L. Smith (1977, 196), and David Young (1966, 155), among many others.

4. James Calderwood refers to "the breakdown of sexual relationships" as "part of a general dissolving of past identities" (1965, 513). Northrop Frye too refers to this theme of "temporarily lost identity" (1965, 76). See also C. L. Barber (1959, 135); Sidney Homan (1981, 88); Leah Scragg (1977, 151); and Thomas F. Van Laan (1978, 109).

5. To see the play within as in some way a mirror of the full play is very common. See Calderwood (1969, 509); Antony B. Dawson (1978, 69); Homan (1981, 95–98); J. Dennis Huston (1981, 108); Howard D. Pearce (1980, 44); and Smith (1977, 203–7). Huston has further observed that the forest action too is a play within the main play, this

one Oberon's (1981, 96). In quite a different spirit, see Homan (1988, 411) and Paul A. Olson (1957, 109).

6. Stephen Greenblatt argues in "Invisible Bullets" that "it is precisely because of the English form of absolutist theatricality that Shakespeare's drama, written for a theater subject to state censorship, can be so relentlessly subversive: the form itself, as a primary expression of Renaissance power, contains the radical doubts it continually produces" (in Peter Erickson and Coppelia Kahn 1985, 297). But see note 8 to the Introduction above.

7. For arguments confirming Bottom's perfection as an ass, see Deborah Baker Wyrick (1982, 444), David Young (1966, 157), and Martin Esslin ([1961] 1969, 286). For this same view within the context of a marriage of extremes, see Ronald F. Miller (1975, 263) and Millar MacLure (1983, 26–27). However, William Willeford (1964, 141–42) sees a significant degree of psychological complexity within this "marriage" idea. For Elizabeth's resonance, see Louis Adrian Montrose (1986); from a different point of view, Marion A. Taylor (1973); also Annabel Patterson's suggestion that Bottom's festive energy may be related to a particular discontent at that historical moment (1989, 54–70).

8. William C. Carroll argues that this union of Bottom and Titania not only represents the "merging of opposites" (143), but embodies a "fear of the monstrous" in a play which, perhaps for this reason, suppresses the erotic (1985, 142). Michael D. Bristol makes the interesting point (given Bottom) that "carnival is not anti-authority" (1985, 213), but it is not always used to consolidate hierarchical order in the Renaissance; it may sometimes be unassimilable, or even provide an alternative positive vision to that of the dominant class (1985, 197–200). Mikhail Bakhtin discusses the close relationship between high and low discourse, as well as its social implications, esp. in Bakhtin 1981, 270–87, and in Bakhtin 1984, 146–50.

9. For the idea that *Pyramus and Thisby*, by exposing itself as illusion, exposes the full play as well, see among others Huston (1981, 96), Marjorie B. Garber (1974, 83ff.), and Young (1966, 37).

10. Or, as Young sees it, "ever more comprehensive circles" (1966, 91). See also Richard Cody (1969, 141) and, for an incorporation of the metadramatic stance into these parallels, Huston (1981, 104–9). The pervasiveness of this emphasis on metadrama is further suggested by Young's idea that Bottom and Titania represent different dramatic types: Bottom is clown and mummer; Titania, a "literary symbol and heroine" (1966, 15). They therefore represent two contrasting styles of acting, a contrast that again heightens the audience's consciousness of acting per se (1966, 48).

11. It is generally assumed that *A Midsummer Night's Dream* formed part of an aristocratic marriage entertainment, and is in this way mirrored by its play within (see Kenneth Muir 1978, 77; Paul N. Siegel 1953, 139; and Young 1966, 104). The analogy between the theater audience and the stage audience has been noticed, for example, in Young (1966, 91), Pearce (1980, 44), Calderwood (1965, 507–10), Leo Salingar (1974, 283–85), Dawson (1978, 69–70), and Huston (1981, 102).

12. Sidney Homan argues similarly that, as a result of Puck's final speech, "Our own reality is suspect as a fraud, a dream" (1981, 411).

Chapter Two. Awakening: The Sword of Prajna in the Visual Arts and in *Richard III*

1. Foucault 1979, 40. This view of Renaissance knowledge is consistent with the assumptions of those historians of art who have commanded universal respect in the

modern period. See, for example, the studies by E. H. Gombrich (1972), Erwin Panofsky (1960), and Edgar Wind (1958).

2. For a summary of the structuralist defense of the assumptions underlying synchronic history in the arts, see Roston 1987, 4–5.

3. Roy Strong discusses how illusionist theater in the Jacobean period makes this paradox visible by showing the scenery in the process of changing, such that part of appropriate audience reaction "was admiring man's ability to create these illusions" (1984, 157). For a fuller discussion of this paradox in the visual arts, see Appendix A.

4. Kubovy 1986, 83. That our conscious choice to be in collusion with the artist is a precondition for our pretense of belief, is one of Michael Kubovy's points in discussing illusionism. Roy Strong makes a similar observation for the illusionist stage (1984, 156). It seems to me to apply equally to other forms of realism, of which illusionism is an extreme case. Kubovy summarizes his study of perspective in language that is at some points congruent with the Buddhist view: "Taking my analysis of the effects of perspective as a point of departure, one might argue that the Renaissance artists were exploring the nature of egocentrism and ways of using perspective to free oneself from one's special vantage point. To do so is a sign of one's ability to transcend egocentrism" (1986, 171). The Buddhist's dissolution of the ego as a precondition for playing in it seems a closely related idea.

5. In *Renaissance Self-Fashioning,* Stephen Greenblatt interprets this painting, as well as its relationship to drama, very similarly (1980, 17–21, 27).

6. Jonathan Dollimore suggests the possibility of undermining established authority in his introduction to *Political Shakespeare:* although the ruling order may promote subversion in order to strengthen itself, "once installed [this subversion] can be used against authority as well as used by it" (1985, 12). Stephen Greenblatt is somewhat more cautious: "Through improvisation we pass, only partially and tentatively, to a sense that in the very acts of homage to the great formal structures, there open up small but constant glimpses of the limitations of those structures, of their insecurities, of the possibility of their collapse" (1980, 231 n. 11). Both of these writers, however, assess the likelihood of subversion from the point of view of power relations; neither is concerned with the idea of changing consciousness, such that subversion could be expressed in terms different from those offered by the authority structure or the culture to be subverted.

7. Roy Strong's Tate Gallery catalog *The Elizabethan Image* is a treasury of reproductions of such paintings.

8. This idea of the monarch's entrapment in his own image of power or perfection has become almost a commonplace of new historicist and feminist criticism. Jonathan Goldberg asserts it with reference to James: "The king was subjected, shaped, imposed upon, by the language in which, and with which, he attempted to impose himself on others, to shape their minds to match his" (1983, 20). Louis Adrian Montrose applies the same idea to Elizabeth: she "was as much the creature of her image as she was its creator" (1986, 86). Lisa Jardine sees the queen's personal situation very similarly, but with the crucial political difference that her image is not wholly of her creation, nor mainly in her interest (1983, 169–74). Leonard Tennenhouse approaches the problem of a split and entrapped monarchic identity in part by developing the theory of the monarch's two bodies (1986, 79ff.).

9. This comparison is of course encouraged by the reference to Romano in *The Winter's Tale,* however problematic such an evaluation of Romano might be. On the difficulty of categorizing Romano, see Hartt 1958, 12. For mannerism in Shakespeare, one might consult John Greenwood (1988), Arnold Hauser (1965, 8), Wylie Sypher

(1955), Murray Roston (who does not perceive Shakespeare to be a mannerist, but does believe that late in his career he seems to move in that direction, 1987, 239ff.), and Ronald Levao (1985) and Ernest B. Gilman (1978). These last two are not specifically concerned with mannerism, but their ideas about Shakespeare's art include many characteristics commonly associated with this visual style.

10. This portrait of Richard bears a striking resemblance to Gordon Braden's description of the stoic heroes of Senecan tragedy. He discusses their sense of self-sufficiency which is not present in Greek drama (1985, 32–33). "The basic plot of a Senecan play is that of inner passion which bursts upon and desolates an unexpecting and largely uncomprehending world, an enactment of the mind's disruptive power over external reality" (1985, 39). Seneca is seen to be fascinated with "heroic villainy" (1985, 46). He depicts "the restless discontent that animates the pursuit of . . . triumph" (1985, 60), the "self's search for a radical, unpredicated independence" (1985, 67).

11. Leonard Tennenhouse has pointed out that an important form of courtiership in Elizabeth's court was "making love to the Queen." He has also observed that Shakespeare was not close to the aristocratic circle, and could not expect advancement from it, let alone promotion within it. In this perspective, Shakespeare was not technically a courtier (1986, 31ff.). However, he needed court approval in order to practice his profession as playwright. If he succeeded in pleasing the court, he might earn special favors (and profits). In this more generalized sense, Shakespeare was indeed playing the courtier's game.

Chapter Three. *The Merchant of Venice* as Sword of Prajna

1. Thomas Moison tries to rescue this play from the charge of incoherence by an appeal to its metatheatrical qualities: *Merchant* shows "the will and power of dramatic art to divert attention from the ideological contradictions it reflects to its own playful alterity." In this way, "the play manages to transcend the issues its text problematizes to render a dramatically, theatrically satisfying experience" (1987, 202).

2. Both Lawrence Danson (1978, 10) and Barber (1959, 168) argue the efficacy of Bassanio's prodigality. It is seen as a precondition to the virtue of generosity.

3. It is common to believe that love is idealized in this play in a way consonant with religion. See, for example, John Burnet ([1930] 1968, 119), Walter F. Eggers (1977, 332), Francis Fergusson (1977, 120–21), Sir Israel Gollancz (1931, 56), and Barbara K. Lewalski (1962, 337–43).

4. This quality is interpreted differently, although to a similarly condemning judgment, by Peter Stallybrass and Allon White: "Viewed as Lenten and closed, the Jew could be seen within early capitalism as a *calculating* enemy of carnival, a repressive bearer of cold rationality and profiteering individualism which ran counter to the communal spirit of free expenditure and careless exuberance characteristic of the festival" (1986, 55).

5. The image of Portia's "golden mesh" of hair, which might suggest that Jessica's outward gold is an image of inner virtue like Portia's, does not occur until the fifth scene after her gilding, at 3.2.122.

6. See Dawson 1978, 4, 13; E. E. Stoll 1927, 312; and Louis Teeter 1938, 187.

7. Willard Farnham's assertions in *The Shakespearean Grotesque* seem useful: "The Vice of the morality play" was seen "as being an unregenerate quality in man that is at work to betray and undo him from within, instead of being a devil that comes against him from without." Professor Farnham discusses this characteristic within the context of other examples of what he calls grotesques, including the gargoyle, whose monstrous

departure from the "representation of normal forms of life . . . always produces strain or struggle that is essentially dramatic" (1971, 39, 11–12). Neil Rhodes refers to similar artifacts in a related way: "Laughter and revulsion . . . are the twin polarities of the grotesque." There are "two kinds of response [to the same image] which are mutually incompatible, and a tension is set up in the image itself between the elements which create one sort of effect and those which create another." Satire and saturnalia coexist with a seriousness related to the sermon form (1980, 20, 7).

Morris Carnovsky argues in this spirit that the audience is ambivalent toward Shylock (1958/59, 41). Danson sees a "double treatment" of both Shylock and Portia (1974, 9). Barber makes a closely related point in *Festive Comedy:* "Shylock is the opposite of what the Christians are; but at the same time he is an embodied irony, troublingly like them. . . . a figure in whom the evils potential in social organization are embodied" (1959, 168). See also Ralph Berry 1985, 46.

8. For the view that Portia is like an actress playing roles, see Berry 1985, 55, Danson 1978, 9, and Kirby Farrell 1975, 163.

9. Even her sexuality, however, is unclear. Leonard Tennenhouse argues that her moments of greatest triumph "require that she be an androgyne" (1980, 66). Lisa Jardine argues the opposite, that a boy disguised as a woman disguised as a man is erotic and that Portia's sexuality is both strong and ambiguous (1983, 20, 30). Perhaps this sexual ambiguity is widespread in the play; both Janet Adelman (1985) and Coppelia Kahn (1985) believe Antonio to be Portia's rival for Bassanio. See also Marianne Novy 1984, 77.

10. Terry Eagleton asserts that Shylock "has forced the Christians into outdoing his own 'inhuman' legalism" (1986, 37).

11. Nevill Coghill observes that "the scene is constructed on a sudden reversal of situation, a traditional dramatic dodge to create surprise and denouement" (1950, 21).

12. J. W. Lever's phrase (1952, 386).

13. E. M. W. Tillyard believes in Portia's full self-consciousness about what she does: she "knows [from the first that] she has Shylock quite within her power (1961, 51). Dawson (1978, 14–15) agrees. Lever argues that in the trial "the moral position taken up by Shylock is driven to its logical implications" by Portia (1952, 386). In a different context, Lewalski suggests a similar perspective: "Portia's final tactic [is] . . . permitting the law to demonstrate its own destructiveness" (1962, 341).

14. Harold C. Goddard believes that we are all implicated (1951, 116). In his view, Shylock is the scapegoat because he reminds the Venetians "of their own unconfessed evil qualities" (1951, 85). Antonio especially "catches his own reflection in his [Shylock's] face" (1951, 88). My argument expands along these general lines to include us in the audience as viewers who see themselves, and to include Portia and the other Venetians with Shylock as reflectors (because embodiments) of an inner nature that we recognize and find unsavory. This argument contrasts with those of Moisan and Dawson. Moisan asserts that the play's "playful alterity" allows it "to divert attention from the ideological contradiction it reflects" (1987, 202). Similarly, Dawson believes that Shylock is reduced "to a stock figure" in order "to draw attention to the theatrical mode itself as a form of presenting reality as unreality or unreality as reality," and that this consciousness of theatricality distances us, "diminishing the threat" (1978, 4). My view has been, rather, that Portia's metadramatic role as lawyer has actually intensified the threat we feel in the audience because it forces us to see our own viciousness in her acts. Orgel's assertion that in this period "theater . . . was assumed to be a verbal medium," above all to be *heard* (1975, 16–17), seems a reinforcement of the importance I have placed on Portia's "reed voice."

15. Lewalski argues that Portia demonstrates the destructive nature of law so that Shylock can see it and be instructed (1962, 341). Eggers asserts, "Shylock is not only a loser, but a winner" (1977, 332).

16. Tennenhouse refers to the cultural specificity of this image of the wealthy patron bankrolling the young courtier (1980, 57).

17. Sigurd Burckhardt observes that Bassanio "now stands before Portia as Antonio stood before Shylock . . . ; she insists on the letter of the pledge . . ." (1962, 260). Lewalski agrees that the "ring episode" is a comic version of the trial (1962, 342).

18. The significance of the forgiveness and giving themes is generally recognized, often with extraordinary optimism. See Danson 1974, 20–21, and on the playfully teasing duet as a mock combat, 1974, 176–77. Lewalski argues indeed that Antonio in his forgiveness and generosity at times "reflects . . . on the role of Christ" (1962, 334).

19. For many years, it remained usual to take these passages at face value. For example, Burnet sees this passage as reaching beyond Plato's *Timaeus* to the Pythagorean view of music as "purgation of the soul" ([1930] 1968, 164). Mark L. Gnerro argues that the parallels between the duet and the Easter liturgy suggest that even in the duet itself, as well as in the passages following, "Shakespeare was aiming to show religious grace inspiring natural goodness and reconciliation" (1979, 20). See also Danson 1974, 187–89.

20. Burckhardt sees this resolution as an idealist confirmation. He believes that this play "asks how the vicious circles of the bond's law can be transformed into the ring of love. And it answers: through a literal and unreserved submission to the bond as absolutely binding" (1962, 243). Therefore, "The ring is the bond transformed, the gentle bond" (1962, 261).

The quite different perspective of Stallybrass and White also gives a negative cast to Shylock, and implies a positive one for Portia. (See note 4 above.) From this perspective his defeat becomes the containment of a threat to carnival. However, this view seems to assume that Portia somehow represents the opposite, the carnival, and if this is true, might she represent the grotesque body as well? This might be a problem. More importantly, if we must assume that Portia is allied with established authority in Venice, must we not also assume that carnival will be short-lived, indeed contained by the very forces that activate it? Must we not assume that because it is activated by authority, it is either cut off completely from the general population that it normally represents, or is a cynical manipulation of the general population's normal expressive outlet? If we pose a Portia who activates carnival values in opposition to Shylock, in other words, this comfort seems as cold as might Shylock's own.

21. This view is in opposition to that of Tennenhouse, who generalizes that in the 1590s "each of Shakespeare's heroines indeed enacts, problematizes, and resolves the issues of how power was distributed in England" (1986, 61).

22. For a discussion of this view of Queen Elizabeth's role, see Jardine 1983, 37–67, 169–174, and Goldberg 1985, 134–35.

Chapter Four. The Cause of Suffering and the Birth of Compassion in *Julius Caesar*

1. This was discussed at the end of the last chapter. For an exposition of the Four Noble Truths, see Trungpa 1973, 151–57. For a brief indication of the Third and Fourth, see the Glossary.

2. Robert S. Miola has argued the ambivalence of our perception of the character Julius Caesar from the perspective of the sixteenth-century tyrannicide debate. James Siemon argues to a similar conclusion from the point of view of the Protestant reformers' attack on images and metaphors which might be mistaken for truth (1985, 125–82). See also David Daiches 1976, 9; Lawrence Danson 1974, 51–53; Ernest Schanzer 1963, 70; and D. A. Traversi 1963, 12. For a diametrical opposition, see for example D. S. Brewer 1952 and J. Dover Wilson 1949, xxiii–xxv.

3. See Northrop Frye 1967, 83. In a similar vein, J. Leeds Barroll (1958) argues that the play is a statement against civil war, and that it takes a Christian view of Roman history.

4. 5.3.41–46 and 5.5.50–51. Kenneth Burke argues that Antony embodies the "Caesar-principle" for the rest of the play (1941, 333–34).

5. Thus Irving Ribner, for example, explains the nature of the full tragedy in these moral terms, and sees an analogy between it and a morality play; both Caesar and Brutus are tragic because each, confronted with a moral choice, chooses wrongly. In his view, the tragedy's emphasis is mainly on "the exact process by which the hero is led to commit his error" (1960, 53). These conventions of private and public morality operate, however, despite the fact that the element of sacredness accorded medieval and Renaissance monarchs is lacking with Caesar, for of course he is neither crowned nor divinely anointed.

6. This is true regardless of whether we see his enactment as Jonathan Goldberg does, i.e., as a deliberate pretense in the service of a good deed (1983, 165), or as Ralph Berry does, as "the priestly slaying of a victim" (1985, 75). However, Berry's argument that these Romans all play roles of "identity," roles in which they believe they truly show and express themselves (1985, 79–83), leads more directly toward the relations between a character's self-image and the specific theatrical form he chooses for his action.

The idea that Brutus ritualizes the murder of Caesar has often been observed. See for example Ralph Berry 1985, 75; Lawrence Danson 1974, 52–63; Leo Kirschbaum 1949, 520–24; and Peter Ure 1974, 24.

7. Because these script manipulations involve both the order figure and the noble rebel, they represent a politically interesting shift in application from Jonathan Goldberg's description of a *king:* "Destiny is what is spoken. The king was subjected, shaped, imposed upon, by the language in which, and with which, he attempted to impose himself on others" (1983, 20). This observation leads Goldberg to the conclusion that the common metaphor of king as actor often "leads us to see the doubleness in performance in the royal view," such that we see the paradox of "subversiveness in absolutist rhetoric" (1983, 120). Shakespeare's Caesar and Brutus, as I see their enactments, complicate their play's political ambiguity by playing out this paradox in the persons of both the authority figure and his challenger.

8. Kenneth Burke calls particular attention to the metadramatic nature of Antony's speech, albeit to a different purpose: "Instead of being a dramatic character *within* the play, he is here made to speak as a critical commentator *upon* the play" (1941, 329–30).

9. Some aspects of this complex metadramatic situation have been used by others to serve other argumentative ends. For instance, Jonathan Goldberg refers to the "inherent theatricalization" to which this play's "images of the nature of political power" call our attention (1983, 185). Leonard Tennenhouse argues more generally that aesthetics are *always* political (1986, 14–16). Antony Dawson believes that the metadramatic emphasis, without reference to its political implications, leads to "a deeper penetration of reality as we know it" (1978, xiv). Sidney Homan feels that the murder's self-reflexiveness calls our

attention to it as the reenactment of a historical event, a reenactment that binds us to the stage audience (1981, 11–12). Ralph Berry, arguing from different premises, also believes that "the roots of the tragic action" in this play "lie in communal identity" (1985, 87).

10. For a related interpretation of Antony, see Rosalie L. Colie (1974, 175) and Northrop Frye (1967, 26–27). R. A. Foakes suggests the pessimistic interpretation to which this view can lead: the "various themes in language and action all suggest a full circle of events in the play, civil war leading to civil war, blood to blood . . ." (1954, 263).

11. Thus G. Wilson Knight sees Brutus as a kind of first draft for the character Macbeth ([1930] 1970, 120). However, Kenneth Burke argues that the ghost represents a version of "the Caesar-persona" ([1941] 1973, 343).

12. Gordon Braden discusses Seneca's stoic ideal in precisely these terms. In it, "the classical drive for esteem is not being suppressed but only redirected toward a more secure and elite kind of self-esteem" (1985, 18). Again, "the philosophically virtuous life becomes a new version of the martial hero's traditional struggle with contingency" (1985, 19). The self is still involved in a power game, but the battlefield is now internalized; it becomes the individual will whose "operative values are, time and again, power and control" (1985, 20).

Brutus's stature in his suicide is a bone of contention among scholars. Hugh M. Richmond asserts that his "complacent equanimity" and "pride" do not make him "a tragic hero" (1968, 103). Norman Council argues that by the last act Brutus's unorthodox view of honor (as guide rather than reward) "has become merely self-protective, isolated from any concern but its own preservation" (1973, 69). On the other side, Richard G. Moulton speaks for several generations: "In his fall he is glorious" (1966, 183). Matthew N. Proser goes so far as to write, "In his death Brutus achieves pure freedom" (1965, 59).

13. Chögyam Trungpa refers in a similar context to the "suicidal approach to reality" (1976, 58).

14. Thomas F. Van Laan argues that all the major characters have inflated self-images, into which they try unsuccessfully to fit themselves—which they try to "play," and that the audience is extremely aware of this fact (1978, 152–53). Peter Ure makes related observations about Brutus (1974, 24).

15. This is a point argued at some length above with reference to the *Pyramus and Thisby* play within *A Midsummer Night's Dream*. With *Julius Caesar*, Shakespeare has moved from subverting the characters in the stage audience by subverting a play within a play, to subverting the theater audience by subverting the whole play.

Chapter Five. The Emptiness of *Différance* and the Six Samsaric Realms in *Antony and Cleopatra*

1. It is not difficult to find scholars who condemn the main characters of this play, and from a variety of points of view. See for example Leo Kirschbaum (1944), J. Leeds Barroll (1958), or Franklin M. Dickey (1966). For the political side of this discussion, with reference to gender and carnival, see Leonard Tennenhouse (1986, 144–46). However, a more complex view of the characters is commoner. Julian Markels argues that this is a play without villains in which "the evil . . . [is] not only within the characters . . . ; it is the other side of their goodness" (1968, 8). Ernest Schanzer writes that the characters' love is seen to be good from one side of our minds, but bad from another (1963, 184). For similarly ambivalent readings, see S. L. Bethell (1944), Janet Adelman (1973), Willard Farnham (1950), Sidney Homan (1981, 182–90), L. C. Knights (1959, 149), A. P.

Riemer (1968, 114), Elmer Edgar Stoll (1928, 163), and D. A. Traversi (1969, 238, and 1963, 194). However, John Coates argues that "Antony as Hercules is able to reconcile these contradictions" (1978, 51).

2. Mark Van Doren speaks for many scholars when he observes that Cleopatra "is herself a consummate actress, and she knows Antony knows it" (1939, 272). See also Janet Adelman (1973, 154), Marianne Novy (1980, 263), Linda Bamber (1982, 55–68), Alvin B. Kernan (1978, 192), Matthew N. Proser (1965, 234), and Mark Rose (1977, 11). Antony Dawson takes this idea one step further, in a direction I will later follow: throughout this play, "the characters manifest a consciousness of *story,* an awareness that they are playing a part in a significant action." In addition, they have "a consciousness of audience, an audience within the play and outside it as well" (1978, 138).

3. The idea of their mythic dimensions is argued by Robert Ornstein (1964, 45), John Danby (1949, 213), and Harold Fisch (1970, 59). Irene Dash sees in Cleopatra a union of sexual and political power (1981, 209). The relationship between "play" and identity is explored by David Daiches (1962, 344), David Horowitz (1965, 46), Susan Snyder (1980, 119), and Barbara C. Vincent (1982, 84). The power of this relationship to achieve some version of self-apotheosis is alleged by Robert Ornstein (1964, 45–46, 97), Mark Rose (1977, 12), Thomas F. Van Laan (1978, 222), and Matthew N. Proser's echo of Sir Philip Sidney: "Art is capable of embracing nature, of redefining it, and giving it transcendence" (1965, 234).

4. Carol Thomas Neely makes this point (1985, 146).

5. This anti-Caesar, anti-Roman view is expressed in various ways by John Danby (1952, 157), Northrop Frye (1967, 74), Sidney Homan (1981, 190), Michael Lloyd (1962, 554), Ricardo J. Quinones (1972, 383), J. L. Simmons (1969, 495), and William Wolf (1982, 330).

6. A. P. Riemer argues that this "state of flux . . . provides the central vision of the play" (1968, 114). Enobarbus's ironic comment after the death of Octavia makes this vision explicit, as Northrop Frye has noticed (1967, 145): there are "tailors of the earth; comforting therein, that when old robes are out, there are members to make new" (1.2. 163–65). Antony's comment on the Nile makes the same point: one knows

> By th' height, the lowness, or the mean, if dearth
> Or foison follow. The higher Nilus swells,
> The more it promises; as it ebbs, the seedsman
> Upon the slime and ooze scatters his grain,
> And shortly comes to harvest.
>
> (2.7.19–23)

The human dimension, the changing fortunes of political, military, and amorous striving, is woven into this texture of universal flux, for which Antony and Cleopatra are the exemplary foreground. For variations on this view, see also Janet Adelman (1973, 145), John Danby (1949, 198–99), Maynard Mack (1977, 125), and Mark Van Doren (1939, 276).

7. Linda Bamber makes this point (1982, 55).

8. For different interpretations of this observation, compare Linda Bamber (1982, 61–66) with Susan Snyder (1980, 116–19).

9. Jonathan Dollimore sees their feelings as "a sexual infatuation" that expresses itself in insecurity, "possessiveness and its corollary, betrayal" (1984, 217).

10. D. A. Traversi believes Antony's love to be presented "as *value*" much as honor is (1969, 236). Julian Markels argues that Antony tries to "encompass both" Rome and Egypt for his fulfillment (1968, 9). J. L. Simmons (1969, 504) and David Daiches (1962, 344) agree.

Many scholars have noticed the dramatic nature of her suicide. See Janet Adelman (1973, 154–55), Antony B. Dawson (1978, 145), David Daiches (1962, 358), Sidney Homan (1970/71, 407, and 1981, 183), and Barbara C. Vincent (1982, 84).

For accounts of their success at transcendence, see Janet Adelman (1973, 111–29), Reuben A. Brower (1971, 353), Harold Fisch (1970, 67), David Horowitz (1965, 44), John Holloway (1961, 102), Julian Markels (1968, 10), John Middleton Murry (1936, 370–79), A. P. Riemer (1968, 114), J. L. Simmons (1969, 49), and Thomas F. Van Laan (1978, 222). See also note 3 above.

11. Among those who believe Cleopatra lifts her play beyond the plane of tragedy are Janet Adelman (1973, 167–68), Dorothy Krook (1969, 199), Howard Felperin (1972, 132), Julian Markels (1968, 10), J. L. Simmons (1969, 509, 570), and J. Dover Wilson (1954, xxxvi).

12. The sensuality of her death has often been noticed. See Marilyn French (1981, 251–64), Robert Grudin (1979, 173), Sidney Homan (1970/71, 407–8, and 1981, 182–83), Leo Kirschbaum (1944, 167), L. C. Knights (1959, 149), Carol Thomas Neely (1985, 161–62), Marianne Novy (1984, 263), Matthew N. Proser (1965, 226), Martha Tucker Rozett (1985), Ernest Schanzer (1963, 125), Susan Snyder (1980, 121), and J. Dover Wilson (1954, xxi).

Antony and Cleopatra's belief that they can transport their luminous sexuality to another plane by inventing and playing "real" roles suggests interesting parallels with the Baroque artistic program of the Counter-Reformation. From about 1580 on, Baroque artists began using the self-undermining meta-art that is exemplified by Annibale Carracci in Appendix A. To the Reformation's primary emphasis on inward spirituality, it offered an alternative, more sensuous vision. The Council of Trent, ending only five months before Shakespeare's birth, determined this agenda. In it, sense stimulation is to be used to inspire an emotional faith in which the will is raised beyond the senses toward God; the artistic equivalent is the use of dynamically emotional realism and illusionism for the purpose of earthly transcendence into the pulsing energy of becoming. This life is not to be taken seriously in itself, yet is to be used as the art is used, as the vehicle by which to rise through this earthly illusion to a higher reality (see Rudolf Wittkower 1973, 21–25) and Andreina Griseri (1967, 4, 11).

In the same way, Clifford Davidson believes Antony to be "miraculously converted into angelic substance" (1980, 52). Robert Grudin argues that Cleopatra's "identification with material pleasures is . . . so complete that it seems to transcend the laws of matter . . . [;] she represents a new and positive sense of the indivisibility of spirit and body, form and matter, and being and change" (1979, 173). Michael Lloyd observes that Charmian's line "'o eastern star!' (5.2.307) as she watches Cleopatra die, may recall the transfiguration of Isis" (1959, 92). The play's theme is then "the statement of the divine humanity which is common to Isis and Cleopatra" (1959, 94).

Although the idea of "levitation" has not been applied to these characters, in this climate the comparison seems appropriate. Levitation involves the spiritualizing of the flesh, such that the intact physical body while still alive is raised above all physical support so that it comes to rest in midair. The sixteenth century had, in fact, its own quite famous real-life exemplification of this idea of the lover's levitation in St. Teresa of Avila, who died in 1582, only about twenty-five years before this play, and was important enough to the leaders of the Counter-Reformation to be canonized by 1622. She believed that her love for Christ was so reciprocated that in a vision she heard him call her his bride. She thought of herself as mystically married to him, and was wont to levitate at the mass. Certainly Bernini's slightly later (1645–52) statue of her during ecstatic levitation, in the Cornaro Chapel of Rome's Church of Santa Maria della Vittoria, emphasizes the erotic aspect of her spiritual rapture. Thus the idea that levitation occurs in the context of a wife's love for her God/husband is perhaps not particularly unusual for the age. It might also be noticed that two of the other great Counter-Reformation saints, canonized with St. Teresa on the same day, Ignatius of Loyola and Philip Neri, were confirmed levitators as well, but always in private. Saint Francis of Assisi was an earlier example; levitation was taken as a sign of spiritual power. For a general account of all this, consult Irving Lavin (1980, 120–44). He asserts that "levitations became a *topos* in the biographies of modern saints." Therefore, "we have from this period a plethora of scenes showing a religious personage suspended in air..." (1980, 119).

As with any such event that seems to contradict our everyday experience, the temptation to be incredulous is high. However, several strands of Renaissance thought were compatible with the idea of levitation, so that to the Renaissance mind an event of this kind might seem miraculous but nonetheless plausible. The concept of the world's and the individual's perfectibility was common. Natural or white magic, the Christian sacraments, and alchemy were all considered to contain methodology for spiritualizing and thus perfecting physical reality of various kinds. The "chemical wedding" of opposites is a common alchemical term that suggests its theoretical relationship to the sacrament of holy matrimony, and Joseph Campbell asserts that the Roman Catholic mass is a kind of magic in which "God, through the power of the words of the consecration, descends into the bread and wine" (1956, 171). The work done on magic by Frances A. Yates, especially in Yates 1964, and by Daniel P. Walker, is now well known. In the field of alchemy, Mircea Eliade is particularly helpful; see both Eliade 1958 and 1978a. Equally useful are Jung 1967a and 1967b.

Shakespeare's contemporary El Greco (1541–1614) also illustrates this orientation toward the flesh. He uses the skills of realism to create elongated figures that are nearly too thin to be of this world; they are almost embodiments of the spiritual life they contain. It is as if everything in his pictures is in a state of becoming. The compositional point of view reinforces this idea. The earthly ground is typically dark; one follows the principal figure's eyes or movement upward; it is in him and in his higher goal that one sees the greatest light. The focal point is above. When the subject is the Resurrection, for example, the Christ leaves this world for the next as if he were blasting off. The lesser figures who had surrounded him below are thrown back by the force of his upward thrust. There is always the feeling of movement, of the embodied spirit restlessly seeking his home in the heavens (see for example the excerpted critical passages in Ioan Horga 1975, 10–13).

As will be argued below, Shakespeare seems to undermine belief in his characters' grand self-imaging. From this perspective, the play might be seen as an opposition to anti-Protestant art. For an argument that sees this self-undermining quality in English and European literature of the period as a parallel to Baroque art, see Frank J. Warnke (1972, especially 65–97).

13. See John M. Bowers (1983) for a discussion of the monument on which this death is staged. Linda Bamber anticipates one of the self-contradictory aspects in this staging, which the following passages explore more fully (1982, 67).

14. The sixth of this cycle of realms is the Animal Realm (see Trungpa 1973, 140). This realm seems less inhabited by Antony and Cleopatra because of their infatuation with a more grandiose scale of becomings.

15. See note 7 to the Introduction for the sources of this observation.

16. See Michael Goldman (1975, 8–16, 92); Goldman (1972, 6–10); and Marianne Novy (1984, 264). See also the interviews with Peter Brook in *Parabola* 6, no. 3 (1981): 60–73 and 4, no. 3 (1979): 46–59.

17. John Greenwood calls attention to the self-reflexive quality of Romano's work in the Palazzo Te, and compares it in a general way both to Shakespeare and to mannerist painting (1988, 22–28). He also considers Enobarbus's references to Cleopatra, particularly including the "barge" speeches, to be mannerist in their "shifting perspectives" (1988, 82)—one reason that our relationship to the play is "complex" (1988, 53).

18. For a full discussion of this issue, see Ken Jones (1989).

19. This observation is not meant to suggest that the court audience had a less important formative influence on Shakespeare's turning toward romance. For discussions of this role, see especially Roy Strong (1984, 156–57) and Leonard Tennenhouse (1986, 97ff.). Strong suggests the relationship between court, perspective, and overt symbolism in which the audience is invited to collude; Tennenhouse suggests the relationship between court and metadrama (1986, 184).

Chapter Six. Prince Hal's Deferral as the Ground of Free Play

1. For a fuller discussion of this idea, see the concluding paragraphs of chapter 1.

2. It is of course not unusual to believe that Hal is in fact judging Falstaff here, and beginning to dissociate himself from his companion. See, for example, Richard L. McGuire (1967) and James Winny (1968, 141). Paul A. Gottschalk (1973/74) argues that there is no change at all in their relationship in this scene.

3. For the idea of Hal as a conscious actor within the play, see James Calderwood (1979, 116), Alvin B. Kernan (1978, 186), and Julian Markels (1968, 63). For the complexity that eludes definition, see Eileen Jorge Allman (1980, 69), William Empson (n.d., 43), Richard A. Lanham (1976, 207), and Ricardo J. Quinones (1972, 326). For an idealized reading of the prince and his life, see J. Dover Wilson (1953, 68).

4. For a variety of interpretations of this often-seen aloofness, see John Danby (1958, 89), E. M. W. Tillyard (1956, 274–81), and James Winny (1968, 131).

5. Or a morally righteous one (the more common older view, for which see Harry Levin's overview [1981] and the more partisan readings of E. M. W. Tillyard [1956, 265] and J. Dover Wilson [1953, 14]). On the unitary structure of the two plays, see also Harold C. Goddard (1951, 116) and Mark Van Doren (1939, 117).

6. For moral categories, Tillyard (1956, 265) and Wilson (1953, 17–20) remain exemplary, although S. I. Bethell's view is broader (1952/53, 92–94). However, Willard Farnham (1971, 68) and Neil Rhodes (1980, 104) see Falstaff as a complex Elizabethan grotesque, and Mikhail Bakhtin (1984, 303–436) discusses in more general terms the background cultural (including class) implications of "the grotesque body" and "the material bodily lower stratum." A long list which includes Sukanta Chaudhuri (1981, 123–25), Harold C. Goddard (1951, 183), Samuel Johnson (1958), Maurice Morgann (1958), and Bernard Spivack (1957) agree that he is too full to be categorized. Empson, for one, sees in him "the comic idealisation of freedom" (n.d., 109); Goddard sees in him "the

highest conception of life we are capable of forming" (1951, 183). This list, and its variety, could be expanded exponentially. For an interesting contemporary feminist view of the character, see Valerie Traub (1989). The standard new historicist view must be Greenblatt 1985.

7. A. C. Bradley (1909, 264), Sukanta Chaudhuri (1981, 126), Harold C. Goddard (1951, 184), and Maurice Morgann (1958, 185–86) agree that Falstaff does not attempt to fool anyone with his lies.

8. For a complex view of the interrelationship between high and low cultures within their different discourse levels, as well as within the enactment of carnival, such that they need not be conceived as being in opposition to one another, see Bakhtin (1981, 270–87, and 1984, 146–50); for a similarly complex account of a closely related issue, royalty's relationship with the fool, see Willeford (1969, chaps. 6–9). On the relationship between character and role with specific reference to this scene, see Robert Weimann (1978, 11–14) and, with reference to Cambyses, Weimann (1978, 158). Paul A. Gottschalk (1973/74, 610–11) and James Winny (1968, 106–9) discuss the parodic nature of these roles within roles, and how this tone privileges the world of play at the expense of external reality. J. I. M. Stewart takes quite a different view of the tone of this play extempore, but also sees Falstaff as a criticism of the king (1949, 138).

9. For further comments on this scene as metadrama, see also Calderwood (1965, 70–73), Sigurd Burckhardt (1968, 148), and Thomas F. Van Laan (1978, 150).

10. Both J. Dover Wilson (1953, 20) and S. L. Bethell (1952/53, 93–94) see Falstaff as a devil-figure. However, there is another side to this scene. His return to life in act 5 is not merely cynical or clever; it is also a kind of resurrection, a refusal to die of this always present counterstroke of disengagement from the conventional, the authorized, the *formulated.* Falstaff's affinity with a comic resurrection here has been noticed by C. L. Barber (1959, 205), by Michael Bristol (1985, 186), and by James Calderwood (1979, 69). The traditional view that the structure of this play is modeled on that of the morality play, a view championed by E. M. W. Tillyard (1956, 265), J. Dover Wilson (1953, 14) and, more recently, Harry Levin (1981, 10), requires modification. To the degree that the morality play *is* a model, indeed, Alan Dessen argues that it is the later morality play, in whose first half the vice makes a criticism of the conventional world that must be taken seriously (1986, 36, 88).

11. James Winny calls Henry the "master-thief" (1968, 141), and observes more generally that "throughout the series [of history plays] the king, whether usurper or rightful heir, sits uneasily on his throne . . ." (1968, 9).

12. William Empson suggests this term (n.d., 45).

13. Stephen Greenblatt (1985, esp. 27–43) makes most of these points. See also Leonard Tennenhouse (1985) and Valerie Traub (1989).

14. Gerard H. Cox argues that because he *seems* to gain nothing, he is in fact the embodiment of true chivalry. "Hal's is a triumph of honor precisely because he is not accorded any public triumph" (1985, 147). Although Cox's view is in quite a different context than mine, it emphasizes the prince's nonattachment to conventional appearances.

15. Paul A. Gottschalk emphasizes the extemporaneous nature of the "playing" in act 2, scene 4 to set it apart from the play-within-a-play convention, which requires a script. He argues that this extemporaneity emphasizes "the primacy of the play world and thus . . . the unreality of the political" (1973/74, 613). I am suggesting that there may also be a further reason for this unusual quality to emerge in this particular play. For example, Zen Master Shunryu Suzuki writes that in this state of mind, "When Buddha comes, you will welcome

him; when the devil comes, you will welcome him. . . . There is no problem" (1970, 42–43). Opposites can coexist.

16. For a fuller discussion of this aloneness quality, see chapter 4 above, as well as Trungpa (1973, 152–53).

Chapter Seven. Further Glimpses of Free Play in *Hamlet* and *King Lear*

1. This play's artistic transparency and its difficulty of interpretation, as well as their source in metadramatic qualities, are commonly noticed. Lionel Abel particularly emphasizes these qualities in the play, and links them to the nature of its main character: "Certainly Hamlet is one of the first characters to be free of his author's contrivances" (1963, 58). In discussing the implications of metatheater, he writes that it specifically denies "any image of the world as ultimate." Instead it implies that any such image is "a projection of human consciousness" (1963, 113). Many others have followed this essential perspective. For example, Robert Weimann argues that in *Hamlet* "Shakespearean mimesis comprehends a self-conscious subversion of authority in representation" (1985, 277). Similarly, James Calderwood asserts that the play "repeatedly insists upon its own fictionality" (1983, 15; see also 1983, 170). Anne Righter sees the play's relationship to reality as metaphoric, and argues (as I shall below in different terms) that this metaphor is "an affirmation of the power of the stage" (1962, 164).

2. There is of course a long and hallowed tradition of seeing dislocation and mystery in the play. See, for example, T. S. Eliot (1960) for the first, and Maynard Mack (1961) for the second.

3. According to Peter Brook, good acting necessarily projects the "reality" of the actor, so that his illusionist representation becomes his own self-enactment, as it does with the actor/character Hamlet. Brook believes that an actor can only enact what he contains within himself (*Parabola* 6, no. 3 [1981]: 60–73). Polonius might be said to exemplify this idea rather broadly: having once played the part of the murdered Julius Caesar (3.2.103–4), in act 3, scene 4 he does so again, in earnest, to Hamlet's purging Brutus.

Michael Goldman believes that this relationship between the actor and his role—that is, acting itself—"is always in some sense the subject of the play" (1975, 92). He extends this idea to a point where it verges on the political: "The leading role or roles of any play act out some version of a half-allowed, blasphemous, and sacred freedom characteristic of the era in which the play was written" (1975, 55).

4. Robert Weimann similarly observes that in the scenes leading up to the mousetrap, and particularly in *Gonzago* itself, we have "a self-conscious vehicle of the drama's awareness of the functional and thematic heterogeneity of mimesis, . . . [a] mimesis of mimesis" (1985, 279). Professor Weimann believes that in this consciousness lies "a self-conscious subversion of authority in representation" (1985, 277) that leads to actual subversion. Although I agree with both his facts and his conclusion, I do not believe that the second follows directly from the first. For the strength of representation seems to me to lie precisely in its self-subversion, and this is true no matter who does the representing, the weak or the strong.

5. Both Nigel Alexander (1971, 115) and P. J. Aldus (1977, 117) have seen that the mousetrap contains the past and the future at once.

6. Stephen Orgel has suggested that in court theater, of which the mousetrap is

certainly an example within the play, "the spectators watched . . . not a play but a queen at a play, and their response would have been not simply to the drama, but to the relationship between the drama and its primary audience, the royal spectator" (1975, 9). With this idea in mind, Claudius's self-casting as the player-king merely intensifies the normal theatrical situation, thereby perhaps emphasizing the further idea that court life is composed of royal games and pretense.

7. The play insists on the metadramatic aspect of the duel. We see its script being written in act 4, scene 7, when Claudius and Laertes plan to poison the sword, as well as to take advantage of Hamlet's "generous, and free" nature, ensuring that Laertes will get the right weapon (4.7.135). In act 5, scene 2, we see Osric present the challenge and set up the rules of the game (5.2.165–69). We hear the lord ask Hamlet if he is ready "to play" (5.2.240). We see the king preside over a ritual handshake between the combatants (5.2.225), and Hamlet ask Laertes formally for pardon before they fight, in a way reminiscent of *Richard II*'s first act. Both Hamlet and the stage directions use the word "play" several times more to describe the way this mock-ritual entertainment is to be presented.

Nigel Alexander suggests the idea of the duel as a sequel to the mousetrap by calling it the conclusion of the pattern begun by the ghost's supposed revelation, a kind of repetition of the mousetrap (1971, 2). James L. Calderwood sees that the duel fuses a common identity between play and reality; he states that in this deadly action "reality invades fiction" (1983, 45). In the same vein, see Ronald Levao (1985, 347).

8. Trungpa writes, "Your suffering is truth; it is intelligent. . . . Confusion and pain are viewed as sources of inspiration" (1976a, 150). Again, "Buddhism promises nothing. It teaches us to be what we are where we are, constantly, and it teaches us to relate to our living situations accordingly" (1976a, 93). "According to Buddha, life *is* pain, life *is* pleasure. . . . There is no need at all to reduce life situations or intensify them" (1976a, 95).

9. Although he places this speech in quite a different dramatic context, Alex Newell (1965) provides a thorough reading of it along the lines I am developing in this paragraph.

10. Trungpa writes that one must acknowledge and surrender to "the raw, rugged, clumsy and shocking qualities of one's ego," but

> we find it very difficult. . . . Although we may hate ourselves, at the same time we find our self-hatred a kind of occupation. In spite of the fact that we may dislike what we are and find that self-condemnation painful, still we cannot give it up completely. If we begin to give up our self-criticism, then we may feel that we are losing our occupation, as though someone were taking away our job. . . . there would be nothing to hold on to. Self-evaluation and self-criticism are, basically, neurotic tendencies which derive from our not having enough confidence in ourselves, "confidence" in the sense of seeing what we are, knowing what we are. . . .
>
> [But] we must surrender our hopes and expectations, as well as our fears, and march directly into disappointment, work with disappointment, go into it and make it our way of life. (1973, 24–25)

In this process, you must be

> willing to give up the company of your shadow, your twenty-four-hours-a-day commentator who follows you constantly, the watcher. . . . This is a very big step. . . . You have to give up the questioner and the answer . . . , the checking mechanism that tells you whether you are doing well or not doing well.

With this self-deception dissolved,

> it is like living among snow-capped peaks with clouds wrapped around them and the sun and moon starkly shining over them. (1976a, 150)

11. However, we must see Hamlet's "How all occasions do inform against me" speech (4.4.32ff.) in the context of act 4, scenes 5 and 7. Ophelia has gone truly mad. Laertes is so eager for revenge that he acts rashly (as presumably Hamlet could), walking into the king followed by "a riotous head" (4.5.102), willing to undermine his honor and sense of fair play by the rapier-poisoning trick. In this context, Hamlet's final self-reproach seems a sign of sanity and integrity. He is right to be deliberate and sure, to endure his self-reproaches instead of capitulating to them and acting rashly. In his one rash act he killed the wrong man, Polonius. But even there he did not sacrifice his integrity, and subsequently he is not rash.

12. Nor does he feel remorse for having killed his old friends Rosencrantz and Guildenstern: "They did make love to this employment, / They are not near my conscience. Their defeat / Does by their own insinuation grow" (5.2.57–59). Like Polonius, they chose to be spies. "'Tis dangerous when the baser nature comes / Between the pass and fell incensed points / Of mighty opposites" (5.2.60–62). Hamlet must follow his destiny, as they theirs. Unfortunately for his old friends, they crossed. But Hamlet did not seek this crossing; rather, his old friends did. They did not guess the largeness of the stakes in the game they joined: the life of the monarch. They took action in ignorance, precisely what Hamlet was never willing to do. Here Hamlet knows fully what is at issue; he therefore deals quickly and effectively (this may mean ruthlessly) with his old friends. He is resolved.

13. A crucial preparation for the heroic path of the bodhisattva—he who will sacrifice himself for the well-being of others—"is the synchronization of body and mind: the body works for the mind and the mind works for the body" (Trungpa 1976a, 107).

14. James Calderwood asserts that Hamlet faces death and negation in the graveyard as a precondition for his later "readiness" (1983, 103). Susan Snyder emphasizes the humor of this recognition: "It is Hamlet's peculiar heroism that he can see the joke very clearly indeed [in the graveyard] and still in the face of absurdity assert the meaning of his own life . . ." (1979, 135).

15. Trungpa describes this state when the watcher has dissolved as follows:

> Having opened, having given up everything without reference to the basic criteria of "I am doing this, I am doing that," without reference to oneself, then other situations connected with maintaining ego or collecting become irrelevant. That is the ultimate morality and it intensifies the situation of openness and bravery: you are not afraid of hurting yourself or anyone else because you are completely open. You do not feel uninspired with situations, which brings patience, . . . and patience leads to energy. . . . There is the tremendous joy of involvement, which is energy. (1973, 100)

16. Trungpa describes compassion

> in terms of clarity, clarity which contains fundamental warmth. . . . You begin to trust yourself. . . . Compassion in this sense is not feeling sorry for someone. It is basic warmth.

> As much space and clarity as there is, there is that much warmth as well, some delightful feeling of positive things happening in yourself constantly. (1973, 97)

17. Trungpa expands on the qualities that accompany mental clarity:

> Because you see situations very clearly, much more clearly than you did before, because you see them as they really are, you know how and where to direct the energy. Previously you imposed your version of reality onto life, rather than seeing things as they are. So when this kind of veil is removed, you see the situation as it is. Then you can communicate with it properly and fully. You do not have to force yourself to do anything at all. There is a continual exchange, a continual dance. It is similar to the sun shining and plants growing. The sun has no desire to create the vegetation; plants simply react to sunlight and the situation develops naturally.

In this natural situation, "your actions become exceedingly accurate because they are spontaneous" (1973, 182). Patience becomes a natural characteristic, but

> patience does not mean forbearance in the sense of enduring pain, allowing someone to torture you at his leisure. The bodhisattva would strike down his torturer and defend himself, which is common-sense sanity. In fact the bodhisattva's blow would be more powerful because it would not be impulsive or frivolous. The bodhisattva has great power because nothing can shake him; his action is calm, deliberate and persevering. Since there is space between himself and others, he does not feel threatened, but he is very careful.... So the bodhisattva can spring out like a tiger and claw you, bite you, crush you. He is not inhibited by conventional morality. ... He is not afraid to subjugate what needs to be subjugated, to destroy what needs to be destroyed, and to welcome that which needs to be welcomed. (1976a, 114–15)

However, this action is not aggressive action, for "aggressive action is generally connected with defending" one's self-image, the identity by which one defines oneself. This kind of "self" is lacking in the realized bodhisattva (1973, 182).

To see Hamlet adopting this spirit is to separate his values from those of his aggressively self-defensive antagonist, as Nigel Alexander has argued (1971, 189–90). It is also to deny that he assumes a "stoic resignation" that closes off his other potentialities, as James Calderwood alleges (1983, 173, 105–6). In his more expansive discussion of the stoic hero in Senecan tragedy, Gordon Braden argues that this hero is "redefining individual freedom as a state of mind" that moves progressively inward toward acceptance of whatever is given (1985, 17). Rather than quarrel with authority, the stoic is indifferent. Yet the belief in one's self-importance is not "suppressed but only redirected toward a more secure and elite kind of self-esteem" (1985, 18). The stoic is as much playing a power game as is the warrior, but his battlefield becomes the will. "The operative values are, time and again, power and control" (1985, 20). In referring to Hamlet's "divinity" speech, Braden theorizes that his stoicism is "Christianized by an unclassically thorough humility before a greater power" (1985, 221).

Although Buddhism believes in no theology and no higher power, and in this respect obviously diverges from Hamlet's belief system (as it is reflected in his references to "divinity" and to "providence"), the psychological analysis that is the core of Buddhist teaching seems closer to Hamlet's character than does Braden's Christianized Stoicism.

Hamlet is hardly indifferent to the authority of Claudius and, I have argued, he is beyond "self-esteem." The Zen Master Shunryu Suzuki writes of the relationship of potentiality to emptiness, "If your mind is empty, it is always ready for anything; it is open to everything" (1970, 21).

18. James Calderwood calls it "a reflex action" (1983, 46).

19. For this view of the royal court, see among others Lisa Jardine (1983, 169–74) and Roy Strong (1984, 21–41).

20. Anne Righter believes that here the stage and theater audiences are combined (1962, 164). P. J. Aldus suggests that *Hamlet* is Horatio's telling of the Hamlet story, so that the ending is also the beginning (1977, 84).

21. Robert Weimann asserts that in this play "Shakespearean mimesis comprehends a self-conscious subversion of authority in representation" (1985, 277). Ronald Levao argues, "The play concludes by making us Hamlet's heirs, ambivalent kings of infinite space" (1985, 366). The play is characterized, in his view, by a late-Renaissance and baroque "need both to question and to affirm" (1985, 369).

22. James L. Calderwood disputes this claim. He accurately observes that "deconstruction is built into [this] play . . . to the extent that *Hamlet* repeatedly insists upon its own fictionality" (1983, 15). Subject and stage, actor and role, audience and theater—three apparently differentiated binaries collapse into each other so that the real seems illusory and illusion is transformed into the only reality there is. Calderwood argues that we must therefore abandon "a metaphysics of 'presence': the conception of an objective, unmediated, real world out there of which we can have direct knowledge" and which might stand in opposition to the world of the play (1983, 190). Within negation, there is an affirmation of the sheer experiential fact of being-in-the-theater. But this is "a theater of discredited illusions" and, "shift about as they will, neither the illusions of *Hamlet* nor its realities can escape their confinement within the master illusion of the play itself" (1983, 196).

It seems to me that Calderwood takes his metadramatically deconstructive view of the play into a cul-de-sac. Using Derridean ideas and vocabulary, he reverses the spirit of Derrida's deconstructive techniques. His interpretation is a denial of "real" significance by affirmation, whereas Derrida affirms by negation. However, Calderwood's reading does show that deconstruction can easily be interpreted as a denial of its positive possibilities; Derrida says again and again that no direct assertion of the affirmative is possible. One is, therefore, without guidance. *Hamlet*, though, seems to show that direct guidance is possible by presenting a character who exemplifies some of the fruitful aspects of emptiness; in his embodiment, they need not be spoken of directly, nor thought of in negative terms.

23. However, this similarity is easily exaggerated. Leonard Tennenhouse argues that although James saw himself figurally as husband, father, even god of England (1986, 153), and although for him purity of blood and family were transcendent political issues (1986, 171–84), Lear himself does not believe in primogeniture but in his own personal power to dispense the monarchy as he will (1986, 137). On the other hand, one might read this difference as a warning to James that the blindness that is a danger in absolutism can lead it to contradict its own beliefs.

24. Tennenhouse reads Lear's trial in this scene as a parody of kingship, demonstrating (to James's presumed satisfaction) how "pollution of blood" turns everything upside down and subverts the patriarchy (1986, 139–40). I prefer to weigh the inevitable upside-downness of the world itself more heavily.

25. Marianne Novy sees this play as using Western female stereotypes, in which a woman is either a devil (Goneril and Regan) or an angel (Cordelia) (1984, 153). See also Marilyn French (1981, 237). Leonard Tennenhouse adds a political dimension to the handling of this gender issue under James: "The unruly woman of Elizabethan comedy was criminalized and the world of inversion and of the carnivalesque took on sinister features"; these qualities are then "unleashed upon the world when patriarchy is absent" (1986, 153). This feminization of the lust for power in *King Lear* thus comes to seem like a typical Jacobean trope.

26. See Kott (1964, 106) for a discussion of Gloucester' pantomime. Professor Kott defines the grotesque in relation to the tragic: "The tragic situation becomes grotesque when both alternatives of the choice imposed are absurd, irrelevant or compromising. The hero has to play, even if there is no game. Every move is bad, but he cannot throw down his cards. To throw down the cards would also be a bad move" (1964, 94). This is basically Gloucester's view of his situation, and probably ours as well, a situation that Kott also calls an "absurdity," as if this word is in significant ways a synonym for the grotesque.

When describing the qualities of a grotesque *character*, Kott speaks of Gloucester's "philosophical buffoonery" (1964, 105) in terms that suggest kinship with Martin Esslin's definition of the absurd in the theater: "The Theatre of the Absurd strives to express its sense of the senselessness of the human condition and the inadequacy of the rational approach by the open abandonment of rational devices and discursive thought" (1964, 6). Kott emphasizes that the essence of the impression Gloucester makes on us in this scene derives from the sheer physical contrast between what we see performed onstage and what Gloucester the character thinks he is performing (1964, 100–109).

27. For Trungpa's discussion of the crucial importance of having a sense of humor about oneself and one's world, see Trungpa 1973, 111–16.

28. Marianne Novy suggests that in kneeling to his daughter for forgiveness, Lear "reverses hierarchies of both age and sex, and suggests their limitations" (1984, 159). Again, with his daughter in his arms at the end, she sees him as a kind of pietà. He begins to take on a female role which, Novy believes, deepens his character (1984, 162–63). Tragically, I might add, this depth is self-destructive; it helps neither Cordelia nor himself.

Epilogue. *The Tempest*

1. A partial list of scholars who concur with this essential view includes Robert Egan (1972, 182, and 1975, 117–19); Martin Esslin (1961, 303); Ernest B. Gilman (1980, 229); Michael Goldman (1972, 148–50); Robert G. Hunter (1965, 242–43); Frank Kermode (1963, 49); Alvin b. Kernan (1982, 151–52); Norman Rabkin (1981, 127); Ann Righter (1962, 207); Gary Schmidgall (1981, 133–34); Thomas F. Van Laan (1978, 251); and David Young (1978, 166). One view of the power of this gesture is given by Harry Berger: "Fiction can fulfill itself only by going beyond itself and invading life . . . [while its] open gestures of self-limitation . . . [reveal] itself as mere make-believe" (1965, 75).

2. Many scholars have observed the collapsing together of levels of "reality" in this speech. For example: Reuben A. Brower (1951, 115–16), Antony B. Dawson (1978, 166), Robert Egan (1972, 179), Frank Kermode (1954, lxxiii), Alvin B. Kernan (1974, 144–45), and Clifford Leech (1978, 59).

3. Gary Schmidgall makes this point about the revels speech (1981, 251–53), but his emphasis concerning this storm scene is on its role as prologue to the full play (1981, 161–73).

4. Alvin B. Kernan feels that Shakespeare's work generally is like *Las Meninas* in giving us an image of "the artist creating art" that changes our emphasis "from the thing known to the process of knowing" (1978, 176). Although agreeing that there is a comparison to be made, I am arguing that these two emphases are reciprocally reinforcing rather than mutually exclusive.

5. Sidney Homan is not alone in asserting that Prospero "must stand as surrogate for the playwright himself" (1981, 204).

6. There is no reason to assume that Prospero's relationship with the author-function means that he is in some way also meant as an analogy for the biographical William Shakespeare. Harry Levin's suggestion (1969, 51) that the character is "a portrait of the artist" in the abstract seems close to what I mean.

7. Descriptions of King James in these terms, suggesting an analogy with Prospero, are given in Jonathan Goldberg (1986, 3–32), Stephen Orgel (1986, 50–64), and Leonard Tennenhouse (1986, 153, 171–74). Patrick Grant (1979, 76) and Frances A. Yates (1975, 19) argue for an even closer identification between the character and the king.

For the idea that Prospero acts like a good ruler who teaches virtue to his subjects, see for example Michael Goldman (1972, 124–27, 137–50), F. D. Hoeniger (1956, 37), G. Wilson Knight (1948, 217, 244), and Michael Platt (1982, 239–41).

8. James L. Calderwood argues that "if we seek the originating transcendental signified—the nontheatrical reality which the play [*The Tempest*] presumably represents—we shall find merely a further play of illusions, an infinite immortal regress from theater to theater, play to play, illusion to illusion" (1987, 194). Precisely, *if* we seek "the originating transcendental signified." But if we seek nothing and accept the regress, it becomes sufficient, it becomes us, it becomes whatever "reality" is. As Shunryu Suzuki writes, "True being comes out of nothingness, moment after moment. Nothingness is always there, and from it everything appears" (1970, 109). Again, "The bird both exists and does not exist at the same time. . . . What appears from emptiness is true existence" (1970, 110). This may seem strange to our ordinary way of thinking, but "if you can just sit and experience the actuality of nothing in your [meditation] practice, there is no need to explain" (1970, 109).

9. We might imagine the same effect from gazing into the mirrors at the back of the room in *Las Meninas,* in which, it may be, we are figured as the royal couple; we may also be aware of standing outside the painting, in which case we are implicitly in the gaze of their reflection.

10. For this view, as well as its political implications, see Lorie Jerrell Leininger (1980).

11. With the difference that a Buddhist surrenders *to* nothing, and does not surrender in hope of a reward. He or she just does it.

12. Jan Kott (1987, 74) and Paul Brown (1985, 49–71) are two of those who see this similarity.

13. These curses, in turn, let Prospero know he must remain on guard. As Stephen Greenblatt argues for Harriot's American Indians and for Shakespeare's Falstaff (1985, 18–47), so here it can be argued that subversive thinking is given voice that it may be recognized, understood, its threat contained. On this colonialist theme, see also Greenblatt

(1988b, 129–63), Paul Brown (1985), and Annabel Patterson (1989, 11, 156). All three of these writers see some version of the "radical ambivalence at the heart of colonialist discourse" (Brown 1985, 66); its complexity is discussed below.

14. This is, of course, a common practice of victors, including colonizers, as Walter Benjamin points out (1986b, 681–82). Indeed, Prospero's reference to Caliban's mother Sycorax as having been "banish'd" to this island from "Argier" (1.2.265–66) might suggest family origins in the slave trade, another self-undermining historical subtext which, as we would expect, Prospero suppresses. Jan Kott notices the "Argier"– North African connection (1987, 70).

15. This may be another version of giving subversives their voice so that they may more easily be contained, a parallel to the play's treatment of Caliban. Both Stephen Orgel (1986, 62) and Kirby Farrell (1989, 188) see the situation in this way.

16. This view differs from that of several scholars who read this scene more pessimistically. Robert Egan thinks the revels speech to express "nihilistic despair" (1975, 109). Douglas L. Peterson sees a similar sense of "futility" (1973, 241), and Cosmo Corfield (1985) essentially agrees. It seems to me that this disagreement rests at bottom on different ways of conceiving experience—on whether power can be given up for positive reasons, in a positive frame of mind.

Others argue for our greater objectivity: Andrew V. Ettin (1977, 280) believes us to see what Prospero does not: that the other characters are not reformed. Howard Felperin (1978, 66) and Jan Kott (1964, 163–205) agree in the main. Whether or not it is justified, this reading seems to me to be irrelevant to the approach I am developing here, since I am examining the inconsistencies within Prospero rather than the accuracy of his reading of others.

17. Again, Stephen Orgel makes this point (1986, 62–63).

18. For the colonialist implications of this play, see Thomas Cartelli (1987) and Meredith Anne Skura (1989), as well as note 13 above.

19. The relationship between anxiety and royal politics is explored by Stephen Greenblatt (1988b) and by Stephen Orgel (1986). The reciprocity between demystifying power relations and the achievement of power is explored by Jonathan Dollimore (1984, 8, 22) and by David Scott Kastan (1986), for both of whom the royal discourse of theater is inherently subversive of the royalty it expresses.

20. See the description of court theater in Stephen Orgel (1975, 9–11).

21. Just as, from a political view, Jonathan Dollimore concludes. Although Renaissance thinkers were not radical in our modern sense, their implications are subversive. For example, Machiavelli "demystifies power in order that the powerful may rule more effectively, yet he has the effect of undermining the very basis of power itself" by exposing how power works (Dollimore 1984, 22).

Appendix A. The Sword of Prajna in the Visual Arts of the Continent

1. The uniquely self-conscious artist who, in the early twelfth century along a border of the great tympanum at Autun, chiseled out his inscription, "Gislbertus hic fecit," may be taken as the exception who proves the rule, the single reminder of the self-reflexive quality implicit in resemblance which has elsewhere been effaced by medieval art.

2. For one clear account of the nature of this ubiquitous medieval style, as well as its

relationship to some of the developments that led into the Renaissance, see Roston (1987, 195–205).

3. Anthony Blunt makes explicit the common assumption: "In the time of Leonardo . . . realism had been fully established" ([1940] 1963, 32).

4. Joseph Forte (1987) has fully described the effects of this restoration. See especially p. 106.

5. The intention of the present argument is to show a particular effect to be inherent in the art of resemblance, regardless of differences in epoch and style. Therefore, a discussion of the relations between the various Renaissance, mannerist, and baroque styles of the sixteenth century seems to be irrelevant here, as does the scholarly debate about the extent to which Romano should be categorized as a mannerist. But see Egon Verheyen (1977, 45–48) for the conflicting views on this subject.

6. Verheyen (1977, 20–23, 43, 51–54); see also Gian Maria Erbesato (1981, 15).

7. Verheyen writes, "The room is not only a masterwork of illusionistic painting but also of acoustics" (1977, 37). "It allows one to become part of it, to participate in the battle between the gods and the giants . . ." (1977, 38). Frederick Hartt amplifies the same observations, believing that the viewer is so caught up in the room as to experience a horror or fear similar to that depicted in the giants themselves ([1958] 1981, 154–56). This latter view Verheyen disputes, observing that in Vasari's second edition of the *Lives* he "backed down from his earlier statement" that this room induces fear in the viewer (1977, 54). See also Greenwood's discussion of illusionism in this room (1988, 13–16).

8. Hartt ascribes "certain fairly ludicrous aspects" of the giants' composition to Romano's assistant Rinaldo Mantovano, with his "brutal ignorance of the art of drawing"; in the same sentence, however, he concedes that "the total effect of the room is overpowering" ([1958] 1981, 156). It is questionable whether one can have it both ways. Verheyen argues that Rinaldo was "able to assimilate Giulio's design to such a degree that his intentions were actually realized" (1977, 50).

9. The relationship of Carracci's achievement in this gallery to the style that we call baroque is not part of our concern here, fascinating though the topic is.

10. Rudolf Wittkower describes the Farnese Gallery as "the crowding within a relatively small space of . . . [a] great variety of illusionist painting, the overlapping and superimposition of many elements of the over-all plan," in which "all this decoration is contrived as if it were real" (1973, 66).

11. Leatrice Mendelsohn shows that, typically for the time, Benedetto Varchi in his *Due Lezzioni* of 1547 justifies imitative art primarily on the basis of "the aspiration of the image toward a 'truth beyond reality'" (1982, 33). See especially pp. 29–33 and 41–43 for an analysis of the interaction between literary and visual artists and their response to Plato's attack on mimesis.

Appendix B. Shakespeare's Access to Renaissance Practices in the Visual Arts

1. For a fuller discussion of the deconstructive and political implications of this style, see chapter 2 above.

2. In Roy Strong (1969) see illustrations #2 (p. 10) and #26 (p. 19) for William Scrots and his circle; #35 (p. 25) for Antonio Mor; and for Robert Peake, compare #80 (p. 41) with #108 (p. 56).

3. For a summary of the major details of Elizabethan literature's indebtedness to Italian literature and culture, see Harold B. Segel (1974, 38–39).

4. Lewis W. Spitz (1972, 10–11) provides a brief but graceful summary of late fifteenth- and early sixteenth-century humanism in England (including the Colet-Erasmus-More circle) of which the Elizabethan age is the great conclusion.

5. For Nicholas Hilliard, see Erna Auerbach (1961, 203–13), Roy Strong (1969, 50) and Wolfgang Stechow (1966, 169–71), the latter particularly for his Italian references. For Paolo Giovanni Lomazzo's listing of Italian artists, see Lomazzo ([1598] 1966, 15, 20, 23, 214). Ernest B. Gilman (1978, 52) argues that English knowledge of Continental experiments with the witty use of perspective was extensive, in spite of its anti-Roman Catholic, anti-Italian prejudices, its "lack of a studio tradition, and Elizabeth's own indifference to the visual arts." (See Gilman 1978, 49–66 for his full survey.)

6. Erna Auerbach (1961, 14). See also Auerbach (1961, 254) and Roy Strong (1969, 48).

7. In the same spirit, Clark Hulse asserts that "English connoisseurs of art learned about Alberti at about the same time as they did Zuccaro . . ." (1981, 197–98).

Glossary of Buddhist and Buddhist-Related Terms

For a much expanded discussion of those terms that derive specifically from Tibet or Sanskrit, as well as a large number of terms not included here, see the Nalanda Translation Committee 1986, 211–59.

Awakening: The process of becoming aware, or the state of being aware, of the true nature of **confusion** and **samsara**.

Compassion: A state of being, the best expression of which is the fact of mirroring another's **confusion**, such that this other person **awakens** to it.

Confusion: Any of the many forms of belief in a solid **self** and/or world—that is, in a particular kind or version of the **self** and/or the world (see **ego**). Sometimes referred to as **ignorance**.

Desire: A manifestation of **confusion** in which we identify certain ideas, things, or experiences as pleasure-producing (that is, as confirming our existence), and which we therefore wish to "have." Sometimes referred to as **passion**.

Dharma: The truth, or the teaching or practice of the truth, free of the **confusions** of **ego** (free of preconceptions about the nature of ourselves and the world). The *Hridayasutra* (Heart sutra) tells us that the ultimate **dharma** is that there is no **dharma**.

Ego: The concept of an independent and continuously existing **self,** with particular character and personality traits and a particular place in the world, in which we conventionally believe. Because we find it frightening not to believe in our existence, we marshal the full powers of human intelligence to defend its "reality." This concept, therefore, can be extremely subtle. Within the Buddhist community, one of its forms might be belief in one's own enlightenment.

Emptiness: See **sunyata.**

Four Noble Truths: Meditating under the Bodhi Tree, the Buddha realized that (1) we continually suffer in this life; (2) that the cause of this suffering is our belief in **ego** and the **desires** that come from this belief; (3) that this suffering can be ended with an attitude of goal-lessness and nonstriving; and (4) that the way of achieving this attitude is to follow the path of meditation.

Identity: A conventional term that I often use in this book to indicate our tendency to compress ourselves into an idea of a particular **self,** into a self-definition or self-image. In this usage, belief in a personal **identity** is a form of **confusion.**

Ignorance: See **confusion**.

Lineage: Those who follow or belong to a particular tradition in the transmission of particular Buddhist teachings. For example, the Dalai Lama is the leader of the Gelukpa lineage.

Mahayana: A form of Buddhism emphasizing the teaching of **sunyata** and the giving up of the goal of individual enlightenment. Its main centers, with a great variety of styles and practices, are in northern Asia, in Tibet and the lands nearby (for example, Nepal, Bhutan, India), and in the Far East (for example, in Japan, Korea, China).

Nirvana: The state of being in this mundane world, but without the **confusions** of **ego,** such that one is outside pleasure and suffering, outside cause and effect, outside time and rebirth.

Nonattachment: The state of being **egoless** and **desireless**. Having no belief in a particular personal definition or **identity,** one needs no self-confirmation, hence is **attached** to nothing, either within oneself or outside oneself.

Passion: See **desire**.

Prajna: That aspect of human intelligence that can see through the **confusion** of **samsara** as if it were transparent, and can thereby see it for what it is.

Renunciation: Like the state of **nonattachment;** nothing within or without has value for the **self** because nothing is needed. (Therefore, everything can be delightfully itself.) **Renunciation** is not the product of asceticism so much as of revulsion; it simply occurs; it cannot be forced by an act of will.

Samsara: The state of **confusion** in which, because one believes in **ego,** one is driven by the endlessly self-perpetuating cycle of **desire** into continuous dissatisfaction and suffering. (Note that **samsara,** like **nirvana,** occurs in this world. Their difference is in how this world, and oneself, is perceived. In this sense, **nirvana** is the other side of the same coin as **samsara**; a person in **nirvana** sees the same objects and faces the same situations as does a person in **samsara**, but experiences them differently. Thus the two states are not said to be opposed to one another, but rather to be interdependent.)

Self: See **ego**.

Six Realms: Six psychological styles of acting out and perpetuating the pain of **samsara** in this world and life. We all participate in each of these styles, though one or another may seem dominant in a particular individual. See chapter 5.

Skillful Means: An action, performed by one who sees the truth behind (or in) **confusion**, which indicates to someone else how to "see" in this way.

Sunyata: A state of conceptual **emptiness**, hence **desireless** and goal-less; it is a state in which full being (**nirvana**) is possible.

Sutra: A written record of a teaching given orally by the Buddha.

Theravada: A major form of Buddhism, with many styles and practices. It emphasizes the way to individual enlightenment. It is centered in Southeast Asia (for example, Burma, Cambodia, Sri Lanka, Thailand, and Vietnam).

List of Works Cited

Abel, Lionel. 1963. *Metatheatre: A New View of Dramatic Form*. New York: Hill and Wang.

Adams, Hazard, and Leroy Searle, eds. 1986. *Critical Theory since 1965*. Tallahassee: Florida State University Press.

Adelman, Janet. 1973. *The Common Liar*. New Haven: Yale University Press.

———. 1985. "Male Bonding in Shakespeare's Comedies." In *Shakespeare's Rough Magic,* edited by Peter Erickson and Coppelia Kahn, 73–103. Newark: University of Delaware Press.

Aldus, P. J. 1977. *Mousetrap: Structure and Meaning in "Hamlet."* Toronto: University of Toronto Press.

Alexander, Nigel. 1971. *Poison, Play, and Duel. A Study in "Hamlet."* Lincoln: University of Nebraska Press.

Allman, Eileen Jorge. 1980. *Player-King and Adversary: Two Faces of Play in Shakespeare*. Baton Rouge: Louisiana State University Press.

Ashley, Leonad R. N. 1980. "Floreat Florio." *SN* 30:49.

Atkins, G. Douglas. 1983. *Reading Deconstruction. Deconstructive Reading*. Lexington: University Press of Kentucky.

Auerbach, Erna. 1961. *Nicholas Hilliard*. Boston: Boston Book and Art Shop.

Bakhtin, Mikhail. 1981. *The Dialogic Imagination*. Translated by Caryl Emerson and Michael Holquist. University of Texas Press Slavic Series no. 1. Austin: University of Texas Press.

———. 1984. *Rabelais and His World*. Translated by Helene Iswolsky. Bloomington: University of Indiana Press.

Bamber, Linda. 1982. *Comic Women, Tragic Men. A Study of Gender and Genre in Shakespeare*. Stanford, Calif.: Stanford University Press.

Barber, C. L. 1959. *Shakespeare's Festive Comedy*. Princeton: Princeton University Press.

Barroll, J. Leeds. 1958. "Antony and Pleasure." *JEGP* 57:708–20.

———. 1958. "Shakespeare and Roman History." *MLR* 53:327–43.

A. L. Beier. 1985. *Masterless Men: The Vagrancy Problem in England 1560–1640*. London: Methuen.

Benjamin, Walter. 1986a. "The Author as Producer." In *Reflections*, edited by Peter Demetz. Translated by Edmund Jephcott. New York: Schocken.

———. 1986b. "Theses on the Philosophy of History." In *Critical Theory Since 1965*, edited by Hazard Adams and Leroy Searle, 680–85. Tallahassee: Florida State University Press.

Berger, Harry. 1965. "The Renaissance Imagination: Second World and Green World." *Centennial Review* 9:36–78.

Berry, Ralph. 1985. *Shakespeare and the Awareness of the Audience.* New York: St. Martin's.

Bethell, S. L. 1944. *Shakespeare and the Popular Dramatic Tradition.* Durham, N.C.: Duke University Press.

———. 1952/53. "The Comic Elements in Shakespeare's Histories." *Anglia* 71:82–101.

Blunt, Anthony. [1940] 1963. *Artistic Theory in Italy 1450–1600.* London: Oxford University Press.

Blyth, Reginald Horace. 1960. *Zen in English Literature and Oriental Classics.* New York: Dutton.

Bowers, John M. 1983. "'I am Marble-Constant': Cleopatra's Monumental End." *HLQ* 46:283–93.

Braden, Gordon. 1985. *Renaissance Tragedy and the Senecan Tradition.* New Haven: Yale University Press.

Bradley, A. C. 1909. "The Rejection of Falstaff." In *Oxford Lectures on Poetry,* 247–73. London: Macmillan.

Brewer, D. S. 1952. "Brutus' Crime: A Footnote to *Julius Caesar.*" *RES,* n.s. 3:51–54.

Bristol, Michael D. 1985. *Carnival and Theater. Plebeian Culture and the Structure of Authority in Renaissance England.* New York: Methuen.

Brower, Reuben A. 1951. *The Fields of Light.* New York: Oxford University Press.

———. 1971. *Hero and Saint. Shakespeare and the Graeco-Roman Heroic Tradition.* Oxford: Oxford University Press.

Brown, Patricia Fortini. 1988. *Venetian Narrative Painting in the Age of Carpaccio.* New Haven: Yale University Press.

Burckhardt, Sigurd. 1962. "*The Merchant of Venice:* The Gentle Bond." *ELH* 29:239–62.

———. 1968. *Shakspearean Meanings.* Princeton: Princeton University Press.

Burke, Kenneth. [1941] 1973. "Art in Behalf of the Play." In *The Philosophy of Literary Form,* 3d ed., 329–43. Berkeley: University of California Press.

Burnet, John. [1930] 1968. *Essays and Addresses.* Freeport, N.Y.: Books for Libraries Press.

Calderwood, James. 1965. "*A Midsummer Night's Dream:* The Illusion of Drama." *MLQ* 26:506–22.

———. 1971. *Shakespearean Metadrama.* Minneapolis: University of Minnesota Press.

———. 1979. *Metadrama in Shakespeare's Henriad.* Berkeley: University of California Press.

———. 1983. *To Be and Not To Be. Negation and Metadrama in "Hamlet."* New York: Columbia University Press.

———. 1987. *Shakespeare and the Denial of Death*. Amherst: University of Massachusetts Press.

Campbell, Joseph. 1956. *The Hero with a Thousand Faces*. New York: Meridian.

Carnovsky, Morris. 1958/59. "Mirror of Shylock." *Tulane Drama Review* 3:35–45.

Carroll, William C. 1985. *The Metamorphoses of Shakespearean Comedy*. Princeton: Princeton University Press.

Cartelli, Thomas. 1987. "Prospero in Africa: *The Tempest* as Colonialist Text and Pretext." In *Shakespeare Reproduced,* edited by Jean E. Howard and Marion F. O'Connor, 99–115. New York: Methuen.

Chaudhuri, Sukanta. 1981. *Infirm Glory: Shakespeare and the Renaissance Image of Man*. Oxford: Clarendon.

Coates, John. 1978. "'The Choice of Hercules' in *Antony and Cleopatra*." *ShS* 31:45–52.

Cody, Richard. 1969. *The Landscape of the Mind*. Oxford: Clarendon.

Coghill, Nevill. 1950. "The Basis of Shakespearian Comedy." In *Essays and Studies 3, New Series,* edited by G. Rostrevor Hamilton, 1–28. London: John Murry.

Cohen, Walter. 1985. *Drama of a Nation*. Ithaca, N.Y.: Cornell University Press.

Colie, Rosalie L. 1974. *Shakespeare's Living Art*. Princeton: Princeton University Press.

Conze, Edward, ed. and trans. 1959. *Buddhist Scriptures*. New York: Penguin.

Corfield, Cosmo. 1985. "Why Does Prospero Abjure His 'Rough Magic'?" *ShQ* 36:31–48.

Council, Norman. 1973. *When Honour's at the Stake*. New York: Barnes and Noble.

Coward, Harold G. 1990. *Derrida and Indian Philosophy*. Albany: State University of New York Press.

Cox, Gerard H. 1985. "'Like a Prince Indeed': Hal's Triumph of Honor in *1 Henry IV.*" In *Pageantry in the Shakespearean Theater,* edited by David M. Bergeron, 130–49. Athens: University of Georgia Press.

Daiches, David. 1962. "Imagery and Meaning in *Antony and Cleopatra.*" *English Studies* 43:343–58.

———. 1976. Introduction to *Julius Caesar*. London: Edward Arnold.

Danby, John. 1949. "The Shakespearean Dialectic: An Aspect of *Antony and Cleopatra.*" *Scrutiny* 17:196–213.

———. 1952. *Poets on Fortune's Hill*. London: Faber.

———. 1958. *Shakespeare's Doctrine of Nature*. London.

Danson, Lawrence. 1974. *Tragic Alphabet: Shakespeare's Drama of Language*. New Haven: Yale University Press.

———. 1978. *The Harmonies of "The Merchant of Venice."* New Haven: Yale University Press.

Dash, Irene G. 1981. *Wooing, Wedding, and Power: Women in Shakespeare's Plays*. New York: Columbia University Press.

Davidson, Clifford. 1980. "*Antony and Cleopatra:* Circe, Venus, and the Whore of Babylon." In *Shakespeare: Some Contemporary Approaches,* edited by Harry R. Garvin, 31–55. East Brunswick, N.J.: Associated University Presses.

Dawson, Antony B. 1978. *Indirections: Shakespeare and the Art of Illusion*. Toronto: University of Toronto Press.

Derrida, Jacques. 1986a. "Différance." Translated by Alan Bass. In *Critical Theory Since 1965,* edited by Hazard Adams and Leroy Searle, 120–136. Tallahassee: Florida State University Press.

———. 1986b. "Structure, Sign and Play in the Discourse of the Human Sciences." Translated by Alan Bass. In *Critical Theory Since 1965,* edited by Hazard Adams and Leroy Seale, 83–94. Tallahassee: Florida State University Press.

———. 1989. "How to Avoid Speaking." Translated by Ken Frieden. In *Languages of the Unsayable,* edited by Sanford Budick and Wolfgang Iser, 3–70. New York: Columbia University Press.

Dessen, Alan C. 1986. *Shakespeare and the Late Moral Plays.* Lincoln: University of Nebraska Press.

Dickey, Franklin M. 1966. *Not Wisely But Too Well.* San Marino, Calif.: Huntington Library.

Dollimore, Jonathan. 1984. *Radical Tragedy. Religion, Ideology and Power in the Drama of Shakespeare and his Contemporaries.* Chicago: University of Chicago Press.

Dollimore, Jonathan, and Alan Sinfield, eds. 1985. *Political Shakespeare. New Essays in Cultural Materialism.* Ithaca, N.Y.: Cornell University Press.

Eagleton, Terry. 1986. *William Shakespeare. Rereading Literature.* Oxford: Blackwell.

Egan, Robert. 1972. "This Rough Magic: Perspectives of Art and Morality in *The Tempest.*" *ShQ* 23:171–82.

———. 1975. *Drama Within Drama: Shakespeare's Sense of his Art.* New York: Columbia University Press.

Eggers, Walter F., Jr. 1977. "Love and Likeness in *The Merchant of Venice.*" *ShQ* 28:327–33.

Eliade, Mircea. 1958. *Yoga: Immortality and Freedom.* Translated by Willard R. Trask. The Bollingen Series 56. Princeton: Princeton University Press.

———. 1978a. *The Forge and the Crucible.* Translated by Stephen Corrin. Chicago: University of Chicago Press.

———. 1978b. "The Myth of Alchemy." *Parabola* 3, no. 3 (August): 8.

Eliot, T. S. 1960. "Hamlet and his Problems." In *The Sacred Wood,* 95–103. New York: Barnes and Noble.

Empson, William. N.d. *Some Versions of Pastoral.* Norfolk, Conn.: New Directions.

Erbesato, Gian Maria. 1981. *Il Palazzo Te di Mantova.* Novara: Instituto Geografico De Agostini.

Erickson, Peter, and Coppelia Kahn, eds. 1985. *'Shakespeare's Rough Magic.* Newark: University of Delaware Press.

Esslin, Martin. [1961] 1969. *The Theater of the Absurd.* Garden City, N.Y.: Anchor.

Ettin, Andrew V. 1977. "Magic into Art: The Magician's Renunciation of Magic in English Renaissance Drama." *TSLL* 19:268–93.

Farnham, Willard. 1950. *Shakespeare's Tragic Frontier.* Berkeley: University of California Press.

———. 1971. *The Shakespearean Grotesque.* Oxford: Clarendon.

Farrell, Kirby. 1975. *Shakespeare's Creation. The Language of Magic and Play.* Amherst: University of Massachusetts Press.

———. 1989. *Play, Death, and Heroism in Shakespeare*. Chapel Hill: University of North Carolina Press.

Felperin, Howard. 172. *Shakespearean Romance*. Princeton: Princeton University Press.

———. 1978. "Romance and Romanticism: Some Reflections on *The Tempest* and *Heart of Darkness;* or, When Is Romance No Longer Romance?" In *Shakespeare's Romances Reconsidered*, edited by Carol McGinnis Kay and Henry E. Jacobs, 60–76. Lincoln: University of Nebraska Press.

Ferguson, Margaret W., Maureen Quilligan, and Nancy J. Vickers, eds. 1986. *Rewriting the Renaissance. The Discourse of Sexual Difference in Early Modern Europe*. Chicago: University of Chicago Press.

Fergusson, Francis. 1977. *Trope and Allegory. Themes Common to Dante and Shakespeare*. Athens: University of Georgia Press.

Fields, Rick. 1986. *How the Swans Came to the Lake. A Narrative History of Buddhism in America*. Boston: Shambhala.

Fisch, Harold. 1970. "*Antony and Cleopatra:* The Limits of Mythology." *ShS* 23:59–67.

Foakes, R. A. 1954. "An Approach to *Julius Caesar*." *ShQ* 5:259–70.

Forte, Joseph. 1987. "The Riddle of Mantegna." *Arts and Antiques*, May, 64–71, 106.

Foucault, Michel. 1973. *The Order of Things. An Archaeology of the Human Sciences*. New York: Vintage.

———. 1980. *Power/Knowledge. Selected Interviews and Other Writings 1972–1977*. Edited by Colin Gordon. Translated by Colin Gordon, Leo Marshall, John Mepham, and Kate Soper. New York: Pantheon.

———. 1986. "What Is an Author?" Translated by Donald F. Bouchard and Sherry Simon. In *Critical Theory Since 1965*, edited by Hazard Adams and Leroy Searle, 138–48. Tallahassee: Florida State University Press.

French, Marilyn. 1981. *Shakespeare's Division of Experience*. New York: Summit Books.

Frye, Northrop. 1965. *A Natural Perspective*. New York: Harcourt.

———. 1967. *Fools of Time: Studies in Shakespearean Tragedy*. Toronto: University of Toronto Press.

Frye, Roland Mushat. 1980. "Ways of Seeing in Shakespearean Drama and Elizabethan Painting." *ShQ* 31:323–42.

Gadol, Joan. 1969. *Leon Battista Alberti, Universal Man of the Early Renaissance*. Chicago: University of Chicago Press.

Garber, Marjorie B. 1974. *Dream in Shakespeare: From Metaphor to Metamorphosis*. New Haven: Yale University Press.

Geanakoplos, Deno John. 1961. *Greek Scholars in Venice*. Cambridge: Harvard University Press.

———. 1976. *Interaction of the "Sibling" Byzantine and Western Cultures in the Middle Ages and Italian Renaissance (330–1600)*. New Haven: Yale University Press.

Gill, Joseph, S.J. 1961. *The Council of Florence*. Cambridge: Cambridge University Press.

———. 1965. *Personalities of the Council of Florence*. New York: Barnes and Noble.

Gilman, Ernest B. 1978. *The Curious Perspective. Literary and Pictorial Wit in the Seventeenth Century*. New Haven: Yale University Press.

———. 1980. "'All eyes': Prospero's Inverted Masque." *RenQ* 33:214–30.

Girard, René. 1973. "Lévi-Strauss, Frye, Derrida and Shakespearean Criticism." *Diacritics* 3, no.3: 34–38.

Gnerro, Mark L. 1979. "Easter Liturgy and the Love Duet in *MV* V, I." *AmN&Q* 18, no. 2:19–21.

Goddard, Harold C. 151. *The Meaning of Shakespeare*. Chicago: University of Chicago Press.

Goldberg, Jonathan. 1983. *James I and the Politics of Literature*. Baltimore: Johns Hopkins University Press.

———. 1985. "Shakespearean Inscriptions: The Voicing of Power." In *Shakespeare and the Question of Theory,* edited by Patricia Parker and Geoffrey Hartman, 116–137. New York: Methuen.

———. 1986. "Fatherly Authority: The Politics of Stuart Family Images." In *Rewriting the Renaissance,* edited by Margaret W. Ferguson, Maureen Quilligan, and Nancy J. Vickers, 3–32. Chicago: University of Chicago Press.

———. 1986. "Textual Properties." *ShQ* 37, no. 2:213–17.

Goldman, Michael. 1972. *Shakespeare and the Energies of Drama*. Princeton: Princeton University Press.

———. 1975. *The Actor's Freedom: Toward a Theory of Drama*. New York: Viking.

Gollancz, Sir Israel. 1931. *Allegory and Mysticism in Shakespeare*. London: George Jones.

Gombrich, E. H. 1972. *Symbolic Images: Studies in the Art of the Renaissance*. New York: Praeger.

Gottschalk, Paul A. 1973/74. "Hal and the 'Play Extempore' in *1H4*." *TSLL* 15:605–14.

Grant, Patrick. 1979. *Images and Ideas in Literature of the English Renaissance*. Amherst: University of Massachusetts.

Greenblatt, Stephen. 1980. *Renaissance Self-Fashioning. From More to Shakespeare*. Chicago: University of Chicago Press.

———. 1985. "Invisible Bullets: Renaissance Authority and its Subversion." In *Political Shakespeare,* edited by Jonathan Dollimore and Alan Sinfield, 18–47. Ithaca, N.Y.: Cornell University Press.

———, ed. 1988a. *Representing the English Renaissance*. Berkeley: University of California Press.

———. 1988b. *Shakespearean Negotiations. The Circulation of Social Energy in Renaissance England.* Berkeley: University of California Press.

Greenwood, John. 1988. *Shifting Perspectives and the Stylish Style. Mannerism in Shakespeare and his Jacobean Contemporaries.* Toronto: University of Toronto Press.

Griseri, Andreina. 1967. *Le Metamorfosi del Barocco.* Torino: Giulio Einaudi.

Grudin, Robert. 1979. *Mightly Opposites. Shakespeare and Renaissance Contrariety*. Berkeley: University of California Press.

Guenther, Herbert V., and Chögyam Trungpa. 1988. *The Dawn of Tantra*. Edited by Michael Kohn. Boston: Shambhala.

Guilhamet, Leon. 1975. "*A Midsummer Night's Dream* as the Imitation of an Action." *SEL* 15:257–71.

Hartt, Frederick. [1958] 1981. *Giulio Romano.* New Haven: Yale University Press. New York: Hacker.

Hauser, Arnold. 1965. *Mannerism: The Crisis of the Renaissance and the Origin of Modern Art.* Vol. 1. Translated by L. Eric Mosbacher. New York: Knopf.

Hawkes, Terence. 1985. "Telmah." In *Shakespeare and the Question of Theory,* edited by Patricia Parker and Geoffrey Hartman, 310–32. New York: Methuen.

Hoeniger, F. D. 1956. "Prospero's Storm and Miracle." *ShQ* 7:33–38.

Holloway, John. 1961. *The Story of the Night.* London: Routledge and Kegan Paul.

Homan, Sidney. 1970/71. "When the Theater Turns to Itself." *New Lit Hist* 2:407–17.

———. 1981. *When the Theater Turns to Itself. The Aesthetic Metaphor in Shakespeare.* Lewisburg: Bucknell University Press.

Horga, Ioan. 1975. *El Greco,* trans. Andrea Gheorghiţoiu. London: Abbey Library.

Horowitz, David. 1965. *Shakespeare: An Existential View.* London: Tavistock.

Howard, Jean E., and Marion F. O'Connor, eds. 1987. *Shakespeare Reproduced. The Text in History and Ideology.* New York: Methuen.

Hulse, Clark. 1981. *Metamorphic Verse. The Elizabethan Minor Epic.* Princeton: Princeton University Press.

Hunter, Robert G. 1965. *Shakespeare and the Comedy of Forgiveness.* New York: Columbia University Press.

Huston, J. Dennis. 1981. *Shakespeare's Comedies of Play.* New York: Columbia University Press.

Jameson, Frederic. 1981. *The Political Unconscious. Narrative as a Socially Symbolic Act.* Ithaca, N.Y.: Cornell University Press.

Jardine, Lisa. 1983. *Still Harping on Daughters. Women and Drama in the Age of Shakespeare.* Totowa, N.J.: Barnes and Noble.

Johnson, Samuel. 1958. "Preface to Shakespeare." In *Shakespeare Criticism, A Selection 1623–1840,* edited by D. Nichol Smith, 77–117. London: Oxford University Press.

Jonas, Hans. 1963. *The Gnostic Religion: The Message of the Alien God and the Beginnings of Christianity.* 2d ed. Boston: Beacon.

Jones, Ken. 1989. *The Social Face of Buddhism. An Approach to Political and Social Activism.* London: Wisdom.

Jung, C. G. 1967a. *Alchemical Studies.* Translated by R. F. C. Hull. Vol. 13 of *Collected Works.* 2d ed. Princeton: Princeton University Press.

———. 1967b. *Psychology and Alchemy.* Translated by R. F. C. Hull. Vol. 12 of *Collected Works.* 2d ed. Princeton: Princeton University Press.

Kahn, Coppelia. 1981. *Man's Estate. Masculine Identity in Shakespeare.* Berkeley: University of California Press.

———. 1985. "The Cuckoo's Nest: Male Friendship and Cuckoldry in *The Merchant of Venice.*" In *Shakespeare's Rough Magic,* edited by Peter Erickson and Coppelia Kahn, 104–12. Newark: University of Delaware Press.

Kastan, David Scott. 1986. "Proud Majesty Made a Subject: Shakespeare and the Spectacle of Rule." *ShQ* 37, no. 4:459–75.

Kermode, Frank. 1954. Introduction to *The Tempest.* Cambridge: Harvard University Press.

———. 1961. "The Mature Comedies." In *Early Shakespeare,* edited by John Russell Brown and Bernard Harris, 211–27. Stratford-on-Avon Studies 3. New York: St. Martin's.

———. 1963. *Shakespeare: The Final Plays.* London: Longmans, Green.

Kernan, Alvin B. 1974. "This Goodly Frame, The Stage." *ShQ* 25:1–5.

———. 1978. "Shakespeare's Essays on Dramatic Poesy: The Nature and Function of Theater within the Sonnets and the Plays." In *The Author in His Work*, edited by Louis L. Martz and Aubrey Williams, 175–96. New Haven: Yale University Press.

———. 1979. *The Playwright as Magician.* New Haven: Yale University Press.

———. 1982. "Shakespeare's Stage Audiences: The Playwright's Reflections and Control of Audience Response." In *Shakespeare's Craft,* edited by Philip H. Highfill, Jr., 138–55. Carbondale: Southern Illinois University Press.

Kirschbaum, Leo. 1944. "Shakespeare's Cleopatra." *ShAssnBull* 19:161–71.

———. 1949. "Shakespeare's Stage Blood and its Critical Significance." *PMLA* 64:517–29.

Knight, G. Wilson. [1930] 1970. *The Wheel of Fire.* London: Methuen.

———. 1948. *The Crown of Life.* London: Methuen.

Knights, L. C. 1959. *Some Shakespearean Themes.* London: Chatto and Windus.

Kott, Jan. 1964. *Shakespeare Our Contemporary.* Translated by Boleslaw Taborski. Garden City, N.Y.: Doubleday.

———. 1987. *The Bottom Translation.* Translated by Daniel Miedzyrzecka and Lillian Vallee. Evanston, Ill.: Northwestern University Press.

Krook, Dorothy. 1969. *Elements of Tragedy.* New Haven: Yale University Press.

Kubovy, Michael. 1986. *The Psychology of Perspective and Renaissance Art.* Cambridge: Cambridge University Press.

Lanham, Richard A. 1976. *The Motives of Eloquence: Literary Rhetoric in the Renaissance.* New Haven: Yale University Press.

Lavin, Irving. 1980. *Bernini and the Unity of the Visual Arts.* New York: Oxford University Press.

Leech, Clifford. 1978. "Masking-Unmasking in the Last Plays." In *Shakespeare's Romances Reconsidered,* edited by Carol McGinnis Kay and Henry E. Jacobs, 40–59. Lincoln: University of Nebraska Press.

Leininger, Lorie Jerrell. 1980. "The Miranda Trap. Sexism and Racism in Shakespeare's *Tempest*." In *The Woman's Part,* edited by Carolyn Ruth Swift Lenz, Gayle Greene, and Carol Thomas Neely, 285–94. Urbana: University of Illinois Press.

Lenz, Carolyn Ruth Swift, Gayle Greene, and Carol Thomas Neely, eds. 1980. *The Woman's Part. Feminist Criticism of Shakespeare.* Urbana: University of Illinois Press.

Levao, Ronald. 1985. *Renaissance Minds and Their Fictions. Cusanus, Sidney, Shakespeare.* Berkeley: University of California Press.

Lever, J. W. 1952. "Shylock, Portia and the Values of Shakespearean Comedy." *ShQ* 3:383–86.

Levin, Harry. 1969. "Two Magian Comedies: *The Tempest* and *The Alchemist*." *ShS* 22:47–58.

———. 1981. "Falstaff's Encore." *ShQ* 32:5–17.

Lewalski, Barbara K. 1962. "Biblical Allusion and Allegory in *The Merchant of Venice.*" *ShQ* 13:327–43.

Lloyd, Michael. 1959. "Cleopatra as Isis." *ShS* 12:88–94.

———. 1962. "Art and the Game of Chance." *JEGP* 61:548–54.

Lomazzo, Paolo Giovanni. [1598] 1966. *A Tracte Containing the Artes of Curious Painting.* Translated by Richard Haycocke. New York: Da Capo.

Loy, David. 1987. "The Cloture of Deconstruction: A Mahayana Critique of Derrida." *International Philosophical Quarterly* 27, no. 105:59–80.

———. 1988. *Nonduality: A Study in Comparative Philosophy.* New Haven: Yale University Press.

Mack, Maynard. 1961. "The World of *Hamlet.*" In *Shakespeare: Modern Essays in Criticism,* edited by Leonard Dean, 237–57. New York: Oxford University Press.

———. 1977. "Mobility and Mutability in *Antony and Cleopatra.*" In *Twentieth-Century Interpretations of "Antony and Cleopatra,"* edited by Mark Rose, 125– 31. Englewood Cliffs, N.J.: Prentice-Hall.

MacLure, Millar. 1983. "Spenser's Images of Society." *Dalhousie Review* 63, no. 1:22–33.

Magliola, Robert. 1984. *Derrida on the Mend.* West Lafayette, Ind.: Purdue University Press.

Markels, Julian. 1968. *The Pillar of the World.* Columbus: Ohio State University Press.

McGuire, Richard L. 1967. "The Play-Within-the-Play in *1 Henry IV.*" *ShQ* 18:47–52.

McPeek, James A. 1972. "The Psyche Myth and *A Midsummer Night's Dream.*" *ShQ* 23:69–79.

Mendelsohn, Leatrice. 1982. *Paragoni: Benedetto Varchi's Due Lezzioni and Cinquecento Art Theory.* Ann Arbor, Mich.: UMI Research Press.

Miller, Ronald F. 1975. "*A Midsummer Night's Dream:* The Fairies, Bottom, and the Mystery of Things." *ShQ* 26:254–68.

Miola, Robert S. 1985. "*Julius Caesar* and the Tyrannicide Debate." *RQ* 38, no. 2:271–89.

Moisan, Thomas. 1987. "Which is the merchant here? and which the Jew? Subversion and recuperation in *The Merchant of Venice*." In *Shakespeare Reproduced,* edited by Jean E. Howard and Marion F. O'Connor, 188–206. New York: Methuen.

Montaigne, Michel de. 1948. "To the Reader." In *Selections from the Essays of Montaigne,* translated and edited by Donald M. Frame, 3. New York: Appleton.

Montrose, Louis Adrian. 1986. "*A Midsummer Night's Dream* and the Shaping Fantasies of Elizabethan Culture: Gender, Power, Form." In *Rewriting the Renaissance,* edited by Margaret W. Ferguson, Maureen Quilligan, and Nancy J. Vickers, 65–87. Chicago: University of Chicago Press.

Morgann, Maurice. 1958. "From An Essay on the Dramatic Character of Sir John Falstaff, 1777." In *Shakespeare Criticism. A Selection 1623–1840,* edited by D. Nichol Smith, 153–89. London: Oxford University Press.

Moulton, Richard G. [1893] 1966. *Shakespeare as a Dramatic Artist.* New York: Dover.

Muir, Kenneth. 1954. "*Pyramus and Thisbe:* A Study in Shakespeare's Method." *ShQ* 5:141–53.

———. 1978. *The Sources of Shakespeare's Plays.* New Haven: Yale University Press.

Murry, John Middleton. 1936. *Shakespeare.* London: Jonathan Cape.

Nalanda Translation Committee. 1986. *The Life of Marpa the Translator.* Boston: Shambhala.

Neely, Carol Thomas. 1985. *Broken Nuptials in Shakespeare's Plays.* New Haven: Yale University Press.

Nellist, John S. 1967. *British Architecture and its Background.* London: Macmillan.

Newell, Alex. 1965. "The Dramatic Context and Meaning of Hamlet's 'To Be Or Not to Be' Soliloquy." *PMLA* 80:38–50.

Nichol, D. M. 1979. *The End of the Byzantine Empire.* Foundations of Medieval History Series. New York: Holmes and Meier.

Novy, Marianne. 1980. "Shakespeare's Female Characters as Actors and Audience." In *The Woman's Part,* edited by Carolyn Ruth Swift Lenz, Gayle Greene, and Carol Thomas Neely, 256–69. Urbana: University of Illinois Press.

———. 1984. *Love's Argument. Gender Relations in Shakespeare.* Chapel Hill: University of North Carolina Press.

Olson, Paul A. 1957. "*A Midsummer Night's Dream* and the Meaning of Court Marriage." *ELH* 24:95–119.

Orgel, Stephen. 1975. *The Illusion of Power. Political Theater in the English Renaissance.* Berkeley: University of California Press.

———. 1986. "Prospero's Wife." In *Rewriting the Renaissance,* edited by Margaret W. Ferguson, Maureen Quilligan, and Nancy J. Vickers, 50–64. Chicago: University of Chicago Press.

Ornstein, Robert. 1964. "The Ethic of the Imagination: Love and Art in *Antony and Cleopatra.*" In *Shakespeare. The Tragedies,* edited by Alfred Harbage, 31–46. Englewood Cliffs, N.J.: Prentice-Hall.

Panofsky, Erwin. 1960. *Renaissance and Renascences in Western Art.* Stockholm: Almquist and Wiksell.

Parker, Patricia, and Geoffrey Hartman, eds. 1985. *Shakespeare and the Question of Theory.* New York: Methuen.

Patterson, Annabel. 1989. *Shakespeare and the Popular Voice.* Cambridge: Blackwell.

Pearce, Howard D. 1980. "A Phenomenological Approach to the *Theatrum Mundi* Metaphor." *PMLA* 95:42–57.

Peterson, Douglas L. 1973. *Time, Tide and "Tempest."* San Marino, Calif.: Huntington Library.

Platt, Michael. 1982. "Shakespeare's Apology for Poetic Wisdom." In *Shakespeare and the Arts,* edited by Cecile Williamson Cary and Henry S. Limouze, 231–44. Washington, D.C.: University Press of America.

Proser, Matthew N. 1965. *The Heroic Image.* Princeton: Princeton University Press.

Purdon, Noel. 1974. *The Words of Mercury.* Salzburg: Institut für Englische Sprache und Literatur.

Quinones, Ricardo J. 1972. *The Renaissance Discovery of Time.* Cambridge: Harvard University Press.

Rabkin, Norman. 1981. *Shakespeare and the Problem of Meaning.* Chicago: University of Chicago Press.

Radhakrishnan, Sarvepalli. 1940. *Eastern Religions and Western Thought.* 2d ed. London: Oxford University Press.

Reynolds, Graham. 1974. *The Raphael Cartoons.* London: Victoria and Albert Museum.

Rhodes, Neil. 1980. *Elizabethan Grotesque.* Boston: Routledge and Kegan Paul.

Ribner, Irving. 1960. *Patterns in Shakespearian Tragedy.* London: Methuen.

Richmond, Hugh M. 1968. "Brutus and the End of the Play." In *Twentieth-Century Interpretations of "Julius Caesar,"* edited by Leonard F. Dean, 103–4. Englewood Cliffs, N.J.: Prentice-Hall.

Riemer, A. P. 1968. *A Reading of Shakespeare's "Antony and Cleopatra."* Sydney: Sydney University Press.

Righter, Ann. 1962. *Shakespeare and the Idea of the Play.* London: Chatto and Windus.

Rose, Mark. 1977. Introduction to *Twentieth-Century Interpretations of "Antony and Cleopatra,"* edited by Mark Rose, 1–13. Englewood Cliffs, N.J.: Prentice-Hall.

Roston, Murray. 1987. *Renaissance Perspectives in Literature and the Visual Arts.* Princeton: Princeton University Press.

Rozett, Martha Tucker. 1985. "The Comic Structure of Tragic Endings: The Suicide Scenes in *Romeo and Juliet* and *Antony and Cleopatra.*" *ShQ* 36, no. 2:152–64.

Said, Edward. 1983. *The World, the Text, and the Critic.* Cambridge: Harvard University Press.

Salingar, Leo. 1974. *Shakespeare and the Tradition of Comedy.* Cambridge: Cambridge University Press.

Schanzer, Ernest. 1963. *The Problem Plays of Shakespeare.* New York: Schocken.

Schaub, Uta Liebmann. 1989. "Foucault's Oriental Subtext." *PMLA* 104, no. 3:306–17.

Schmidgall, Gary. 1981. *Shakespeare and the Courtly Aesthetic.* Berkeley: University of California Press.

Schneidau, Herbert N. 1976. *Sacred Discontent: The Bible and Western Tradition.* Baton Rouge: Louisiana State University Press.

Schwartz, Murray M., and Coppelia Kahn, eds. 1980. *Representing Shakespeare. New Psychoanalytic Essays.* Baltimore: Johns Hopkins University Press.

Scott, James C. 1985. *Weapons of the Weak.* New Haven: Yale University Press.

Scragg, Leah. 1977. "Shakespeare, Lyly, and Ovid." *Shakespeare Survey* 30:125–34.

Segel, Harold B. 1974. *The Baroque Poem.* New York: Dutton.

sGam.po.pa. 1986. *The Jewel Ornament of Liberation.* Translated by Herbert V. Guenther. Boston: Shambhala.

Shakespeare, William. 1974. *The Riverside Shakespeare.* Edited by G. Blakemore Evans. Boston: Huughton Mifflin.

Siegel, Paul. 1953. "*A Midsummer Night's Dream* and the Wedding Guests." *ShQ* 4:139–44.

Siemon, James R. 1985. *Shakespearean Iconoclasm.* Berkeley: University of California Press.

Simmons, J. L. 1969. "The Comic Pattern in *Antony and Cleopatra.*" *ELH* 36:493–510.

Sinfield, Alan. 1983. *Literature in Protestant England, 1560–1660.* Totowa, N.J.: Barnes and Noble.

Skura, Meredith Anne. 1989. "Discourse and the Individual: The Case of Colonialism in *The Tempest.*" *ShQ* 40, no. 1:42–69.
Smith, Stephen L. 1977. "*A Midsummer Night's Dream:* Shakespeare, Play and Metaplay." *Centennial Review* 21:194–209.
Snyder, Susan. 1979. *The Comic Matrix of Shakespeare's Tragedies.* Princeton: Princeton University Press.
———. 1980. "Patterns of Motion in *Antony and Cleopatra.*" *ShS* 33:113–22.
Spitz, Lewis W. 1972. *The Northern Renaissance.* Englewood Cliffs, N.J.: Prentice-Hall.
Spivack, Bernard. 1957. "Falstaff and the Psychomachia." *ShQ* 8:449–59.
Spriet, Pierre. 1980. "Regard et verbe: La metamorphose du heros dans quelques pièces de Shakespeare." In *La Metamorphose dans la poesie baroque française et anglaise,* edited by Gisele Mathieu-Castellani, 203–9. Tübingen: Gunter Narr.
Stallybrass, Peter, and Allon White. 1986. *The Politics and Poetics of Transgression.* Ithaca, N.Y.: Cornell University Press.
Stechow, Wolfgang. 1966. *Northern Renaissance Art 1400–1600.* Englewood Cliffs, N.J.: Prentice-Hall.
Stewart, J. I. M. 1949. *Character and Motive in Shakespeare.* New York: Barnes and Noble.
Stoll, Elmer Edgar. 1927. *Shakespearean Studies.* New York: Macmillan.
———. 1928. "Cleopatra." *MLR* 23:145–63.
Strong, Roy. 1969. *The Elizabethan Image: Painting in England 1540–1620.* London: Tate Gallery.
———. 1984. *Art and Power. Renaissance Festivals 1450–1650.* Berkeley: University of Calfornia Press.
Stroup, Thomas B. 1978. "Bottom's Name and his Epiphany." *ShQ* 29:79–82.
Stubblevine, James H. 1979. *Duccio di Buoninsegna and his School.* Princeton: Princeton University Press.
Summers, Joseph H. 1984. *Dreams of Love and Power. On Shakespeare's Plays.* Oxford: Clarendon.
Suzuki, Shunryu. 1970. *Zen Mind, Beginner's Mind.* Edited by Trudy Dixon. New York: Weatherhill.
Sypher, Wylie. 1955. *Four Stages of Renaissance Style.* Garden City, N.Y.: Doubleday.
Taylor, Gary. 1989. *Reinventing Shakespeare.* New York: Weidenfeld and Nicolson.
Taylor, Marion A. 1973. *Bottom, Thou Art Translated. Political Allegory in "A Midsummer Night's Dream."* Amsterdam: Rodopi NV.
Teeter, Louis. 1938. "Scholarship and the Art of Criticism." *ELH* 5:173–94.
Tennenhouse, Leonard. 1980. "The Counterfeit Order of *The Merchant of Venice.*" In *Representing Shakespeare,* edited by Murray M. Schwartz and Coppelia Kahn, 54–69. Baltimore: Johns Hopkins University Press.
———. 1985. "Strategies of State and Political Plays: *A Midsummer Night's Dream, Henry IV, Henry V, Henry VIII.*" In *Political Shakespeare,* edited by Jonathan Dollimore and Alan Sinfield, 109–28. Ithaca, N.Y.: Cornell University Press.
———. 1986. *Power on Display. The Politics of Shakespeare's Genres.* New York: Methuen.

Tillyard, E. M. W. 1956. *Shakespeare's History Plays.* London: Chatto and Windus.

———. 1961. "The Trial Scene in *The Merchant of Venice.*" *REL* 2, no. 4:51–59.

Traub, Valerie. 1989. "Prince Hal's Falstaff: Positioning Psychoanalysis and the Female Reproductive Body." *ShQ* 40, no. 4:456–74.

Traversi, D. A. 1963. *Shakespeare: The Roman Plays.* Stanford, Calif.: Stanford University Press.

———. 1969. *An Approach to Shakespeare.* . Vol. 1. 3d ed. Garden Ciy, N.Y.: Anchor.

Truax, Elizabeth. 1980. "Lucrece! What hath your conceited painter wrought?" In *Shakespeare: Contemporary Critical Approaches,* edited by Harvey Garvin, 13–30. Lewisburg, Pa.: Bucknell University Press.

Trungpa, Chögyam. 1969. *Meditation in Action.* Boulder, Colo.: Shambhala.

———. 1973. *Cutting Through Spiritual Materialism.* Edited by John Baker and Marvin Casper. Boulder, Colo.: Shambhala.

———. September 1974. "Seminar on Vipasyana." Transcript of a seminar given in Barnet, Vermont.

———. 1976a. *The Myth of Freedom and the Way of Meditation.* Edited by John Baker and Marvin Casper. Boulder, Colo.: Shambhala.

———. 1977. *Born in Tibet,* as told to Esme Cramer Roberts. Boulder, Colo.: Shambhala.

———. 1978a. *Glimpses of Abhidharma.* Boulder, Colo.: Prajna Press.

———. 1975, 1976b, 1978b, and 1979. Transcripts of Vajradhatu seminaries.

Ure, Peter. 1974. "Character-Roles from Richard III to Hamlet." In *Elizabethan and Jacobean Drama,* edited by J. C. Maxwell, 22–43. Liverpool: Liverpool University Press.

Van Doren, Mark. 1939. *Shakespeare.* New York: Holt.

Van Laan, Thomas F. 1978. *Role-Playing in Shakespeare.* Toronto: University of Toronto Press.

Vasari, Giorgio. 1965. *The Lives of the Artists.* Translated by George Bull. Harmondsworth: Penguin.

Verheyen, Egon. 1977. *The Palazzo del Te in Mantua: Images of Love and Politics.* Baltimore: Johns Hopkins University Press.

Vincent, Barbara C. 1982. "Shakespeare's *Antony and Cleopatra* and the Rise of Comedy." *ELR* 12:53–86.

Von Simson, Otto. 1948. *Sacred Fortress: Byzantine Art and Statecraft in Ravenna.* Chicago: University of Chicago Press.

Waage, Frederick O. 1980. "Be Stone No More: Italian Cinquecento Art and Shakespeare's Last Plays." In *Shakespeare: Contemporary Critical Approaches,* edited by Harvey R. Garvin, 56–87. Lewisburg: Bucknell University Press.

Walker, Daniel P. 1958. *Spiritual and Demonic Magic From Ficino to Campanella.* London: Warburg Institute, University of London.

Warnke, Frank J. 1972. *Versions of Baroque: European Literature in the Seventeenth Century.* New Haven: Yale University Press.

Weimann, Robert. 1978. *Shakespeare and the Popular Tradition in the Theater: Studies in the Social Dimension of Dramatic Form and Function.* Edited by Robert Schwartz. Baltimore: Johns Hopkins University Press.

———. 1985. "Mimesis in *Hamlet*." In *Shakespeare and the Question of Theory,* edited by Patricia Parker and Geoffrey Hartman, 275–91. New York: Methuen.

White, John. 1979. *Duccio: Tuscan Art and the Medieval Workshop.* New York: Thames and Hudson.

Willeford, William. 1969. *The Fool and His Scepter.* Evanston, Ill.: Northwestern University Press.

Wilson, J. Dover. 1949. Introduction to *Julius Caesar.* Cambridge: Cambridge University Press.

———. 1953. *The Fortunes of Falstaff.* Cambridge: Cambridge University Press.

———. 1954. Introduction to *Antony and Cleopatra.* Cambridge: Cambridge University Press.

Wind, Edgar. 1958. *Pagan Mysteries in the Renaissance.* New Haven: Yale University Press.

Winny, James. 1968. *The Player King.* New York: Barnes and Noble.

Wittkower, Rudolf. 1952. *The Drawings of the Carracci . . . at Windsor Castle.* London: Phaidon.

———. 1973. *Art and Architecture in Italy, 1600–1750.* Harmondsworth: Penguin.

Wolf, William D. 1982. "'New Heaven, New Earth': The Escape from Mutability in *Antony and Cleopatra.*" *ShQ* 33:328–35.

Woudhuysen, Henry. 1982. "Renaissance Routines." *TLS,* 18 June, 678.

Wunderlich, Hans Georg. 1983. *The Secret of Crete.* Translated by Richard Winston. Athens: P. Efstathiadis and Sons.

Wyrick, Deborah Baker. 1982. "The Ass Motif in *The Comedy of Errors* and *A Midsummer Night's Dream."* *ShQ* 33:432–48.

Yates, Frances A. 1964. *Giordano Bruno and the Hermetic Tradition.* Chicago: University of Chicago Press.

———. 1975. "Magic in Shakespeare's Last Plays." *Encounter* 44, no. 4 (April): 14–22.

Young, David. 1966. *Something of Great Constancy. The Art of "A Midsummer Night's Dream."* New Haven: Yale University Press.

———. 1978. "Where the Bee Sucks: A Triangular Study of *Doctor Faustus, The Alchemist,* and *The Tempest."* In *Shakespeare's Romances Reconsidered*, edited by Carol McGinnis Kay and Henry E. Jacobs, 149–66. Lincoln: University of Nebraska Press.

Ziegler, Georgianna. 1985. "Parents, Daughters, and 'That Rare Italian Master': A New Source for *The Winter's Tale.*" *ShQ* 36, no. 2:204–12.

Index

Note: Numerals in bold type refer to the pages of illustrations.

Abhidharma, 67–68
Alberti, Leon Battista, 214
Antony and Cleopatra, 24, 114–44, 146, 147, 165, 239–40n.12; and Buddhism, 24, 114, 128–34, 143–44
Autun and Gislbertus, 250n.1

Baroque: as style, 226; in *Antony and Cleopatra,* 239–40n.12; in *Hamlet,* 247n.21
Benjamin, Walter, 40–41
Bernini, Gianlorenzo, 240n.12
Bettes, John, and studio, 64
Bodhisattva, 245n.13, 246n.17
Brecht, Bertolt, 41
Brunelleschi, Filippo, 214
Buddha, Sakyamuni, 30, 66
Buddhism, 13–14; and belief, 20–21, 66, 93, 134; and deconstruction, 16, 20, 25, 71, 197, 221–22; and Jacques Derrida, 16–17, 19–21, 49, 74, 109, 131–34, 197, 229–30n.7; and Michel Foucault, 19; and literary criticism, 14–16; and political interpretation of texts, 15–21
Buddhist view: of adversarial/nonadversarial (oppositional/nonoppositional) attitudes, 18, 22, 30–31, 36, 39, 41, 68, 87, 111, 143–44, 152, 155, 158–59, 165–66, 182, 198, 242–43n.15; of aggression, 70, 74, 158–59, 178–79, 182, 246n.17; of enlightenment, 31–32, 109–10; of flux and impermanence, 35–36, 48, 109, 114, 119–21, 157, 164; of freedom, 27, 31–32, 39, 48, 144, 146, 157, 182, 186

Carnival, 43, 44, 150, 153–54, 230n.8, 231n.8, 233n.4, 235n.20, 242n.8, 248n.25
Carpaccio, Vittore, 212–13, 217; *The Miracle of St. Tryphon,* 212–13
Carracci, Annibale, 102; at the Farnese Palace, 220–21, 226
Carraci brothers, the, 227
Cause of suffering, 20. *See also* Four Noble Truths: Second
Cervantes, Miguel de: *Don Quixote,* 53, 57
Charles V, 141, 218
Cimabue, 203
Clouets, the, 225
Compassion, 111–13, 178, 188, 245–46n.16
Correggio, 225
Council of Trent, 239n.12

da Vinci, Leonardo, 212, 224, 225
Deconstruction: and Shakespeare, 21; and theater, 71, 94, 137
de Critz, John, 226
de' Medici, Cosimo, 208
de' Medici, Lorenzo, 208, 211
Derrida, Jacques: and Buddhism, 16–17, 19–20, 24, 94, 131–34, 143–44, 163, 166–67, 192, 197–98, 229–30n.7; and deconstruction, 16, 20, 143, 247n.22;

INDEX 271

and deferral, 24, 25, 134, 146–49, 154–55, 157, 160–62, 165–68, 173, 196, 198; and "différance," 15, 24, 26, 49, 134, 149, 165; and free play, 20, 24, 31, 49, 131–34, 137, 146–50, 163; and identity, 20, 131–34, 150, 154; and language and meaning, 19–20, 131–34, 148–49, 196, 247n.22; and "presence" and "absence," 16–17, 24, 109, 113, 133, 148–49, 154, 157, 168, 171, 173, 175, 178, 182, 197–99, 229–30n.7, 247n.22

Desire, 24, 31–32, 33, 36, 44, 49, 70, 77, 96, 107–8, 110–11, 113, 114, 121–23, 127–30, 132, 134, 143, 144, 146, 151, 153, 158–59, 163, 178, 183. *See also* Passion

Dharma, 20, 21

Donatello, 214

Duccio di Buoninsegna, 61, 203–8, 221; *Madonna in Trono con il Bambino e Sei Angeli*, 204, 207; *Maestà*, 204, **205**, 207; *Madonna di Crevole*, 204, **206**, 207

Dürer, Albrecht, 225

Ego/egolessness, 76, 108–11, 114, 146, 172–73, 175, 179–80, 184–86, 244–45nn. 8, 10, 13, and 15

Elizabeth, Princess, 194

Elizabeth I, 23, 73, 93, 106, 182; and *A Midsummer Night's Dream,* 46–47; and Titania, 43–44; and visual arts, 60–61, 64–65, 223–26; as Gloriana, 182; her court, 56

Emptiness and fullness, 20, 24, 29, 109–10, 134, 145, 151, 157, 179, 181–82, 187, 197–99, 247nn. 17 and 22, 249nn. 8 and 11. *See also* Sunyata

Florio, John, 194, 224

Fontainebleau, 224

Foucault, Michel: and the art of resemblance, 22, 52–55, 57, 60, 61, 66, 192–94, 200, 203; on authorship, 17; and Buddhism, 19–20, 144; and Derrida, 16, 19–20; and individual power in society, 17–19, 60, 95, 150; and truth, 17, 19, 151–52

Four Noble Truths: First, 23, 96; Second, 23, 96, 113, 114, 128–30, 143; Third, 24, 111, 113, 130–31, 146–47, 244–45n. 10; Fourth, 235n.1

Francis I, 223, 224

Gheeraerts circle, 226

Giotto, 203–4, 208

Gonzaga family, 141, 142, 214, 217–20; Ludovico, 218

Gower, George, 64

Greco, El, 240n.12

Greenblatt, Stephen: and Jacques Derrida, 16, 148; and Michel Foucault, 18; and the new historicism, 18–19, 60; and individual power in society, 18–19, 59–60, 196; and interpretation, 14; and theater and subversion, 27, 40, 64, 148

Hamlet, 25, 168–82, 196; and Buddhism, 25, 172–75, 177–182

Hardwick Hall, 224

Henry, Prince of Wales, 226

Henry IV, Part One, 24–25, 146–67, 168, 173, 180, 182, 196, 226; and Buddhism, 24–25, 146–47, 155, 157, 163–67

Henry IV, Part Two, 149, 161, 166, 196

Henry VIII, 56, 60, 223, 225

Hilliard, Nicholas, 22, 225, 226, 252n.5; *Portrait of Elizabeth,* 61, **62**, 64, 67, 86; as Elizabethan portrait style, 65, 72, 159; *A Treatise on the Arte of Limninge,* 225

Holbein, Hans, the Younger, 22, 223, 225; *The Ambassadors,* 56–59, 64, 66, 67, 72, 75, 76, 86, 104, 207–8, 212; Basel altar panels, 223; *Portrait of William of Warham,* 223–24

Hridayasutra (Heart sutra), 20, 30–31

Ignatius of Loyola, St., 240n.12

Ignorance, 178

Interpretation. *See* Reading

James I, 25–26, 60, 64, 142–43, 182–83, 193, 196, 198, 226, 247n.23, 248n.25

Jonson, Ben, 224
Julius Caesar, 23–24, 96–113, 130, 143, 165; and Buddhism, 23–24, 96, 107–13

Kagyü lineage, 13, 29
King Lear, 25, 182–90, 197; and Buddhism, 25, 182, 184, 186–88, 190

Leicester, earl of, 226
Levitation, 239–40n.12
Literature and visual arts, 65, 105, 251n.11
Lomazzo, Paolo Giovanni, 225, 226
Longleat House, 224

Mahayana, 13, 229n.7
Mannerism, 66, 223, 225, 226; and Shakespeare, 232–33n.9, 241n.17, 251n.5
Mantegna, Andrea, 102, 214, 216–18, 219, 221, 225; *La Camera degli Sposi,* 214, **216,** 217–18
Marxism and consciousness, 17, 60, 95, 144
Mary I, 224
Masaccio, 102, 203, 213–14; Brancacci Chapel, 214; *The Trinity,* 214, **215**
Medieval iconographic style in visual arts, 60–65, 223–24. *See also* Duccio; Ravenna
Meditation, 41–42, 131
Merchant of Venice, The, 23, 74–95, 96, 112–13, 143, 164; and Buddhism, 23, 74–77, 93–95
Michelangelo, 224, 225, 226
Midsummer Night's Dream, A, 22, 27–51, 55, 57, 59, 66, 72, 74, 76, 86, 92, 138, 144; and Buddhism, 22, 27–51, 57, 60, 66
Mimesis. *See* Foucault, Michel: and the art of resemblance
Minoan art, 200–201, 213
Montaigne, Michel de, 194, 213
Mor, Antonio, 225, 251n.2

Neri, St. Philip, 240n.12
Nirvana, 19, 29–30, 32, 47–48, 96, 110–11, 133, 181–82, 185, 198–99

Nonattachment/attachment, 31, 36, 48, 60, 72, 143, 146, 148–56, 161, 164, 166, 185–86, 188

Oliver, Isaac, 225, 226

Paleologian Renaissance, 203
Palladio, Andrea, 224
Parmigianino, 225
Passion, 69, 74, 178. *See also* Desire
Peake, Robert, 64, 223, 224, 226, 261n.2
Piazza Armerina, 201
Pollock, Jackson, 41
Pompeii, 201
Prajna, 51, 58, 74, 200
Primataccio (or Primaticcio), Francesco, 224

Rape of Lucrece, The, 224
Raphael, 225, 226
Ravenna, 60, 64, 201–3, 208; Justianian and Theodora, 64, 201–2, 213; Theodora, **63;** Galla Placidia, 201; S. Vitale, 201–3
Reading: and audience response, 16, 75–76, 92; and Buddhism, 14–16, 77; and desire, 132, 134; as intervention, 14–15, 92–93; as political act, 15–16; as presence in absence, 134–37; as process, 74; as reinvention, 15, 181; as transaction with text, 15
Renunciation, 59, 108, 143, 185, 187
Richard II, 158, 161, 244n.7
Richard III, 22–24, 67–73, 74, 76, 86, 92, 93, 96, 100, 138, 144, 233n.10; and Buddhism, 22–23, 67–71, 74
Romano, Giulio, 102, 218–20, 221, 224, 225, 232n.9, 241n.17, 251nn. 5, 6, 7, and 8; *Sala dei Giganti,* 138, **139–40,** 141, 143, 193, 218–20
Rossi (or Rosso), Fiorentino, 224, 225

Samsara, 47–50, 60, 70, 74, 93, 96, 107, 110–11, 114, 123, 133, 158, 164–65, 173–74, 185, 198–99; Six Realms of, 24, 128–31, 132, 173–74, 241n.14
Scrots, William, 224, 225, 251n.2

Shakespearean metadrama: and Derrida and Buddhism, 21, 137, 197; as subversion, 25, 66, 72, 112–13, 143, 165, 168, 182, 198–99, 243 nn. 1, 3, and 4; and visual arts, 65–66, 219, 220, 223–27

Shakespearean self-deconstruction, 21–22, 25, 143, 198–99, 223; and Buddhism, 22, 24–26, 66, 67, 197–99; and emptiness, 22, 24, 25, 145, 198

Shakespearean texts. *See* individual titles

Shute, John, 224

Skillful means, 25, 40, 163–64, 175, 179, 245 n.13, 246 n.17

Smythson, Robert, 224

Southampton, circle of, 224

Spenser, Edmund, 65, 226

Sunyata, 17, 19, 24, 110, 134, 163, 187, 198. *See also* Emptiness

Tantra, 13

Tempest, The, 25–26, 191–96, 198; and Buddhism, 25–26, 192, 194, 197

Teresa, St., 239–40 n.12

Theravada, 13

Titian, 225

Transparency of artistic illusion: and the Buddhist view, 49–51, 55, 57, 58, 59, 66, 94, 157, 197, 200, 221–22, 232 n.4, 249 n.8; and concepts, 59, 93–95, 157; and free play, 47; and meaning in the theater, 25–26, 51, 55, 92, 102–4, 143, 157, 166, 170–71, 181, 243 nn. 1, 3, and 4, 243–44 n.6, 247 n.22, 248 n.1, 249 n.8; and meaning in the visual arts, 138, 141, 232 n.4; and meaning in the world, 25, 157, 165, 169, 181; and meditation, 41–42, 249 n.8; and power in the theater, 38, 45–47, 49, 72, 112–13, 142–43, 157, 165–66, 169–72, 179, 182, 191–94, 196–98; and power in the visual arts, 51–61, 64, 138–41, 200–204, 207–8, 211–22

Trungpa, Chögyam, Rinpoche, 13, 14; on bodhisattva, 245 n.13, 246 n.17; on cessation of suffering, 146, 244–45 n.10; on compassion, 111–12, 188, 245–46 n.16; on ego/egolessness, 76, 109, 146, 179–80, 245 n.15; on emptiness/fullness (sunyata), 111, 153, 187, 198; on enlightenment, 31–32, 109, 131; on freedom, 39, 144, 186; on illusion of solidity, 35–36, 58–59, 68–70, 93, 110; on life as play, 94, 110, 131–32, 185; on meditation, 42, 59, 131; on nirvana, 29–30; on prajna, 51, 58; on renunciation, 59, 143–44, 186; on samsara, 93–94; on samsara/nirvana interdependence, 48–49, 110–11, 198–99, 244 n.8; on six realms of samsara, 128–32, 173–74; on skillful means, 163–64, 179–80

Uccello, Paolo, 208–12, 213, 221; *Battle of San Romano,* 208, **209,** 211–12; *Sir John Hawkwood,* **210,** 211–12

Varchi, Benedetto, 251 n.11

Vasari, Giorgio, 203–4, 208, 211–12, 218, 225, 251 n.7

Velázquez, Diego, 22; *Las Meninas,* 53–54, 55, 57, 66, 67, 72, 192–93, 212, 221, 249 nn. 4 and 9

Vignola, 224

Winter's Tale, The, 219, 224

Wollaton Hall, 224

Zuccaro, Federigo, 225